Picture Book Storytelling

Literature Activities for Young Children

Janice J. Beaty
Elmira College

Harcourt Brace College Publishers

Fort Worth Philadelphia San Diego New York Orlando Austin San Antonio
Toronto Montreal London Sydney Tokyo

In memory of my husband
Dale H. Janssen
A remarkable storyteller

Publisher	Ted Buchholz
Acquisitions Editor	Jo-Anne Weaver
Developmental Editor	Tracy Napper
Project Editors	Clifford Crouch
	Annelies Schlickenrieder
Production Manager	Jane Tyndall Ponceti
Senior Art Director	Diana Jean Parks
Electronic Publishing Coordinator	Jill Stubblefield
Electronic Publishing Supervisor	Michael Beaupré
Cover Photographer	Donna Buie
Photographs	Janice Beaty
Action chants & verses	Janice Beaty
Illustrations	Jill Sacherman
Music	Donna Zeigler

Thanks to all of our cover models (Josh, Ryan, Ashley, Kristen, and Victoria) and the Trinity Lutheran Children's Center. A special thanks to Scott Lennox for reading "Maebelle's Suitcase" by Tricia Tusa.

ISBN: 0-15-500486-7

Library of Congress Catalog Card Number: 93-83613

Copyright © 1994 by Harcourt Brace & Company

Address editorial correspondence to: 301 Commerce Street, Suite 3700
Fort Worth, Texas 76102

Address orders to: 6277 Sea Harbor Drive
Orlando, Florida 32887
1-800-782-4479, or 1-800-433-0001 (in Florida)

PREFACE

Children's picture books have long held a special place in the hearts of children, parents, and teachers. For many youngsters picture books are their first encounter with the grownup world of reading, writing, drawing, and books. Such a coming together is a joyous one, indeed. But for other youngsters the encounter does not seem to happen because there are no picture books in the home, or no teacher in the preschool or kindergarten who takes the time to make it happen. *Picture Book Storytelling* has been written for the children and adults in both instances.

It presents the glorious world of children's picture books as the tip of an immense iceberg of learning. And it presents this learning in young children's terms of play, projects, and games. "What else can you do with a book besides read it?" *Picture Book Storytelling* tells how to sing it, dance it, whisper it, make puppets of it, shine flashlights around it, make food from it, write stories about it, send post cards from it, pretend to be a hero with it, and several hundred other original endeavors.

Teachers and parents learn how to choose good picture books, how to read or tell them to children, and how to extend the excitement of each book with activities, experiences, and projects. Nearly two hundred carefully selected picture books are described, from classics like *Gilberto and the Wind* to absurd adventures like *Gregory the Terrible Eater;* from the traditional *Noah's Ark* to the far-out *Professor Noah's Spaceship;* from the wheelchair-bound *The Balancing Girl* to the astounding African-American *Amazing Grace.* Teachers learn how to bring children together with picture books like *The Best Peanut Butter Sandwich in the Whole World* by actually making peanut butter (and butter, and bread!), and how to overcome fear by taming *The Beast in the Bathtub.*

All of the picture books included are storybooks rather than nonfiction, so that children can hear them or tell them as tales. But the categories of the tales in each chapter reflect the current interests of children and early childhood curriculum themes such as: self-image, families, friends, pets, dramatic play, dinosaurs, food, space, the environment, music, and beauty. The use of storytelling picture books to motivate emergent writing, and of predictable books to support emergent reading assists teachers in implementing the *whole language* philosophy. Children learn to re-enact favorite fairy tales as they investigate their own place in the world. Teachers and children together learn to give rather than take from the good Earth through stories about its creatures.

Teachers find that the excitement of picture books in a young child's world can blossom into amazing classroom interests when teachers adopt the presentation techniques put forth in *Picture Book Storytelling.* Let this book do the same for you!

❧ Acknowledgments

My love for and knowledge about children's literature and storytelling has been growing for much of my life. I owe this great passion of mine to many people and places: those that helped in my collecting of folktales on the island of Guam in the 1960s, and on San Salvador Island in the Bahamas in the 1970s and 1980s ; the wonderful oldstory tellers in the Bahamas; my writing of children's books for Pantheon Books in New York; my twenty years of teaching children's literature at Elmira College, Elmira, New York; and Dr.Frank Brady who got me started teaching children's literature. I am especially grateful for the five years traveling to Mark Twain locations across the country with my late husband, Dale H. Janssen, a tale teller with the mark of the master. This book also owes much to my business partner, Ann Gilchrist who read the manuscript and commented with insight; to Dr. Linda Pratt, a colleague and reading specialist who offered excellent ideas; to Donna Zeigler, a colleague who not only knows children's literature, but can put it to music (!); to Bonny Helm, a colleague and great nursery school storyteller; to Ben Otten at McGraw Bookstore, Elmira College; to Debbie at My Bookstore in Pensacola; to Peg at Bookmarks in Elmira; to Holly at Hurricane Books in Gulf Breeze, Florida; to Bruce at Becky Thatcher Bookstore in Hannibal, Missouri; to the many teachers and children in the Head Start programs I have worked with for twenty years; to Jill Sacherman, my daughter-in-law who did the outstanding illustrations; to the editors Jo-Anne Weaver and Tracy Napper, and finally to the reviewers Joanne Bernstein (Brooklyn College), Susan Hepler, and Susan Neuman (Temple University).

BRIEF CONTENTS

CONTENTS

10 Rhythms and Rhymes

Photo and Illustration Credits

Appendix

Index of Authors

Index of Books

Index of Multicultural Books

Index of Book Extension Activities

General Index

Picture Book Storytelling

Literature Activities for Young Children

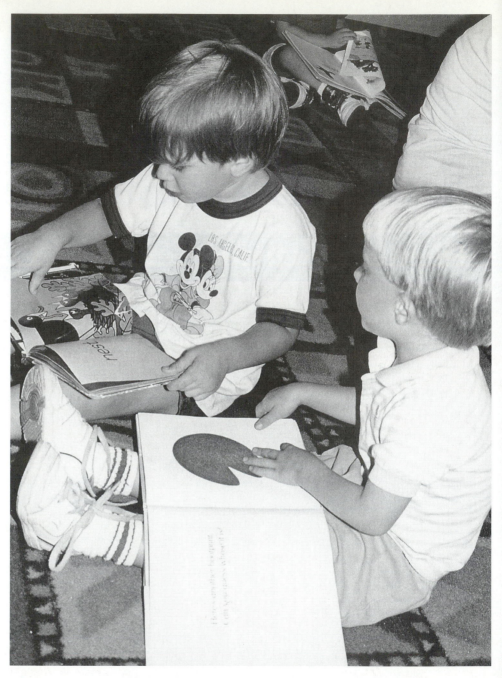

STORIES FOR TELLING AND LISTENING

Action Chant

What can you do with a story?
A tale full of fancy and fun?
You can build a block house,   *(stack with fists)*
You can paint a pink mouse,   *(swish hands up and down)*
You can rip,   *(tear with hands)*
You can rap,   *(clap)*
You can run!   *(run in place)*

What else can you do with a story?
A tale that is timeless and true?
You can put on a mask,   *(cover eyes with hand)*
You can finish a task,   *(pound with fist)*
You can broom,   *(sweep with hands)*
You can bloom,   *(raise arms overhead)*
You can boo!   *(shout "Boo!")*

But what can you do with a story?
When the tale is both ghastly and grim?
You can frighten a ghost,   *(jump)*
You can munch on some toast,   *(hand to mouth, chew)*
You can groan,   *(make groaning noise)*
You can growl,   *(say "Grrrr!")*
You can grin!   *(fingers at mouth corners)*

❧ Why Storytelling?

Storytelling has been with us since the beginning of human experience. Before there was art there were stories. Before there was writing there were stories. Even before religion became formalized there were stories. Stories told people who they were, why they were here, how they fit into the scheme of things. Stories explained natural phenomena: the sun, the moon, the seasons, the weather. They told people how to behave—and how not to behave. They explained. They entertained. They moralized. They passed along history and new ideas. Stories could be happy, exciting, fearsome, hilarious, or tragic. They were everything that people were, for the human species has always lived in narrative: a stream of consciousness within, that eventually had to be expressed aloud.

At first stories were told orally, then pictorially, and finally in writing. Some were sung by bards, others acted out in amphitheaters, town squares, and on stages. As civilization developed, so did the means for telling stories. Oral tales became books; books became films; films became videos. Yet oral storytelling never disappeared. A tale well told by a single teller has always had the power to captivate an audience, to touch something deep within the human species. Stories are a part of us. Storytelling reaches into a core of our being and satisfies the spirit.

Today oral storytelling is experiencing an extraordinary revival. As we search for our roots and try to preserve folkways, storytellers of all sorts have come forth. They are teachers, librarians, parents, grandparents, video stars, history buffs, folklore buffs, authors, professional storytellers, and even children. Some who have become nationally known through their storytelling videotapes include Jay O'Callahan from Martha's Vineyard, African-Americans Jackie Torrence and Joe Ferguson, librarian and writer Caroline Feller Bauer, Irish storyteller Maggi Peirce, Native American Gayle Ross, children's writer Diane Wolkstein, "Beauty and the Beast" storytellers Martha Hamilton and Mitch Weiss, and many more.(See references.)

Storytellers tell their tales at folk festivals, at family reunions, in theaters, in libraries, on television, in colleges and universities, in the home, and in the classroom. They are people with a story to share, with an anecdote to impart, with a love for an audience (even an audience of one!) They could be you.

This text invites you to participate in telling or reading stories to your children. It will help you learn to choose appropriate stories, and then to tell or read them in ways that will make a difference in children's lives.

✿ Why Storytelling for Young Children?

The earliest stories, the folk tales, myths, and legends of antiquity, were told for adults. Children were often a part of the audience, but the tales were not directed at them specifically. Children's personal stories came instead at bedtime, when the adult caregiver wanted to lull the child to sleep. Today, on the other hand, we often view storytelling as an activity exclusively for children, although professional tellers make a point of gearing their tales for adults as well.

Nevertheless, it is most important that we involve young children in listening to stories and telling them themselves as early as possible. The years from three to six are crucial ones in children's development. Not only are children shooting up physically and mentally during these years, but also emotionally as they develop attitudes about themselves that may last a lifetime, and creatively as their uniqueness in expression becomes apparent. Greater changes in children occur during these years than at almost any other period of development.

We as teachers and parents of young children need to take advantage of these crucial years of growth to bring youngsters together with activities that will make a difference in their lives. Storytelling is such an activity.

> Noting the rapid decline of language skills over the past two generations, child psychologists and educators are now actively championing storytelling as an ideal method of influencing a child to associate listening with pleasure, of increasing a child's attention span and retention capacity, of broadening a child's vocabulary, and of introducing a child to the symbolic use of language. (Maguire, 1985, 13)

This text has, then, as its primary goal, *teaching adults to tell or read stories to young children in order to develop within the children:*

1. A love for stories, books, and reading

2. A good feeling about themselves as learners and as emergent readers, writers, and speakers

3. The creativity to make up stories of their own

4. The inventiveness to tell, write, and dramatize stories from picture books

A tall order, it seems, but not really, as far as stories and youngsters are concerned. Stories attract children's attention because young children live in a story. They are at a developmental stage in which pretending about themselves and the world around them is dominant. They make up things as they go along. Once their interest is piqued, young children tend to respond strongly to the characters in the stories they hear. Societies down through the ages seemed to know this and, in fact, have taught children such things as moral values and acceptable behavior through the actions of storybook characters.

Our own society has only begun to realize the power of oral stories to mold behavior, motivate interest, and accelerate learning in young children. Yet most current research on children's learning has pointed out: that "children who have listened to stories and poems from an early age experience the most success in school." (Friedberg & Strong, 1989, 46) If storytelling can perform such wonders, then it behooves us as teachers of young children to make it a part of every facet of our curriculum.

Thus this text has as a second goal, helping adult storytellers and story readers learn how to:

1. Choose appropriate stories and books for young children;

2. Learn how to tell a story orally from a picture book;

3. Learn how to read a story with expression;

4. Learn which picture books are better told aloud and which are better read aloud;

5. Create activities for children based on stories;

6. Promote children's emergent reading, writing, speaking, and dramatizing through involvement with picture book stories.

The chapters to follow describe in detail how to accomplish these goals both for adults and for children. The young children described here are three to six year olds: youngsters in preschool and kindergarten. This is the age group for which the majority of picture books have been created.

✣ Whole Language and Emergent Literacy

Should you as a storyteller or story reader be involved in teaching preschool and kindergarten children how to read such stories and even to write them? Not so many years ago such a question would be answered with a resounding "No!" Today we know better. It is not that you will be teaching young children to read and write—it is that the children themselves will be emerging into reading and writing with or without your help.

The real question is: Is reading and writing taught or is it learned? Until recently it was generally assumed that children had to be taught to read and write. How else could they learn? But, as more and more preschoolers entered kindergarten already knowing how to read and sometimes to write, without having been taught by anyone, linguists, reading specialists, and child development researchers began taking another look. To the surprise of many, researchers found that many children learned to read and write by themselves in the same way they learned to talk.

> Because children naturally interact with print in functional and meaningful ways, children can read and write in their own ways before entering school and continue to learn through authentic reading and writing lessons. (Mills and Clyde, 1991, 58)

We now realize that preschool children in modern society are flooded with printed materials if they have access to television programs, supermarkets, fast-food restaurants, picture books, cereal boxes, computer games, and even printed slogans on T-shirts. We now understand that young children are born with the drive to make sense of their world and to give meaning to the things they encounter in their environment. One of the important things they encounter is language in all its forms.

We have long known that children learn to speak their native language naturally by listening to it spoken around them, by trying it out themselves, and eventually, by extracting the rules for putting words together. Their first efforts are rudimentary with one-word utterances in babytalk. But with practice (not adult teaching), and maturity, they finally become fluent. Now we understand that the same development can also occur with reading and writing.

> In both oral and written language systems, children construct personally meaningful rule systems based on their developing understandings of oral and written language surrounding them in their daily life experiences. (Schrader & Hoffman, 1987, 9)

From such personally constructed rule systems, preschool children teach themselves to talk and begin teaching themselves how to read and write if encouraged. How far they progress depends upon the amount of environmental print that they encounter, their maturity, and the expectations of the adults around them that encourage them to develop in this direction. Their progress does not require that adults must "teach" them. Young children will learn naturally by playing around with the words, symbols, and ideas that they encounter. They can extract meaning on their own and apply it naturally if encouraged by the adults in their environment. The picture book activities in this text give children the opportunity to hear and use language in fun ways in order to promote this natural emergence of speaking, reading, and writing skills.

What we as educators have learned from this research is that speaking, reading, and writing (and even drawing) need to be looked at holistically. They are all elements of one whole communication system that young children can develop naturally with appropriate materials and encouragement. Such development in young children is known as *emergent literacy.* The philosophy behind this holistic view is called *whole language.*

This text subscribes to such a whole language philosophy of teaching and learning: that speaking, reading, and writing are best learned in an integrated and natural manner through actual use in real situations and with real materials. As Edelsky, et al. point out in *Whole Language, What's the Difference?,* "reading and writing are learned through really reading and writing (not through doing reading and writing exercises)" and that whole language teachers "use genuine texts—children's literature, recipes, song lyrics, dictionaries, and so on." (Edelsky, et al., 1991, 8)

Picture Book Storytelling is based on this whole language point of view, and supports it by describing children's literature books (not basal readers) and hands-on activities (not lessons or worksheets) to support young children's natural acquisition of speaking, reading, and writing.

Setting Up the Classroom Learning Environment

To support children's natural acquisition of language as described above, the early childhood classroom can best be arranged into learning centers or activity areas that children can choose and use on their own. (See Beaty, 1992.) Such classrooms may include the following areas: Block Center, Computer Center, Manipulative/ Math Center, Story Center, Sound Center, Writing Center, Art Center, Music Center, Science Center, Dramatic Play Center, and Large Motor Center. Many of the story activities discussed in the chapters to follow will take place in a Story Center as described in detail in Chapter 12, "Picture Book Storytelling and You."

Those activities that encourage children to emerge naturally into writing can take place in a *Writing Center* if you have set it up with writing tools and print materials as follows:

• *Writing Center*

The Writing Center should contain a table and chairs—or better still, a child-sized desk. A roll-top desk with pigeon-holed compartments is a natural stimulus for writing. Children are excited to be sitting at such a grown-up desk. You may need to have a sign-up sheet for turns at the desk as you do for turns at the computer. The compartments of such a desk should be filled with writing and printing tools and implements:

Pencils: regular pencils, primary-sized pencils, soft color pencils, and erasers that fit over their tops.
Pens: ball-point pens of the "rolling writer" type.
Markers: felt-tip markers of various sizes and colors
Pencil sharpeners: regular, fastened-down sharpener; small hand-held sharpeners of different types.

Paper clips: container of large paper clips.
Stapler: child-sized stapler and staples.
Rulers: several wooden and plastic rulers.
Scissors: several pairs.
Hole punch: several hole punchers and large brads for fastening.
Rubber stamps: alphabet letters, rubber animal stamps, dinosaur stamps, flower stamps, and so on; address stamps, stamp pads with different colors of ink.

The drawers of such a desk should be filled with:

Paper: blank typing paper, light-colored construction paper, carbon paper.
Pads and tablets: small multicolor pads, writing tablets, pads with self-sticking pages.
Notebooks: spiral notebooks, secretary's dictation notebooks, loose-leaf notebooks.
Stationery: various kinds of note paper and matching envelopes; regular white envelopes.
Cards: three by five cards of various colors.
Paste: rubber cement, glue, cellophane tape.
Peel-offs: blank peel-off labels, peel-off stickers with pictures and designs; large peel-off alphabet letters; address labels.
Stamps: cancelled stamps of various kinds. (Beaty, 1992, 151–152)

In addition, you should feature a typewriter: either a primary typewriter or a standard adult typewriter which is easier to use than a child's toy typewriter. Perhaps a parent can donate an old manual typewriter to the program. A computer can also be featured here, whether or not you have a separate Computer Center. As businesses and families upgrade their computers to the latest models, the old machines can be donated to a child development center if you make your wants known. A chalkboard and chalk, and even a sand table have their place in the Writing Center, where children can experiment with all kinds of materials for making scribbles, mock writing, and letters.

If such an adult-style center for three- to six-year-old children sounds strange to you, consider the message that activity areas say to children: the Block Center, filled with blocks, says: "Come and build." The Story Center, filled with books, says: "Come and read or listen." The Sound Center, filled with communication tools, says: "Come and speak or listen." If we want young children to emerge into writing, then we must provide them with a similar center filled with writing tools that say to the children: "Come and write."

• *Sound Center*

Just as children need a print-rich environment to emerge naturally into reading and writing, so they also can benefit from a sound-rich environment in which they are surrounded by the sounds of the language: spoken words from such diverse areas as storytelling, story reading, story dramatization, telephone conversations, tape recorders, and videos. All these will encourage children's development of the spoken language and help them make the connection between spoken and written language. (Pratt, 1992) Undoubtedly language sounds can be heard throughout your classroom every day, but a Sound Center is something different. A Sound Center is a small learning activity area where *personal language sounds* are produced and listened to.

The *Sound Center* is a new addition to preschool and kindergarten classroom learning centers. It should be located somewhere near the Story Center, so that the book and story activities done with a group can spill over easily into personal sound activities. The Sound Center should contain a small table or low counter for equipment such as a tape recorder and microphone, a walkie-talkie, head sets with a jackbox attached to the tape recorder, a small automated filmstrip viewer or a small television/VCR combination, a small feltboard and feltboard stories, a toy microphone, and two toy telephones, cellular phones, or a child-sized toy telephone booth. In addition there can be a "sound booth" made from a commercial puppet theater or a large cardboard carton. The center should be small, accommodating not more than four children at a time, so that personal language activities can be practiced easily by individuals.

Children will be doing both real and pretend activities. They can call one another on the toy phones or walkie-talkies. They can listen to tapes of stories from picture books on the head sets. They can view and listen to book filmstrips and videos. They can make up their own feltboard stories with feltboard characters from picture books you have read. They can tape record their own stories. Pretend activities can also include having a TV news broadcast with an announcer, covering fast-breaking news with a toy video camera, reporting from space in an imaginary space shuttle, giving the news and weather as a radio announcer.

If your program cannot afford the equipment mentioned, make your own and have the children pretend it is real. Although commercial toy camcorders are available in plastic, it is easy to make your own video camera from a shoebox and paper tissue tube. Walkie-talkies can be made like tin-can telephones. Tie a string from a puncture in the bottom of one tin can to the puncture in the bottom of another. One child can talk through the open end of his can while the other listens to the vibrations of the words with the open end of his can against his ear when the string is stretched taut.

Commercial toy catalogs offer "network news kits" containing props such as toy microphone, weather chart, pointer, clock, and signs. With imagination you can make your own. Signs can read "QUIET" or "ON THE AIR" or "RECORDING IN PROGRESS." The only real piece of equipment necessary is a cassette tape recorder with microphone, head set (earphones) and blank tapes.

Such a Sound Center is an exciting support for the book reading and storytelling activities you will be doing in the Story Center by providing children with the tools to make up and record their own oral stories.

✿ Why Picture Book Storytelling?

Young children's picture books are the sources for the stories described in this text. Whereas many storytellers make up their own tales or tell stories without books at hand, in this case it is important for young children to see the actual books from which the stories are told or read, and to handle the books themselves afterwards, in order eventually to learn to read them. To develop this love for stories, books, reading, writing, and speaking, youngsters need to make the connection that the stories they are hearing come from books: picture books that they can look at and someday learn to read.

When you *tell* children a particular story, you will not be showing them the illustrations from the picture book, but you should have the book available for them to look at afterwards. When you *read* a story to individuals or groups, you will be showing them the pictures as you turn the pages, but be sure the book is also available to be handled by children after you have read it. That is the reason for this text's focus on children's picture books: to bring together children and books.

While storytelling and story reading are among the primary techniques for bringing children together with books, the story alone can't do it. It may be the most gripping and suspenseful tale the children have ever heard, but its impact for promoting the love of books and reading will be lost if there is no book available afterwards.

A Head Start teacher who told Marie Hall Ets' story *Gilberto and the Wind* had her children on the edge of their seats, intent on hearing about Gilberto's next encounter with the unpredictable wind. After hearing this delightful tale the children were able to stand outside their classroom door to feel the wind on their faces. What an experience for three- and four-year-olds! Afterwards the teacher mentioned that they could find the book that the story came from in the school library down the hall if they were interested when they visited the library next week. What a letdown! These threes and fours were terribly interested, but to wait for "library day" next week was too much to ask. Have the book available immediately. Next week is too late!

That books themselves are crucial in children's natural emergence of literacy becomes clear in much of the research on early reading. Child-development specialist Judith Schickedanz, in her book *More Than the ABCs: The Early Stages of Reading and Writing,* states: "Children who learn to read naturally before entering school usually have extensive story-reading experience. Similarly, researchers have found that experiences with books during the preschool years is related to successful literacy development during the elementary school years." (1986, 37–38)

She feels that as young children first become acquainted with books, they learn:

1. how books work

2. print should make sense

3. print and speech are related in a specific way

4. book language differs from speech

5. books are enjoyable
(Schickedanz, 1986, 38–39)

Bringing children together with enjoyable picture books is therefore more than just a pleasurable activity in the preschool and kindergarten. It is a crucial ingredient for children's emergent literacy and their success in learning to read in the elementary grades that follow.

However, not every picture book is an appropriate source of stories for children aged three to six. Some picture books are intended for older children, some for infants and toddlers. A few may showcase an artist's illustrations and have little appeal to young children. Others present facts or concepts without using narrative. How can you tell which is which? How will you know what books are suitable for your particular children? The chapters to follow give valuable suggestions for choosing picture books to fit the needs of tellers, readers, and listeners. The books included in this text are primarily storybooks rather than nonfiction. Nonfiction books are included only if written in narrative form.

✿ Is It Telling or Reading?

Is there much difference between storytelling and story reading, you may wonder? Indeed, there is. In its broadest sense "storytelling" (as used in this book's title) is a generic term that includes story reading. In its narrower sense, "storytelling" means telling a story orally in your own words without reading it aloud from a book. This text promotes both storytelling and story reading from children's picture books.

Most preschool and kindergarten teachers tend to read stories to children from picture books. A lesser number learn stories from books or other sources and then tell them to children in their own words. Although storytelling may seem more difficult to perform than simply story reading from a book, this is not necessarily the case. Both methods require teacher preparation in order to achieve the best results with children.

Both storytelling and story reading are promoted in this text as important presentation techniques. Some stories are much better told than read. Others are more meaningful if they are read from the book. For example, the classic picture book *Goodnight Moon,* by Margaret Wise Brown, shows a little boy bunny saying goodnight to objects in his room. Simple rhyming phrases accompany the illustrated pages that show a room growing progressively darker. Children love the rhyming words such as "a comb and a brush, and a bowl full of mush." They also need to see the darkening room to appreciate what is happening. This particular book should be *read* aloud rather than *told.*

On the other hand, Tomi Ungerer's classic story *Crictor* about the pet boa constrictor who catches a thief, makes just as good a tale for telling (especially with a long, slinky, fake-snake-prop), as it does for reading to children. In either case you can show them Ungerer's wonderfully snakey drawings.

AUTHORS
of **INTEREST**

TOMI UNGERER, born in Strasbourg, France, grew up during the violent times of World War II and the occupation of France. After traveling through Europe and the United States, he settled in New York City. His books often reflect his philosophy of accepting unconventional people and their actions. *Crictor* is set in France, as are several of his children's books. (Hurst, 1990, 124)

The chapters to follow help readers and tellers determine the best way to present picture books to their children, either through reading or telling, or both. There are distinct advantages for using each method.

✣ Advantages of Storytelling

1. Frees teller to use creative techniques to engage children's attention; makes teller more animated.

2. Makes teller more aware of audience's reactions; attention is on children, not on book; easier to keep children's attention.

3. Makes story more personal to teller and therefore to children.

4. Makes teller put more of him/herself into the story (facial expressions, inflections in voice, and so forth) because of projecting self rather than reading words. (Janssen & Beaty, 1988, 43)

5. Allows teller to tailor stories to children's attention span and interest.

    There are numerous advantages to *telling* a story. This method:

6. Stimulates audience to make own mental images rather than relying on book illustrations.

7. Serves as a model for children to emulate in telling their own stories.

✣ How Can You Choose a Story for Telling?

Although all picture books are created to be read and looked at, many also make excellent sources for storytelling as well. The following criteria will help you to select books from your own Story Center shelves that you can tell as well as read to your children.

Books for storytelling should contain (one or more):

1. ORDER: Plot incidents that happen in a set order, easily remembered.

2. CHARACTERS: One or two characters who speak.

3. REPETITION: Repetition of a word, a phrase, or an incident.

4. PUPPET: A story for which you have a puppet or other book object.

5. LENGTH: A good story too long for reading to the youngest children that can be condensed by telling

Picture books that contain one or more of the above criteria may be just what you are looking for to begin your storytelling enterprise. Most storytellers enjoy developing a repertoire of good stories they can tell, almost by heart. They are stories that both teller and listeners love to experience again and again. When the stories come from children's picture books, the books themselves become beloved objects to storytellers and audience alike after the telling is finished. Here are some examples of books that satisfy one or more of the above criteria:

1. ORDER: Plot incidents that happen in a set order, easily remembered. Example: *Caps for Sale* (1968), by Esphyr Slobodkina

This classic story of the peddler selling gray caps, brown caps, blue caps, and red caps which he carries on top of his head until a troupe of monkeys steals them all, is a story that beginning tellers can easily make their own. By remembering the the order of five brief incidents: shaking fingers, shaking both hands, stamping foot, stamping both feet, and throwing cap to the ground, the teller can bring this favorite story to life as often as desired.

2. CHARACTERS: One or two characters who speak. Example: *John Brown, Rose and the Midnight Cat* (1977), by Jenny Wagner, Ron Brooks, illustrator

This is a touching story of the widow Rose who lives alone with her dog John Brown until the Midnight Cat appears. Rose wants to bring the cat inside, but her jealous dog does not. They talk to one another each day until Rose becomes ill and only the Midnight Cat can restore her health. Storytellers can make the tale as long or short as they want by using a particular number of days or incidents, as well as the dialog between Rose and John Brown.

3. REPETITION: Repetition of a word, a phrase, or an incident. Example: *The Doorbell Rang* (1986), by Pat Hutchins

This modern story with humorous overtones tells the tale of mother who makes a plate of cookies that have to be shared with an increasing collection of children every time the doorbell rings. But "nobody makes cookies like Grandma" is the repetitive phrase that saves the day till Grandma finally appears with a plateful of her own cookies. Children can enjoy listening for who will come through the door next, each time the doorbell rings.

AUTHORS
of INTEREST

PAT HUTCHINS lives in London with her artist husband. She often gets her ideas for books by listening to her own children Morgan and Sam. She writes and illustrates her own books, treating double-page spreads as one picture, with orange and green as predominant colors. (Hurst, 1990, 159)

4. PUPPET: A story for which you have a puppet or other book object.
Example: *Keep Your Mouth Closed, Dear* (1966), by Aliki Brandenberg

Since alligator hand puppets are easy to come by (or to make with a bag), this story lends itself to telling rather than reading. It is the story of little alligator Charles who accidentally swallows something every time he opens his mouth: the soap, a wooden spoon, a sponge, his father's hat, a can of baby powder, Father's alarm clock, and finally the hose to the vacuum cleaner which empties his stomach at last. A clever storyteller can use a hand or make a hand puppet that "swallows" each of the items as the story progresses. Child listeners can help by popping the items into "the alligator's mouth" and taking them out again at the end. Pretend items are just as much fun if real ones are not available.

Give each child control of an item.

5. LENGTH: A good story too long for reading to the youngest children that can be condensed by telling it.
Example: *Oh, Kojo! How Could You!* (1984), by Verna Aardema, Marc Brown, illustrator

Written in folk tale style, this delightful African story combines the various aspects of a formula tale (from trickery and tasks to repetition of phrases and sounds), as it sends Kojo, a magic son, to try to outwit Ananse, the trickster. Children love the story, but preschoolers often find it too long for their limited attention spans. Yet it lends itself especially well to oral telling because the teller can control its length by shortening the episodes and involving the audience directly when they get restless by mentioning the River-that-Gurgles and having the listeners respond with the river sound: "Pon-pon-pon-PON-sa."

🎋 How Can You Prepare a Story for Telling?

Once you have chosen your story for telling, the next step is preparation. You will need to learn the story first of all, and then deliver it in a manner to interest and excite the children. To "learn" a story does not mean to memorize it. It is not necessary to tell the story by heart. It is *your words* you will be using, not only the author's words. Guidelines to help you prepare a story for telling include:

1. Read the story through more than once, noting characters, dialog, and plot.

2. Decide which characters to include and how to speak for them.

AUTHORS *of INTEREST*   VERNA AARDEMA from Michigan converts African folklore into stories for children after a great deal of research. She has been writing since she was eleven years old, even during her twenty-five years as an elementary teacher. (Hurst, 1990, 3)

3. Decide how to begin the story to catch the children's attention.

4. Decide on three to five incidents of the story to dramatize with your voice.

5. Decide how the ending of the story can be made dramatic. (Beaty, 1992, 139)

Then you must practice telling the story: to yourself under your breath, to a mirror to see how you look, to a tape recorder to hear how you sound, to someone in your family, to a passenger in your car—however and whatever seems practical to you. No matter how you practice and learn the story, your children are going to enjoy the results and so will you.

The Doorbell Rang is a simple story to begin with. As you read the story to yourself, you will note there are three main characters who speak: Ma and the children Victoria and Sam. Ma bakes a dozen cookies, so Victoria and Sam will each have six cookies to share between them. Each time the doorbell rings before anyone can eat, other children come in, making fewer cookies to share:

1. Tom and Hannah from next door (three cookies each)

2. Peter and his brother (two cookies each)

3. Joy and Simon and their four cousins (one cookie each)

On the final ring no one wants to answer the door because there aren't enough cookies for anyone else, but when they do answer, in comes Grandma with a huge new plate of cookies to share. The different characters always repeat the same words about the cookies: "They look as good as Grandma's"; "They smell as good as Grandma's." Then Ma always says: "No one makes cookies as good as Grandma."

🕉 How Can You Deliver Your Story?

You may want to begin the story as you sit with the children around you by showing them the book itself, and then putting it aside as you say: "Today I am going to *tell* you this story in my words, rather than *read* the story from the book." As soon as they are quietly attentive you can begin.

As teller you don't have to memorize the names of the children from the book, for your children will become more excited to hear *their own names* instead. Each time you tell the story, change the names and the order of the children to create suspense. You may want to "ring the doorbell" as many times as it takes to include all of the children in your group. *The Doorbell Rang* makes a good large-group story for this very reason: children wait for their names to be called with great eagerness. Whether or not you use the particular *number* of cookies to be shared is not important unless you are stressing this aspect of sharing in your curriculum. Then the story can be a teaching experience for learning how to "divide up" a number of items.

Children whose names are called can also participate in the telling by speaking a line of dialog themselves: "They look as good as Grandma's"…"They smell as good as Grandma's." You can create further interest by "ringing the doorbell" in some clever or distinctive way: use a real buzzer; or make a ringing, buzzing, or ding-dong sound with your voice; or by pointing to a child listener who must then "ring" the bell with his or her own voice.

The surprise at the end is of course Grandma herself with her plate of cookies. Some storytellers create great suspense at the end of stories like this by waiting... doing nothing after the doorbell rings...until audience anticipation is built up to the bursting point before the story is finally concluded. You may also want to conclude this story by having all of your listeners shout out the last line together: "No one makes cookies as good as Grandma!"

If your children enjoy this story, they may want to make it real someday by baking their own cookies and dramatizing the narrative. It is also an excellent story to tell whenever there is something to share. You, of course, can substitute "cookies" with another item if this seems appropriate, because once you have told a story you have made it your own.

Because it is important for the children to understand that this story comes from a picture book, you will want to *read* the story as well, perhaps to one or two children at a time in your Story Center. However you do it, be sure to display the book on a shelf in the Story Center for the children to look at by themselves. You may even find them playing the doorbell game on their own.

Simple? Yes, storytelling really is simple, especially if you have chosen your story carefully with your own and your children's interests at heart. You and they may enjoy the results so much you may never want to *read* from a book again! Or as Chase Collins tells us in her excellent book on storytelling:

> Storytelling, like learning how to "pump" on a swing, is a matter of finding the force, energy, and delight you were born with. Once you've learned how to kick up your heels, you'll never be left hanging. Once you've got the rhythm of it, know when to bend and when to stretch, you and your child are ready to swing up, out, and back again on what will become one of the most memorable, freeing, exhilarating experiences of your lives. Rainy days, ice storms, frayed ropes will never stop you; in fact, they will inspire you in the quiet art of storytelling. (Collins, 1992, 4)

✤ Advantages of Picture Book "Reading"

You realize, though, that most picture books by their nature are made for reading to children rather than telling. All of the books described in this chapter, for instance, can be *read* aloud as well as *told* to children. But certain books should be read exclusively rather than told, in order for children to understand the story or gain particular value from the book and its illustrations. Reading any picture book to young children:

1. makes them directly aware that the story comes from a book that they may handle afterwards.

2. helps them become aware of the function and use of written language as used in a book.

3. introduces children to literary language and new vocabulary.

4. helps them to understand the story through use of illustrations.

5. helps them develop an aesthetic sense through the quality of the illustrations.

6. helps them learn to love books and want to read them independently.

7. helps them develop a sense of story.

Books that are better read than told will contain:

1. SPECIAL WORDS: Words that must be spoken exactly as they appear on the pages in order to give the book its special quality.

2. SPECIAL PICTURES: Pictures that are necessary to give the words their special meaning.

3. PAGE TURNING: A story whose action is tied to the turning of the pages.

Picture books containing one or more of the criteria above are especially enjoyed by small groups of children or individuals who can sit as close as possible to the teacher as the story is being read. Then they are able to see the book's words and illustrations, and thus able to follow the action. Some examples of such books include:

1. SPECIAL WORDS: Words that must be spoken exactly as they appear on the pages in order to give the book its special quality.
Example: *The Sneetches and Other Stories* (1961), by Dr. Seuss

All of Dr. Seuss's delightful books with their absurd characters and comical illustrations are written in rhyme. They need to be read aloud exactly as they are written in the author's words rather than in a storyteller's words, and with the illustrations shown as the pages are turned. *The Sneetches,* as with Seuss's other stories, is a humorous morality tale, this time about the Star–Belly Sneetches who discriminate against the Plain–Belly Sneetches. Even children who sometimes memorize much of the story want it read from the book over and over, so they can laugh at pictures of the preposterous characters and their hilarious predicaments.

AUTHORS
of **INTEREST**

DR. SEUSS, the pen name for Theodore Seuss Geisel, spent his early career drawing crazy animals for commercial ads. Since 1937 his inventive imagination and creative cartoonist's pen have created dozens of zany book characters (Horton, the Grinch, the Cat in the Hat, Yertle the Turtle) who must cope with an array of human characteristics such as selfishness, swelled heads, arrogance, and discrimination. His books follow a formula of building up tension to the bursting point, and then pricking the balloon. (Hurst, 1990)

Children need to see the illustrations in certain books to understand the story.

2. SPECIAL PICTURES: Pictures that are necessary to give the words their special meaning.
Example #1: *In the Attic* (1984), by Hiawyn Oram, Satoshi Kitamura, illustrator.

This author and illustrator combine to portray a magical world in a little boy's attic, which he visits on a day when he is bored. Children need to see the fantastic pictures of mice colonies, talking tigers, and imaginary worlds that accompany the simplest of texts (such as "I found a family of mice…") in order to understand what is really happening, especially when the boy's mother later protests that they don't even have an attic.

3. PAGE TURNING. A story whose action is tied to the turning of the pages.
Example: *Is Your Mama a Llama?* (1989), by Deborah Guarino; Steven Kellogg, illustrator

This recent picture book that has already become a favorite of preschoolers is also necessary for them to view as they hear the story. As a little llama poses his title question, "Is your mama a llama?" to each animal he meets, the reader must turn the page to discover what the animal's mama really is. Rhyming sentences give additional hints to the listeners who greatly enjoy this animal guessing game.

✤ How Can You Prepare a Story for Reading?

Many teachers assume that it is unnecessary to *prepare* to read a story to children. All they need to do is pick up the book and begin. They may or may not get through the story successfully, especially if they have never seen the book before and have no idea what the words are or what is coming next in the story. Other teachers realize that book reading is not just an activity to fill up time, but instead it is as important in the curriculum as an art or science project; this means that it takes planning and preparation. Guidelines for story reading that have proved helpful to teachers include:

1. Read the book through ahead of time, aloud if possible.

2. Decide how to introduce the book to get the children's attention.

3. Decide what words or dialog to dramatize with your voice.

4. Decide what follow-up activities to use, and prepare them.

Reading the story aloud ahead of time will help prepare you for possible pronunciation problems or tongue twisters. In *The Sneetches* you should be prepared for the rhymes at the ends of every sentence, sometimes with unusual words like "thars" to rhyme with "stars," as well as the tongue twisting sentences such as "this one was that one, or that one was this one, or which one was what one, or what one was who." If you haven't practiced ahead of time, you may very well stumble over words when you read them cold, which would certainly deprive your children of the best of Dr. Seuss.

How will you introduce this book in order to get the children's attention? It is no use to start reading if the children are not listening. An effective introduction for most books is to show children the cover of the book, and then ask a question or make a comment about the cover. For example, you might say: "Did you ever hear of a 'sneetch'? The book I am going to read today is called *The Sneetches*. It has a picture of two sneetches on the cover. Do you see them? What do you think about them? If you look very closely you might see something else: something special on their tummies. Do you see it? You're right: a star. That's what this story is all about. Let's listen."

The one and only character with dialog in this story is the Fix-it-Up Chappie, Sylvester McMonkey McBean. You may want to dramatize his voice by reading his words in gruff, or squeaky, or even smooth tones. Try it ahead of time to see what suits you best.

For a follow-up activity be sure to have several sheets of peel-off stars. You can do whatever you or the children want with them. All sorts of activities are possible. The children can have their own stars which they secretly stick on or take off themselves. When everyone's back is turned, one child or the teacher can try to guess which children have a star on their shirt or belly or forehead. Which is better, having a star on or a star off? Why? You can talk about how the Sneetches with stars or without stars felt, or how your children feel with stars on or stars off. After all, this is a story about discrimination by the Sneetches with stars on their bellies against those with no stars on "thars."

Children can also buy stars with play money from the teacher or another child representing Sylvester McMonkey McBean. A special day can be declared as "Star-On Day" or "Star-Off Day." Children's imagination and creativity can devise other lively schemes if they respond well to *The Sneetches.* Such activities are possible only if teachers prepare for reading stories ahead of time.

A further plus for this story is that its rhyming structure makes it "a predictable book," that is, a story that helps children predict what word or incident is coming next. Once they are familiar with the rhymes in this book, children who are progressing through the stages of emergent literacy may begin to anticipate what comes next, an important ingredient in learning how a book works and in making sense of print. (Schickedanz, 1986, 51–58)

What Else Can You Do With a Story?

Telling stories and reading them to children is just the beginning—just the jumping off place for ideas that will stimulate youngsters to participate in every activity you offer them. The picture books in your classroom are, in fact, dynamic cores of creativity just waiting to explode into every corner of your curriculum.

What Can You Do With a Story Besides Tell It?
Sing it
Whisper it
Shout it
Dance it
Act it out
Guess what happens next
Rename the characters
Tell it to a doll
Tape record it
Videotape it
Make up your own version of it
Make pictures of it
Make up new words for it
Pretend to be a character in it

These ideas are just of few of the activities both teachers and children can perform after the telling of a favorite story. Similar story-extension ideas make up the core of this text. For every story told there are numerous activities teachers and children can become involved with that will lead them on to undreamed of accomplishments. Storytelling, in fact, can be a springboard into an entire early childhood curriculum.

And picture book reading? Does that have its own special schemes?

What Can You Do With a Book Besides Read It?
Make a game of it
Make a puzzle of it
Make puppets of its characters
Make costumes for its characters
Make masks for its characters
Make a shadow play of it
Make a feltboard of it
Make a play of it
Make sound effects for it
Write your own version of it
Identify butterflies with it
Introduce a new topic with it
Build with blocks about it
Cook food from it

It should be obvious by now that merely telling a story or reading a book to your children is only the tip of an immense iceberg of activities awaiting them. The following chapters of this text present such books and stories with suggestions for reading them or telling them to your children, with ideas for follow-up activities, and with possibilities for you and your children's own creativity within the dynamic world of *Picture Book Storytelling*.

REFERENCES CITED

Beaty, J.J. (1992), *Preschool Appropriate Practices*. Fort Worth, Tex.: Harcourt Brace Jovanovich.

Collins, C. (1992), *Tell Me a Story*. Boston: Houghton Mifflin Co.

Edelsky, C., Atwerger, B., and Flores, B. (1991), *Whole Language, What's the Difference?* Portsmouth, N.H.: Heinemann.

Friedberg, B. and Strong, E. (1989), "'Please don't stop there!': The power of reading aloud." In J. Hickman and B.E. Cullinan, *Children's Literature in the Classroom: Weaving Charlotte's Web* (pp. 39–48). Needham Heights, Mass.: Christopher-Gordon Publishers.

Janssen, D.H. and Beaty, J.J. (1988), *Storytelling Mark Twain Style*. Elmira, N.Y.: McGraw Bookstore, Elmira College.

Hurst, C.O. (1990), *Once Upon a Time...An Encyclopedia for Successfully Using Literature with Young Children*. Allen, Tex.: DLM.

Maguire, J. (1985), *Creative Storytelling*. New York: McGraw-Hill Book Co.

Mills, H. and Clyde, J.A. (1991), "Children's Success as Readers and Writers: It's the Teacher's Beliefs That Make the Difference," *Young Children* 46(2) 58.

Pratt, L. (1992), "Providing a Sound Rich Environment." (unpublished paper).

Schickedanz, J.A. (1986), *More Than the ABCs: The Early Stages of Reading and Writing*. Washington, D.C.: National Association for the Education of Young Children.

Schrader, C.T. and Hoffman, S. (1987), "Encouraging Children's Early Writing Efforts," *Day Care and Early Education* 15(2) 9–13.

OTHER STORYTELLING SOURCES

Baker, A. and Greene, E. (1977), *Storytelling Art & Technique*. New York: R. R.Bowker Co.

Barton, B. (1986), *Tell Me Another: Storytelling and reading aloud at home, at school and in the community*. Portsmouth, N.H.: Heinemann.

Barton, B. and Booth, D. (1990), *Stories in the Classroom: Storytelling, Reading Aloud and Roleplaying with Children*. Portsmouth, N.H.: Heinemann.

Bauer, C.F. (1977), *Handbook for Storytellers*. Chicago: American Library Association.

Bosma, B. (1987), *Fairy Tales, Fables, Legends, and Myths: Using Folk Literature in Your Classroom*. New York: Teachers College.

Breneman, L.N. and Breneman, B. (1985), *Once Upon a Time: A Storytelling Handbook*. Chicago: Nelson-Hall.

Burke, E.M. (1990), *Literature for the Young Child*. Boston: Allyn and Bacon.

Champlin, C. and Renfro, N. (1985), *Storytelling with Puppets*. Chicago: American Library Association.

Coody, B. (1992), *Using Literature with Young Children*. Dubuque, Iowa: Wm.C.Brown Co. Publishers.

Denman, G.A. (1991), *Sit Tight, and I'll Swing You a Tail...Using and Writing Stories with Young People*. Portsmouth, N.H.: Heinemann.

Glazer, J.I. (1990), *Literature for Young Children*. Columbus, Ohio: Merrill.

Greene, E. and Shannon, G. (1986), *Storytelling: A Selected Annotated Bibliography*. New York: Garland Publishing, Inc.

Hamilton, M. and Weiss, M. (1990), *Children Tell Stories; A Teaching Guide*. Katonah, N.Y.: Richard C. Owen Publishers, Inc.

Hamilton, M. and Weiss, M. (1991), "A Teacher's Guide to Storytelling," *Instructor* (May) 27-38.

Harrel, J. (1983), *Origins and Early Traditions of Storytelling*. Kensington, Calif.: York House.

Hart-Hewins, L. and Wells, J. (1990), *Real Books for Reading: Learning to Read with Children's Literature*. Portsmouth, N.H.: Heinemann.

Hough, R.A., Nurss, J.R. and Wood, D. (1987), "Tell Me a Story: Making Opportunities for Elaborated Language in Early Childhood." *Young Children* 43(1) 6-12.

Jalongo, M.R. (1988), *Young Children and Picture Books*. Washington, D.C.: National Association for the Education of Young Children.

Routman, R. (1991), *Invitations: Changing as Teachers and Learners*. Portsmouth, N.H.: Heinemann.

Rudman, N.K. (1989), *Children's Literature: Resource for the Classroom*. Norwood, Mass.: Christopher-Gordon.

Sawyer, W. and Comer, D.E. (1991), *Growing Up with Literature*. Albany, N.Y.: Delmar.

Stephens, D. (1991), *Research on Whole Language: Support for a New Curriculum*. Katonah, N.Y.: Richard C. Owens.

Teale, W.H. and Martinez, M.G. (1988), "Getting on the right road to reading: Bringing books and young children together in the classroom," *Young Children* 44 (1) 10-15.

Trelease, J. (1990), *The New Read-Aloud Handbook*. New York: Viking Penguin.

Wason-Ellam, L. (1991), *Start with a Story: Literature and Learning in Your Classroom*. Portsmouth, N.H.: Heinemann.

CHILDREN'S BOOKS

Aardema, V. and Brown, M. (ill.) (1984), *Oh, Kojo! How Could You!* New York: Dial Books for Young Readers.

Brandenberg, A. (1966), *Keep Your Mouth Closed, Dear.* New York: Dial Books for Young Readers.

Brown, M.W. (1947), *Goodnight Moon.* New York: Harper & Row.

Ets, M.H. (1963), *Gilberto and the Wind.* New York: The Viking Press.

Guarino, D. and Kellogg, S. (ill.) (1989), *Is Your Mama a Llama?* New York: Scholastic, Inc.

Hutchins, P. (1986), *The Doorbell Rang.* New York: Mulberry Books.

Oram, H. and Kitamura, S. (ill.) (1984), *In the Attic.* New York: Henry Holt & Co. Inc.

Seuss, Dr. (1961), *The Sneetches and Other Stories.* New York: Random House.

Slobodkina, E. (1968), *Caps for Sale.* New York: Scholastic, Inc.

Ungerer, T. (1959), *Crictor.* New York: Scholastic,Inc.

Wagner, J. and Brooks, R. (ill.) (1977), *John Brown, Rose and the Midnight Cat.* New York: Puffin.

VIDEOTAPES OF STORYTELLERS

American Storytelling: Vol.1, Jackson Gillman, Gayle Ross, Maggi Peirce. New York: H.W.Wilson Co.

American Storytelling: Vol.2, Ron Evans, Diane Wolkstein. New York: H.W. Wilson Co.

American Storytelling: Vol. 3, Heather Forest, Lynn Rubright, Laura Simms. New York: H.W.Wilson Co.

American Storytelling: Vol.4, Jon Spelman, Chuck Larkin. New York: H.W. Wilson Co.

American Storytelling: Vol.5, David Holt, Barbara Freeman and Connie Regan-Blake, Mary Carter Smith. New York: H.W.Wilson Co.

American Storytelling: Vol.6, Ed Stivender, Brother Blue, Jay O'Callahan. New York: H.W.Wilson Co.

American Storytelling: Vol.7, Elizabeth Ellis, Carol Birch, Michael Parent. New York: H.W.Wilson Co.

American Storytelling: Vol.8, Donald Davis, Marcia Lane. New York: H.W.Wilson Co.

Family Circle Presents Storyland Theater. A 4-volume set with tales by Rafe Martin, Laura Simms, and Jay O'Callahan.

Jackie Torrence: Two White Horses. Weston, Conn.: Weston Woods.

Jay O'Callahan: A Master Class in Storytelling. West Tisbury, Mass.: Vineyard Video Productions.

Jump Over the Moon: Storytelling. South Carolina Educational Television, Columbia, S.C. 29250.

Mark Twain Remembers (With Dale Janssen). Elmira, NY: McGraw Bookstore, Elmira College.

Storytelling with Carolyn Feller Bauer. New York: H.W.Wilson Co.

Storytelling with Joe Ferguson: Tips for Storytellers. Mt.Rainier, Md.: Gryphon House.

Tell Me a Story (Martha Hamilton and Mitch Weiss). Ithaca, NY: Beauty & the Beast Storytellers, P.O. Box 6624.

Where Stories Come From (Neil Inness, Jackie Torrence, Pete Seeger). Weston, Conn.: Weston Woods.

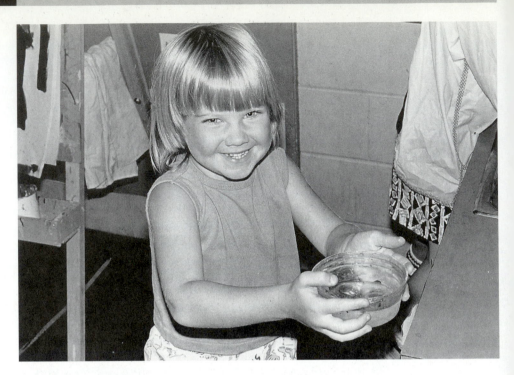

ME, MYSELF AND I TALES

Action Chant

Did you spy,	*(hand shading eyes, turn head)*
Someone shy,	
Try to fly	*(arms outstretched, flapping)*
Way up high?	
Not I!	*(arms at sides, shake head)*
Do you see?	*(hand shading eyes, turn head)*
Someone three,	
Try to ski	*(kneel on one knee)*
On one knee?	
That's me!	*(jump up)*

❧ Building a Positive Self-Image

Young children are highly egocentric beings. From infancy on, they have been a world unto themselves, using tears, laughter, words, and actions to draw attention to themselves alone. This is how the human species is designed to behave. Such self-centeredness serves as a survival mechanism for helpless infants and struggling toddlers. Crying brings feeding, changing, and comforting from adult caregivers. Laughter brings a playful response. Words, they learn, can command and demand.

When those around them respond positively so that the youngsters succeed in satisfying their wants and needs, they come to feel good about themselves. When they are ignored too frequently or responded to harshly, however, young children often begin to doubt their worth and may not develop strong positive feelings about themselves.

As preschoolers or kindergartners who come to your classroom, these children bring such feelings and attitudes with them, along with their own built-in individual natures. But now they are no longer helpless infants and struggling toddlers. Now they must come to understand that there are others like themselves in their world, and that those others have needs to be satisfied as well. Suddenly the focus is no longer on them alone. They must learn to share and care and not always be first. It is an exciting, confusing, and sometimes traumatic time for children.

You, as the leader of such a group, realize that one of your primary goals will be to help the children develop and sustain this positive self-image, this good feeling about themselves as learners and worthy individuals.

❧ Choosing Picture Books to Support Children's Image Development

Picture books can help. The right picture books not only support children's image development, but also lead them to activities that can improve their relations with others and help them to achieve independence.

It is not always easy to choose the best books for young children. A hands-on acquaintance with the books is the best idea. Read the books aloud before you purchase them. Borrow them from the library and try them out with the children first. Become acquainted with new books by favorite authors. Choose books that contain some of these criteria:

1. Simple colorful illustrations
2. Brief text, easily read, so that pages can be turned quickly
3. Possibilities for converting books into puzzles, feltboard characters, or other fun extension activities
4. Topics that are part of your curriculum
5. A story line that lends itself to storytelling

(Beaty, 1992, 134)

How will you choose the appropriate books to support children's development of a positive self-image? Certain books will especially appeal to young children's egocentric natures if they contain:

Familiar characters
Familiar situations
Familiar settings

Young children need to be able to identify with a character or a situation that the character is involved with, or at the very least, with a familiar setting for the action of the story. A human character is best, you may decide, but not necessarily. Young children also relate very well to animal characters that act like people. Sometimes human characters resemble the children themselves too much for them to feel comfortable. Personified animals, on the other hand, are one step removed from real children, yet they can act and talk like children. This permits the child readers or listeners to project themselves freely into the animal character—more freely, perhaps, than they might be willing to do with a child character that reminds them too strongly of themselves. (Lewis, 1981, 124) In addition, preschool children and kindergartners love to pretend. With a talking-animal character, it is all pretending. Four animal-character books that fit this category of feeling good about yourself because of your successful accomplishments of are:

I Like Me!, by Nancy Carlson, 1988
Things I Like, by Anthony Browne, 1989
I Wish I Could Fly by Ron Maris, 1986
Ruby by Maggie Glen, 1990

I Like Me! *(1988), by Nancy Carlson, New York: Viking Penguin.* This small book for the youngest of your children, features a personified little girl pig engaged in dancing, painting, bicycling, reading, tooth-brushing, bathing, eating, roller skating, and making mistakes (falling down, dropping a cake). She speaks in the first person, telling readers what she enjoys doing and how much she likes herself even when she makes mistakes.

+ **Read**   Read the simple one-line text aloud while showing the full page illustrations to your listeners. Simple colorful pictures make it clear what is happening. Children like to hear the character say, "Hi, good-looking!" to herself in the mirror.

+ **Child Discussion**   After hearing the story children can tell what they themselves like to do best.

+ **Pantomime**   Ask a child to act out what he or she likes to do best and have the others try to guess.

+ **Mirror-talking**   Mirrors, both full-length and hand-held, should be available at all times for children's self-image development. After hearing this story, have children tell the mirror what they like to do or what they like about themselves.

+ **First-person Storytelling by Children**   If children show a positive response to this book, in other words, if they ask you to "read it again, teacher," then you should consider initiating storytelling by the children themselves, as well. First person narrative is the simplest form of storytelling for children. After you have read the book more than once, ask for a volunteer to stand up and tell his or her own story about why "I Like Me." Standing up to tell their own stories makes it an actual storytelling experience for children. Teachers can add to the enthusiasm by telling their own "I Like Me" stories.

Things I Like *(1989), by Anthony Browne, New York: Alfred A. Knopf.* Here is another small book for the youngest children about a little boy monkey who speaks in the first person telling how he likes to paint, ride his bike, play, climb, watch TV, and other activities. Each page shows a simple, colorful illustration of the monkey with a single line of text at the bottom.

+ **Read**   Read the book to individuals or a small group and let them comment on the activities that the monkey likes to do.

+ **Monkey Puppet or Stuffed Animal Monkey**   After reading the book to a small group, pass around a puppet or stuffed animal monkey, and have each child ask the monkey and then answer for him what he would like to do in the classroom. Creative children usually have interesting answers for the puppet. Animal hand puppets like this can be purchased as hot pad gloves in kitchen stores or museum gift shops.

+ **Pass-the-Monkey Game**   A pass-the-monkey game can be done on a daily basis, perhaps at circle time in the morning, to have the monkey puppet tell through the words of the child receiving the puppet what different things he sees in the classroom on that particular day that he would like to do, thus acquainting the other children with what activities are available.

+ **First-person Storytelling by Children**   If children like this book, you can encourage children's own storytelling. After you have read the book a second or third time, ask for volunteers to stand up and tell their own story about "Things I Like." This time have child volunteers record their stories in the Sound Center.

I Wish I Could Fly (1986), by Ron Maris, New York: Greenwillow Books. Another simple book for the youngest of preschoolers shows a turtle who meets a series of animals one at a time, and tries to perform like each of them (such as, fly like a bird, dive like a frog, climb like a squirrel, run like a rabbit), with disastrous results, until he finds his own special talent: snuggling inside his shell to keep dry when it rains.

+ Read   Marvelous "sound" words like "Crash! Bang! Wallop! Crunch!" are accompanied by striking double-page illustrations of the turtle and his friends that children need to see in order to understand the words. Read it to individuals or a small group. It is a wild and wonderful romp for children and turtle as both gain new words, experiences, and appreciation for special talents.

+ Pretend   Have your children pretend to be each of the animals by making that animal's motion as shown in the book. Then have the children invent new animal motions. Can the other children guess what new animal each child is demonstrating?

+ Sound Words   Read the book again, and let each child make his/her own sounds for the page where the turtle flops. Have each child tape record his sound words in the Sound Center described in Chapter 1, and then play them back for fun. Can the children make the sounds with their own voices? What other sound-makers could they use to make flopping, crashing, walloping, crunching noises? You may also want to record the story as you read it with the children making the sounds.

+ First-person Storytelling by Children   Here is another book that lends itself to children's telling a story about themselves. Most people wish they could do something they have never done before. After you have read this book more than once, ask for a child volunteer to tell his or her own "I Wish I Could..." story. Children who want can tape-record their stories in the Sound Center, or you can record their stories for them to listen to.

+ Story-writing by Children   If children enjoy telling stories about what they wish they could do, they may also want to write their own illustrated stories. They can begin by drawing a picture of what they wish they could do. For preschoolers who may not be at the representational stage in drawing skills, their scribbles are just as valid as representational drawings. Then have them "write" their story. Most prefer using the same page as their drawing. Preschoolers may make writing-scribbles instead of words for their stories. Child development specialists call this early pre-writing *personal script,* while regular writing is known as *conventional script.* Some kindergartners may have advanced naturally in their writing skills to the level of writing words with conventional script but in an *invented spelling* of their own. For example, some might write "I wish I could fly like a bird," as *I ws I cd fli lk brd* with invented spelling. (Schickedanz, 1986, 71–90; Sansome, 1988, 14–19)

Whatever children do in early writing, it is important that teachers accept it. Scribbling in writing is like babbling in speaking, a beginning level on the way to young children's natural development of literacy. Invented spelling is an advanced form of prewriting that most emergent writers use before they finally come to recognize conventional spelling. Story writing like this is often motivated by the presence of a Writing Center in the room.

If you have set up your classroom with a Writing Center as suggested in Chapter 1, it is only natural for children to write their own stories with the tools and paper provided for them. Have a bulletin board to display their work, or help them to make it into a book of their own.

Ruby (1990), *by Maggie Glen. New York: G.P. Putnam's Sons.* Ruby is the exuberant little stuffed bear who is put together wrong at the toy factory with spotted leopard material and a crooked nose. They stamp her paw "S" meaning "second," but she yells for joy, because for Ruby "S" means "special"! Even when she finds herself in a box full of seconds to be thrown away, Ruby turns the situation around by helping the second bears to escape. Ruby herself escapes to a toy store—where the unimpaired toys push her to the back of the shelf. But little Susie who is shopping with her grandfather chooses Ruby anyway. When they get home Ruby realizes that Susie also has an "S": a silver "S" hanging from a necklace around her neck. "Hooray," exclaims Ruby, "Susie's one of us—a special!"

+ Read   Read this book to children sitting close in order to see the large expressive pictures of Ruby and her bear buddies, as she turns a difficult situation into an advantage. Children with special needs may be able to identify with this special never-give-up little bear.

+ Stuffed Bear Game   Bring in a teddy bear to pass around to children in a small group. When a child gets the bear have her tell what she would do if she were put in a box of "seconds" like Ruby was.

+ Experience Chart Writing   What experiences can a stuffed bear like Ruby have in your classroom? Set your stuffed bear on a chair next to an experience chart (or newsprint paper taped to an easel), and have the children use their imaginations to dream up new adventures for the bear. You can transcribe their dictated stories on pages of newsprint to be read back from time to time. If children like the stories they have created and want them read back often, they may soon be able to "read" it themselves. Be sure to have the children who helped make up the stories sign their names on the newsprint pages.

Choosing Picture Books to Support Children's Relating Well to Others

As you work with young children, you soon come to realize that there is more to developing a child's self-image than reading books about feeling good. A child's self-worth in your classroom often hinges mainly on one factor more than any other, *success:* 1) the success of the child in relating well with others in the classroom, and 2) the success of the child in accomplishing things for him or herself.

If this is a child's first experience with a group of other children, he or she may not succeed at the outset in getting along with the others. She may be too aggressive or too shy. Other children may reject or ignore her. In order to help such a child, you need to be aware that success in relating well to others involves at least two elements:

1. ATTENTION: Getting the attention of others
2. ACCEPTANCE: Accepting others and being accepted by them

• *Getting the Attention of Others*

Successfully getting the attention of other children is not all that easy for some children. What should they do, stand around and look friendly? Push their way into a group activity? Grab someone's toy and run? Picture books can help. Light–hearted picture books featuring attention and acceptance are the best ones to use with children whether or not relationship problems occur. Three popular books that address *attention-getting* on the part of children include:

Milton the Early Riser, by Robert Kraus, Jose Aruego, and Ariane Dewey (ill.), 1972
Even That Moose Won't Listen to Me, by Martha Alexander, 1988
Nobody Listens to Andrew, by Elizabeth Guilfoile; Mary Stevens (ill.), 1973

Milton the Early Riser *(1972), by Robert Kraus; Jose Aruego and Ariane Dewey (illustrators), New York: Windmill Books, Inc. and E.P.Dutton & Co.* Milton is a panda bear who wakes up early, goes out to play, but finds nobody to play with. The "Creeps" and "Nincompoops" and all the other colorful critters are still asleep. Robert Kraus, accompanied by Aruego and Dewey's distinctive artwork, gives children a large-size picture book to enjoy. Even with strange animals it is a world they know well. Like Milton, they too often sing up a storm and mess up their world, but by the time everyone finally wakes up, they have long since gone back to sleep.

+ Read   Large pages full of exotic animal sleepers of every kind and color almost demand that this book be read to individuals or small groups. Children need to spend as much time as necessary gazing at the pictures to discover the snoozing critters tucked away in trees, engulfed in greenery, or dozing amid blossoms.

+ Feltboard   Books with large distinct pictures of the characters and the simple action like this lend themselves to conversion into feltboards. Buy an extra paperback copy of the book, cut out the characters and some of the trees, and mount them on oaktag cardboard. It is best to do this when children are not around to see and copy a book being cut up. Next cut the characters out of the cardboard and fasten an adhesive backing on each: something that will stick the character to the feltboard but pull away easily (such as felt, sandpaper, Velcro). For the board itself, use a commercial board or make your own with felt mounted to cardboard. To make individual boards for single children, use precut felt squares found in sewing centers or hobby shops and glue them to cardboard squares. Children enjoy moving Milton around the board trying to wake up the animal sleepers until finally he "sings up a storm" that shakes all of the critters off the board. Then he must pick them up and try to put the world back together again. Finally the sleepers wake up but Milton himself has fallen asleep. Children love to play the Milton story on a felt board again and again. Partners or small groups like to "sing up a storm" with songs they have learned in the classroom, while the animals are being shaken off the board. Keep the book characters in a separate manila envelope with the cover of the paperback copy mounted on its front for children's easy selection from the Story Center or Sound Center shelf.

+ Stuffed Panda Bear   Bring in a stuffed panda bear and have him tell the story of what happens when he wakes up early. Have your children listeners pretend to be asleep as Milton goes around and tries to wake them. Another day let one of the listeners hold your panda, tell the story, and try to wake the other "sleepers."

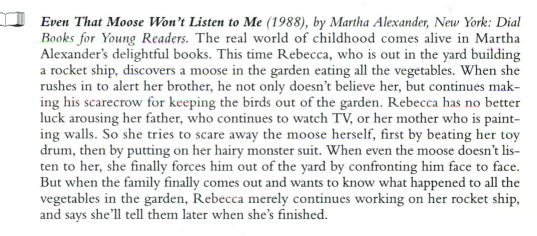

Even That Moose Won't Listen to Me *(1988), by Martha Alexander, New York: Dial Books for Young Readers.* The real world of childhood comes alive in Martha Alexander's delightful books. This time Rebecca, who is out in the yard building a rocket ship, discovers a moose in the garden eating all the vegetables. When she rushes in to alert her brother, he not only doesn't believe her, but continues making his scarecrow for keeping the birds out of the garden. Rebecca has no better luck arousing her father, who continues to watch TV, or her mother who is painting walls. So she tries to scare away the moose herself, first by beating her toy drum, then by putting on her hairy monster suit. When even the moose doesn't listen to her, she finally forces him out of the yard by confronting him face to face. But when the family finally comes out and wants to know what happened to all the vegetables in the garden, Rebecca merely continues working on her rocket ship, and says she'll tell them later when she's finished.

+ Tell   Here is an excellent story for telling aloud first before you read it to the children. Following the criteria for choosing *storytelling* books as mentioned on page 12, this book has a set order of plot incidents easily remembered:

> Rebecca spies the moose
> Rebecca tells her brother
> Rebecca tells her father
> Rebecca tries to scare the moose with her drum
> Rebecca tells her mother
> Rebecca tries to scare the moose with her monster suit
> Finally the moose goes
> The family comes outside

The book also has one or two characters who do most of the speaking, and it has repetition of both the speaking and the incidents. Tellers can make the story their own by using their own words such as "But they just wouldn't listen to me!" If the children like your storytelling, leave the book in the Story Center for them to look at on their own. Will they discover the front and back end-page illustrations that give an added dimension to the wily moose?

+ Vegetable Guessing Game   What vegetables did the moose eat? If your children enjoyed this book, play a vegetable guessing game with them. Cut out pictures of several vegetables from a seed catalog or the fronts of seed packages: beans, beets, lettuce, cabbage, carrots, or use plastic vegetables from the Dramatic Play Center. Make sure the children can identify the vegetables first. Then have them put their hands over their eyes while you remove one of the pictures or vegetables. Then ask them, "Which vegetable did the moose eat?" Make it easy for beginners by having only three vegetables. Add more as the children become good guessers.

+ Plant Seeds   This book is a good lead-in for planting vegetables. Since bean seeds are large and grow quickly, these are good to start with. Each child can plant several in a plastic cup of dirt. Plant a few extra cups in case some seeds do not germinate. The children will want to keep track of the growth of their vegetables, watering them when necessary. As you have noted, these book activities may support either the theme of the text chapter or incidents from the picture book in order to bring children and books together for many purposes.

Nobody Listens to Andrew (1973), by Elizabeth Guilfoile; Mary Stevens, illustrator. New York: Scholastic Books. This paperback reissue of a classic picture book from the 1950s tells the story of Andrew who discovers a bear in his bed, but finds that nobody will listen to him or believe him. When they finally do, pandomonium breaks out as various community helpers arrive with sirens blaring.

+ Read   Children enjoy hearing this story read aloud because of the sound words made by the vehicles and people as they arrive at Andrew's house to deal with the bear. To capture your children's attention at first, tell them the title of the story and then ask them why they think nobody would listen to Andrew. Would *they?* Ask them to guess what they think Andrew had to say. Then start reading. When you come to the sound words, try making the sounds themselves rather than reading the words.

+ Getting Attention   How do your children get the attention of an adult or other family member when they have something to say? Talk with a small group of your

AUTHORS *of INTEREST*   JOSE ARUEGO and ARIANE DEWEY have illustrated many of Robert Kraus's books, but they also write and illustrate their own. Ariane Dewey's favorite book when she was little was a fish catalog from a museum. Jose Aruego, formerly a lawyer, has collaborated with her to produce dozens of books full of their unique animal characters. (Hurst, 1990, 17)

children after reading this book and ask for their personal opinions. Ask how they would try to get the attention of someone else in the classroom. Can they demonstrate? Let a child from your group try to get another child's attention. Then let one of your children try to get another staff member's attention. Does it work? Talk about the results with the group.

• *Accepting Others and Being Accepted by Them*

In addition to getting the attention of others, young children also need to be successful in *accepting others and being accepted by them*. Several picture books speak to this aspect of relating well to others:

Oliver Button Is a Sissy, by Tomie de Paola, 1979
The Balancing Girl by Berneice Rabe; Lillian Hoban, (ill.), 1981
Frederick by Leo Lionni, 1967
Rise and Shine, Mariko-chan!, by Chiyoko Tomoika; Yoshiharu Tscuchida (ill.), 1992

Oliver Button Is a Sissy (1979), by Tomie de Paola, New York: Harcourt Brace Jovanovich. This small-sized book with simple illustrations depicts young Oliver Button who prefers to read, draw pictures, and dance rather than play ball with the boys. The boys at school tease him and write "OLIVER BUTTON IS A SISSY" on the school wall. But his parents send him to dancing school and he eventually tap dances in a talent contest. Although Oliver doesn't win, his classmates are so impressed that they change the sign on the school wall to read "OLIVER BUTTON IS A STAR."

+ Read   The story is more appropriate for your six-year-olds than for preschoolers who seldom show concern over sissy problems. The older children can appreciate the story and even talk about things that they or others like to do that are different.

+ Talent Show   Children who are interested can have a talent show for the others to watch. This can be impromptu with no practicing and no winners or losers. Make a stick microphone and be the master of ceremonies for children who want to sing, dance, play a toy instrument, stand on one leg, balance a block on their head, or any other act they can create on the spot. For children who are shy about performing in front of others, have them record their performance on a tape in the Sound Center.

The Balancing Girl (1981), by Berniece Rabe; Lillian Hoban, illustrator, New York: E.P.Dutton. This story of Margaret, a first grader who uses leg braces, crutches, and a wheelchair, shows how good she is at classroom activities involving balancing. Tommy, who has an acceptance problem, belittles her accomplishments, saying he could do better. The problem is resolved at the school carnival where Margaret's activity makes the most money and Tommy gets his name drawn to be the one to push down Margaret's intricate domino structure.

AUTHORS
of **INTEREST**

MARTHA ALEXANDER has lived and worked across the continent and beyond, from Augusta, Georgia to Hawaii, to Washington State. Her characters are young children expressing the true emotions and realistic dilemmas of childhood. Simple drawings, in pen and watercolor against a white background, show open-mouthed children with the words of a text that is completely dialog in a line or two at the top or bottom of the pages. (Hurst, 1990, 8)

+ Read or Tell   Although this story features older children, preschoolers and kindergartners can still appreciate it. It is an excellent book for illustrating how well a differently-abled child fits into a regular classroom. If the text seems too long for the youngest children, the reader can "tell" the story about Margaret from the pictures. A story like this conveys an important message to the children: that all of them are special human beings with talents.

+ Domino Balancing   It is important to have a set of dominoes on hand after reading this book. Either regular size or giant dominoes standing on end in a line make a challenging and fun balancing game. Children will need to use their best small motor skills to line up the blocks without knocking them over. They may want to draw a name out of a hat as in the story to choose the "pusher." Other balancing activities with blocks, felt-tip markers, and cylinders as shown in the book give additional small motor practice.

+ Crutch Balancing   Bring in a pair of children's crutches and have children take turns trying to walk with them on one leg. Talk about the special skills needed to overcome disabilities.

Frederick (1973), by Leo Lionni, New York: Knopf/Pantheon. One of a number of popular animal fables created and illustrated with unique collage effects by Leo Lionni, Frederick is the tale of a different little mouse who gathers sun rays, colors, and words for the long winter days ahead, rather than the usual corn, nuts, wheat, and straw like his four brother mice. When the food runs out in the winter, Frederick shares his supplies of sunlight, colors, and words to great acclaim as a mouse poet.

+ Read   Here is another picture book children must look at as the teacher reads the words. Be sure the group is small enough to gather close for picture-looking. Can they tell which mouse is Frederick?

+ Collage   After reading the story to a small group, get out collage supplies: torn and cut colored construction paper, tissue paper, buttons, seeds, pipe cleaners, dried corn kernels, dried flowers, scissors, paste, felt-tip markers of rainbow colors, and backing paper. Older children who do representational art may want to recreate Frederick's world. Others can make up their own world.

+ Poetry Reading   If children respond well to Frederick's poem about the seasonal mice, they may want to hear other poems about seasons by human poets. *Stopping by Woods on a Snowy Evening* (1978), is a most unusual picture book rendition of Robert Frost's famous poem with white-on-gray double-page woodland pictures by Susan Jeffers. A line or two of poetry for every two pages makes this also a book to look at. Children love to search for the snowy birds and shadowy animals hiding in its pages.

+ Cutting out Snowflakes   Children can cut out snowflakes like some of the Jeffers' book pictures by folding a square of white paper several times to make the smallest square they can, and then cutting off the corners and opening it up.

Rise and Shine, Mariko-chan! (1992) *by Chiyoko Tomioka; Yoshiharu Tsuchida (illustrator), New York: Scholastic, Inc.* Little Mariko-chan is the youngest of her three sisters, but well accepted by them and her Japanese mother, father, and grandmother. Mariko thinks being littlest is best and her mother agrees that it is—for her. The story of this friendly Japanese family as they get up in the morning and prepare for school or work could be any family anywhere where family members respect one another. With the focus on little Mariko, your children can come to feel that being the littlest is a good thing anywhere in the world.

+ Read   Children need to sit close to the reader to see what Japanese children and their customs are like. Are they surprised at how much like an American family they seem? Can they find anything in the illustrations that is different? What do they do when they get up in the morning before coming to your class?

+ Making a Promise   What is a promise? In this story Mariko's mother promises to bring home strawberries on the way home from work. She says, "I promise, promise, double promise." Then she and Mariko linked pinkie fingers to seal the promise. Can your children promise to do something? Would they like to do the saying and link fingers? Let one or two try it each day with something simple such as helping to pick up the blocks or rinsing out the easel paintbrushes.

Choosing Picture Books to Support Children's Being Able to Accomplish Things on Their Own

It is important for young children to accomplish things on their own in order to bolster a good feeling about themselves. Self-help skills are a case in point. Preschool and kindergarten children can dress themselves, put on outside clothing, zip zippers, and even in some cases tie their shoes successfully. Within the classroom they can set tables for snack or meals, pour their own milk, dish out their own food, get out materials and clean up afterward. In addition, children should be able to complete successfully the activities available in the classroom. Encouragement on your part and practice on theirs is what it takes. However, if children have never been encouraged to do things on their own, they may not succeed in these ventures at first. They may not even want to try. You should be aware of the elements that make a difference:

AUTHORS
*of **INTEREST***

TOMIE DE PAOLA is one of the most prolific picture book writers and illustrators in America with more than 200 books to his credit. From his studio in a converted New Hampshire barn he produces a new Christmas book every year, in addition to many more on subjects ranging from witches (*Strega Nona*) to Indian legends (*The Legend of the Bluebonnet*) to food (*Pancakes for Breakfast*). (Hurst, 1990, 44)

1. MATURITY: Growing up physically
2. INITIATIVE: Trying to do things on your own

There are a great many picture books that speak to these elements of children growing up and doing things on their own. To choose them, be sure to consider first of all the criteria for choosing any picture book as mentioned on page 26:

1. Simple, colorful illustrations
2. Brief text
3. Book extension possibilities
4. Curriculum topics
5. Storytelling possibilities

• *Growing Up Physically*

Young children yearn to be as big as their older siblings and friends. They hear their parents tell them to "be a big boy" or "big girl." They see "the big kids" doing all the "neat things" they themselves would like to do, and they can't even reach the light switch! Books that treat this topic of growing up with great gusto include:

Titch, by Pat Hutchins, 1971
Leo the Late Bloomer, by Robert Krause; Jose Aruego, (ill.), 1971
Much Bigger than Martin by Steven Kellogg, 1976

Titch (1971), by Pat Hutchins, New York: Viking Penguin, Inc. This is the first little "Titch" book, and meant for your youngest children, with only a line or two of large print on every page. Titch has a bigger sister and brother who have toys and tools bigger than his. But when it comes to planting, Titch's little seed grows into something bigger than all of them. Pat Hutchins' simple but captivating illustrations make this a book for looking at.

+ Read   This simple book with few words and fine pictures is best for reading to your children, listening to what they say, and then leaving it on the shelf of the Story Center for their own perusal afterward.

After hearing this story children can plant a seed and measure its growth once a week.

+ Measure Height Reading this book can be a stimulus for measuring the growth of things. Start with the children themselves. Measure each child's height by having them stand against a wall with a chart or paper backing in place. Mark and label each child's height with name and date. Several months later repeat the measuring to see if the child has grown.

+ Grow and Measure Plants After reading *Titch* the children can plant fast growing bean seeds in paper cups labeled with their names. Have them measure the growth of their seeds once a week with a ruler. Help them to draw a line the same height on a chart or graph, or help them to cut out a strip of paper the length of their plant and paste it on a labeled chart. Have them compare the measurements each week.

Leo the Late Bloomer *(1971), by Robert Kraus; Jose Aruego (illustrator), New York: Windmill and E.P.Dutton.* Another large colorful Kraus and Areugo book that has become almost a classic, this is the story of little tiger Leo who can't do anything right: neither read, write, draw, eat neatly, or speak. His father is very worried, but his mother assures him that Leo is just a late bloomer. His father watches but Leo doesn't bloom; his father tries not to watch but Leo doesn't bloom. Then in his own good time Leo finally bursts forth in a triumphant blaze of reading, writing, drawing, eating and speaking.

+ Tell The simple plot incidents, the character, and the repetition make this story easy to learn and tell aloud especially if you have an animal hand puppet. If it is a lion or tiger, all the better, but any interesting animal will do. In this case you will be speaking as narrator while your puppet acts out his role of not blooming and finally blooming. The Leo puppet does not speak until the very last words of the story.

AUTHORS
of INTEREST

LEO LIONNI was born in Amsterdam, Holland, and spent much time as a child in the art museum there. He knew he would become an artist when he grew up, and so he did after he moved to New York. From his first book *Little Blue and Little Yellow* made in 1959 for his grandchildren from torn paper because he had no drawing materials with him, to his original animal fables of the 1980s done in crayon, gouache and collage, many of his books express a strong moral. (Hurst, 1990, 74)

+ Read   Leave the book in the Story Center for the children to look at on their own. Read it when they ask you, especially to individuals and small groups who will be entranced with the visual feast of flowers, plants and animals a–blooming.

+ Make Leo's Garden Guessing Game   Buy an extra paperback copy of this book to be cut up for the characters of Leo, the owl, the elephant, the snake, the plover, and the crocodile. Mount them on posterboard disks. Then cut out double posterboard flowers big enough to hide the animal disks, and mount them on a cardboard garden floor. The object of the game is for children players to guess which animal is hidden inside each flower. If a child guesses correctly she gets to keep the animal until the next round. The child who locates Leo gets to hide the animals for the next round. Guessing games like this may start out as blind chance, but soon evolve into memory practice for young children.

 Much Bigger Than Martin *(1976), by Steven Kellogg, New York: The Dial Press.* Sometimes it's fun for the "I" narrator of this story to be Martin's little brother, but most of the time he hates it because the biggest one always goes first and always gets the biggest piece. This little brother tries various schemes to grow much bigger than Martin, but ends up sick from eating too many apples. In the end he finds a way by building a pair of stilts.

+ Read   Children need to see the comical pictures illustrating the text in this story, thus it is better read to individuals and small groups.

+ Make Tin Can Stilts   If children like the story and want to copy Martin's little brother's idea, rather than tall wooden stilts, they can make (with the teacher's help) tin can stilts. Ask children to bring two clean empty cans of the same kind from home with any sharp edges filed down. Holes need to be punched on opposite sides near the top of each can, and a cord or rope looped through the holes and up as far as the child's hand where it is tied to the other end of the loop. The child stands on the cans and holds them onto his feet with the looped cords. Let children practice walking on one can at a time before making a can stilt for the other foot. The youngest children can balance better on tuna cans. These stilts are also available commercially.

• *Trying to Do Things on Your Own*

Figuring out how to do something and then attempting it on your own is not always simple for preschool and kindergarten children. It is so easy for youngsters to fail. It is so easy for them to be blamed for doing something wrong. Thus, children who try on their own and succeed are a shining example for others. That may be why young children enjoy hearing stories about youngsters like themselves who do things successfully on their own. Several picture books feature this theme:

Amazing Grace, by Mary Hoffman; Caroline Binch, illustrator, 1991
Bravo, Tanya, by Patricia Lee Gauch; Satomi Ichikawa, illustrator, 1992
Cleversticks, by Bernard Ashley; Derek Brazell (ill.), 1991

Amazing Grace (1991), *by Mary Hoffman; Caroline Binch (illustrator), New York: Dial Books.* This large format book about Grace, an African-American girl who loves to act out stories, is quickly becoming the popular favorite of children and teachers alike. Large sensitive illustrations showing Grace entranced by her grandmother Nana's stories, Grace as Anansi the spider, Grace as a pegleg pirate with a parrot, or Doctor Grace saving the lives of Ma and Nana, have captivated almost every reader who has picked up the book. When Grace's teacher announces that the class will be putting on the play Peter Pan, Grace instantly knows who she wants to be: Peter Pan. Her classmates have other ideas: Raj says she can't because she's a girl; Natalie says she can't because she's black. But Nana takes Grace downtown on Saturday to the ballet Romeo and Juliet where a black Juliet from Nana's hometown in Trinidad is playing the title role. The next week Grace amazes everyone with her fantastic rendition of Peter Pan. She has learned the great lesson that she can be anything she sets her mind to be.

+ Read   This book deserves a close audience to see the striking illustrations of Grace nearly leap off the pages as she plays her roles with such realism.

+ Dramatize the Story   Put the book in the Dramatic Play Center along with a box of dress-up materials and let the children have fun creating their own characters just as Grace does. Read or tell an *Anansi the Spider* story or let the children view a videotape of *Peter Pan* to stimulate the dressing-up. Who else would they like to be? Children can create their own costumes and props just as Grace does if you provide them with a collection of cardboard pieces, aluminum foil, ribbons, belts, hats, bandanas, scarves, kerchiefs, and broom handles. Children may also want to play the character roles from other stories you have told or read.

Bravo, Tanya (1992), *by Patricia Lee Gauch; Satomi Ichikawa (illustrator), New York: Philomel Books.* Just as Grace loves to act, little Tanya loves to dance—anywhere, everywhere. She and her toy bear Barbara dance in the meadow, by the brook, and in her bedroom. But when it comes to ballet class where Tanya is the littlest, she can't seem to follow the teacher's loud clapping beat. Only when Tanya dances alone in the meadow can she hear the rhythm in the wind. One day the piano player happens to see Tanya dancing in the meadow. She claps and says "Bravo," and

Children enjoy playing with cutout figures of Leo's father who is spying on Leo for signs of blooming.

tells Tanya how she also hears in her music the wind in the trees and the waves on the beach. After that, Tanya listens for the piano music in the dance studio and is able to dance every step.

+ Read   Here is another story that children need to look at as they hear its words. Lovely realistic pictures bring to life the world of little girls in their Saturday morning ballet class. Your children may not understand ballet moves such as *pirouette* and *arabesque,* but they can appreciate the difficulty of a beginner trying to learn a new skill. Young children do not need to understand every word in every book you read. For many, the sounds of the words are more important than the meanings at this point in their development.

+ Do Creative Movement   Take the children outside when the wind is blowing. Can they stand and sway their bodies like the trees are swaying? Can they run with their arms outstretched to the feel of the wind? Then bring in a classical record or tape such as *The Nutcracker Suite, The Sorcerer's Apprentice, In the Hall of the Mountain King,* and have the children sit and listen first, swaying their bodies to the rhythm of the music. Then have them get up and move to the sounds.

+ Invite a Grandma Piano Player   Invite a grandmother who plays the piano to visit the class and play. Have the children move around the floor to the music.

+ Visit a Dance Studio   A nearby college may have a dance studio your children can visit. Often college dance students will volunteer to help young children do creative movement in the studio.

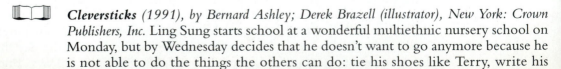

Cleversticks *(1991), by Bernard Ashley; Derek Brazell (illustrator), New York: Crown Publishers, Inc.* Ling Sung starts school at a wonderful multiethnic nursery school on Monday, but by Wednesday decides that he doesn't want to go anymore because he is not able to do the things the others can do: tie his shoes like Terry, write his name like Manjit, button his jacket like Sharon, or tie his painting apron in the back like Anis. His teachers Ms. Smith and Ms. Dhanjal have everyone clap when any of the children accomplishes something on his own. But Ling Sung is tired of clapping for everyone else. Then his cookies slide off his plate and break into pieces that he picks up naturally with two inverted paintbrushes held as chopsticks. Soon everyone is clapping for him and wanting to learn how to do it. His Dad calls him "cleversticks."

+ Read   Children should sit close to see the large double-page illustrations of these animated nursery school children. The text occurs in a line or two of large print at the top of the pages. Some children may try to pick out a word or two of the text, and most will surely laugh at the paintbrush chopstick scene where cookie pieces are bouncing everywhere.

+ Chopstick Practice   Be ready for chopstick practice with your children when you read this popular story. You can bring in real chopsticks for everyone, but children will also want to try inverted paintbrushes as the book shows. Be sure to have enough of the right size brushes. Have the children break their cookies into four pieces to make it easier. Learn how to use chopsticks first yourself at an Asian restaurant, or bring in someone to demonstrate. Do any of the children or their parents know how?

As you read or tell these fascinating stories to your children let them also help you decide what kinds of extension activities they would like to pursue on the road to strengthening their positive self-images.

The book activities included in this chapter and those to follow can also help young children improve in several areas of child development.

ACTIVITIES IN CHAPTER 2 TO PROMOTE CHILD DEVELOPMENT

Emotional

Mirror-talking *(I Like Me!)*

Social

Getting attention *(Nobody Listens to Andrew)*
Making a promise *(Rise and Shine, Mariko-chan)*

Physical

Pantomime *(I Like Me!)*
Sound Center *(I Wish I Could Fly)*
Domino balancing *(The Balancing Girl)*
Crutch balancing *(The Balancing Girl)*

Tin can stilts *(Much Bigger Than Martin)*
Measuring height *(Titch)*
Creative movement *(Bravo, Tanya)*
Chopstick practice *(Cleversticks)*

Cognitive

Pass-the-monkey game *(Things I Like)*
Leo's Garden Guessing Game *(Leo the Late Bloomer)*
Vegetable guessing game *(Even That Moose Won't Listen to Me)*
Planting seeds *(Even That Moose Won't Listen to Me)*
Measuring height; grow and measure plants *(Titch)*

Language

Child discussion *(I Like Me!)*
First-person storytelling *(I Like Me!)*; *(Things I Like)*; *(I Wish I Could Fly)*
Sound Center *(I Wish I Could Fly)*
Story-writing *(I Wish I Could Fly)*
Sound words *(I Wish I Could Fly)*
Stuffed bear game *(Ruby)*
Experience chart writing *(Ruby)*
Poetry reading *(Frederick)*
Dramatics *(Amazing Grace)*
Stuffed panda bear *(Milton the Early Riser)*

Creative

Pantomime *(I Like Me!)*
Monkey puppet *(Things I Like)*
Pretend *(I Wish I Could Fly)*
Felt board *(Milton the Early Riser)*;
Talent show *(Oliver Button Is a Sissy)*
Collage *(Frederick)*
Cutting out snowflakes *(Frederick)*
Creative movement *(Bravo, Tanya)*
Grandma piano player *(Bravo, Tanya)*
Dance studio *(Bravo, Tanya)*

REFERENCES CITED

Beaty, J.J. (1992), *Preschool Appropriate Practices*. Ft. Worth, Tex.: Harcourt Brace Jovanovich.
Frost, R. and Jeffers, S. (ill.) (1978), *Stopping By Woods on a Snowy Evening*. New York: E. P. Dutton.

Lewis, C. (1981), *Writing for Young Children*. Garden City, N.Y.: Anchor Press/Doubleday.

Sansone, R.M. (1988), "SKWL DAS: Emerging Literacy in Children," *Day Care and Early Education,* 16(1) 14–19.

Schickedanz, J.A., (1986), More Than the ABCs: *The Early Stages of Reading and Writing*. Washington, D.C.: National Association for the Education of Young Children.

OTHER CHILDREN'S PICTURE BOOKS ABOUT *ME, MYSELF, AND I*

Carle, E. (1984), *The Mixed-Up Chameleon*. New York: Harper & Row.

Caseley, J. (1991), *Harry and Willy and Carrothead*. New York: Greenwillow Books.

Daly, N. (1987), *Not so Fast Songololo*. New York: Viking Penguin, Inc.

Hutchins, P. (1971), *Happy Birthday, Sam*. New York: Viking Penguin, Inc.

Hutchins, P. (1983), *You'll Soon Grow into Them Titch*. New York: Viking Penguin, Inc.

Havill, J. (1989), *Jamaica Tag-Along*. Boston: Houghton Mifflin Co.

Jensen, V.A. (ill.) (1977), *Sara and the Door*. Reading, Mass.: Addison-Wesley Publishing Co.

Johnson, D. (1992), *The Best Bug To Be*. New York: The Macmillan Co.

Kraus, R. and Aruego, J. (1974), *Herman the Helper*. New York: Windmill Books and Simon & Schuster.

Lester, H. (1985), *It Wasn't My Fault*. Boston: Houghton Mifflin.

Lloyd, Errol. (1978), *Nini at Carnival*. New York: Thomas Y. Crowell.

Mathers, P. (1985), *Maria Theresa*. New York: Harper Collins.

McKissack, P.C. (1988), *Mirandy and Brother Wind*. New York: Alfred A. Knopf.

Pomerantz, C. (1989), *Flap Your Wings and Try*. New York: Greenwillow Books.

Scott, A.H. (1989), *Someday Rider*. New York: Clarion Books.

Wells, R. (1988), *Shy Charles*. New York: Dial Books.

Williams, V.B. (1983), *Something Special for Me*. New York: Mulberry Books.

Yashima, T. (1955), *Crow Boy*. New York: Viking Penguin, Inc.

3

FAMILY FROLICS

Action Chant

Mommy likes to water ski,	*(Arms forward; fists clenched)*
Daddy likes to swim;	*(Swim in place with arms)*
Tracy likes to snorkel,	*(Hold nose; turn head)*
Watch her kick her fins!	*(Kick one leg back)*
Uncle has a surf board,	*(Legs flexed; arms out; rock)*
Auntie a ski jet,	*(Squat; arms forward; fists)*
Grandpa likes to parasail,	*(Arms overhead; fists clenched)*
Me? I won't get wet!	*(Hug self and shake)*

✺ Families of Young Children

Young children are very much a product of their families. The way they talk, walk, and dress; their behavior; their health; even their likes and dislikes are strongly influenced by the families they come from. Large or small, rich or poor, single-parent, dual-career, culturally-diverse, or blended (families come in all kinds and makeups these days)—it is the child's family that is the most important influence in his or her life.

Just as you accept the child as a worthy person—no matter what she looks like, no matter how she talks, no matter what her ethnic background—so must you also accept her family. Her family is as much a part of her makeup as, say, the clothes she wears. Whether you like them is beside the point. Whether you agree with the family's behavior or lifestyle is also not the question. The child is a representative of her family, and you must accept them as you do her.

In doing so, you affirm for the child her place in the world. Your actions say to her, "I can connect with your family, just as I can connect with you." On the other hand, if your actions show that you do not accept her family or that you ignore them, it is very confusing for the young child. She is a part of them, and now she is trying to become a part of your class, a totally new world. The two should not be disconnected. This can tear a child in two. There should be communication, participation, and affirmation involving the roles each of you play in the child's life.

These roles are different. You are not the child's mother or father. You are not her principal caregiver. You are not even her most important teacher. Yours is a secondary, not a primary role, but a significant one, nevertheless. Together you and the child's family can assist and support the growth and development of the youngster who has come to your program.

Respecting a child's family enhances the child's self-esteem. Polly Greenberg, one of the original designers of Project Head Start's parent involvement component, believes that it is not the *amount of instruction* that schools give parents on how to "teach" their children, nor is it the *amount of parent involvement* in the schools that is critical, but instead: *"It seems to be the amount of respect given to the the parent that is relevant to children's attitudes… Knowing that her family and her school agree on who she is supposed to be simplifies the child's evolving self-image struggles."* (Greenberg, 1989, 62–63)

Greenberg's message to teachers of young children is this: *"We can reach out for and show respect for all of our children's families. This is part of enhancing the children's self-respect (self-esteem), which in turn leads to greater learning."* (Greenberg, 1989, 66).

✂ Home-Lending Library

Many teachers would like to build good connections with the families of their children, but do not know how to start. Picture books can help. Books and the use of them can bring teachers and families together just as they bring teachers and children together. Picture books tend to be pleasurable and non-threatening. The use of them in the classroom and then in the home can be the beginning of a positive relationship between school and home. And as Greenberg points out: *"When a member of a child's family takes part in his school life in a positive manner, even briefly and infrequently, the child's self-esteem appears to soar. Such positive participation sends a signal to the child: The family endorses this other world..."* (Greenberg, 1989, 62)

Teachers can promote this home-school interaction by providing a home-lending library of paperback picture books for children to borrow. Have a duplicate collection of the favorite classroom books for children to borrow at the end of the day. Children can borrow them one at a time and then return them the next day. Invite parents and grandparents to come in and listen with the children when you read a book or tell the story from a book. Invite them to read to the children themselves. Send home a newsletter on a monthly basis that tells the names of the books their children are using at the moment, and gives directions for some of the book extension activities they can make or do. Lend this textbook to parents if they show an interest in engaging in book activities. Treat your duplicate collection of paperback books as consumable items to be renewed every year. Then at the end of the year, let each child get to keep one or more of the books from the collection. In this way family members can also help bring children and books together.

Home-school activities can also be reciprocal. Ask parents to lend your program one of their children's favorite picture books. You or they can then read it to the children. What other books do their children like? You may want to order them for your classroom if they fit your needs. Be careful not to concentrate only on a few families in case only a few respond. Encourage all of your children's families to participate. If they look to you for suggestions of picture books to buy for their children, you can develop a bibliography for them from this text, or help to set up a book fair at your school where they can buy books.

✂ Families and Emergent Literacy

Research has found that parents play a crucial role in their children's development of literacy. (Morrow, 1989) According to Leichter (1984), families at home influence their children's development of the ability to read and write in three ways:

1. Interpersonal interaction

2. Physical environment

3. Emotional and motivational climate

Parents need to interact with their children during a literacy experience: that is, they need to read books to them, tell stories, read labels of food products or ask children to identify food products during grocery shopping, or read signs to children and ask them to identify signs. During book-reading, the adults need to interact with their listeners, asking children to "guess what comes next," or "what would you do if that happened to you?"

Then the home environment itself should be conducive to reading and writing. Educators talk about a "print-rich environment" in the classroom, meaning that the room is full of print: books, signs, labels, etc. Such an environment can be replicated at home, as well. Literacy materials such as books, newspapers, magazines, letters, cards, and calendars should be available and used by the family members. Parents of young children can have fun labeling the items in a child's bedroom, for instance, with the child's help. They can help set up a children's library corner in their room or some other accessible part of the house with books on a low shelf that children can reach. If the parents cannot afford to buy children's picture books, they can borrow them from your program or the public library. Children enjoy helping to select their own books at the library.

Finally, the emotional and motivational climate of the home should be conducive to reading and writing. Children should see their parents and older siblings reading books, magazines and newspapers for pleasure. They should see them writing letters and greeting cards. They should be encouraged to "read" and "write" on their own from materials available. Even families that concentrate on television can have cable channel program magazines available and encourage their children to look at them. In fact, reading material should be available throughout the home: in the living room, family room, playroom, kitchen, bedroom, and bathroom.

How is it with the families of your children? Do they engage in reading activities at home? Do they read or tell bedtime stories to their children? Are there books and other reading and writing materials available? Ask parents about this. Visit the homes yourself if parents agree. It is important for you to become aware of the environments from which your children come. Some teachers are uneasy about home-visiting, but taking a picture book along to share with the family is a wonderful ice-breaker. Then you can invite a family member to reciprocate by bringing a picture book of theirs to school to share with the children. When teachers come to understand their children's home environments, they can work even better with children at school.

✿ Picture Books About Families and Family Members

This chapter focuses on picture books about families and family members. The ideas presented can be used both in school and in the home. The five categories of books discussed here come from the books themselves, the kinds of picture books being published today about children and their families:

Mothers
Fathers
Brothers and Sisters
Grandparents
Differently-aligned Families

• *Mothers*

Mothers worry about their children, and children worry about their mothers. There is obviously great mutual concern in this closest of relationships throughout the lives of those involved. Children's picture books reflect this concern in many ways. Here are some of the books:

My Mom Travels a Lot, by Caroline Feller Bauer; Nancy Winslow Parker (ill.), 1981.
A Chair for My Mother, by Vera B. Williams, 1982.
Tucking Mommy In, by Morag Loh; Donna Rawlins (ill.), 1987.
My Mama Needs Me, by Mildred Pitts Walter; Pat Cummings (ill.), 1983.
Blueberries for Sal, by Robert McCloskey, 1948.

 My Mom Travels a Lot *(1981), by Caroline Feller Bauer; Nancy Winslow Parker (illustrator), New York: Frederick Warne.* Written from the point-of-view of the daughter left behind, this little book states on every other page "the good thing about it" and "the bad thing about it" (Mom's travels), with an illustration for each "thing." The dog, the Daddy, and the little girl do things on their own somewhat differently from Mom. But the best thing about it occurs on the last page: "she always comes back!"

+ Read   Young children should cuddle close to the reader for this small book to see the illustrations of what is good and bad about Mom being gone.

+ Child Discussion   Children need to talk about this rather scary occurrence after hearing the story. What else might be good if Mom were away? What else might be bad? Where do they think that this Mom went on her trips? Why did she go?

+ Suitcase   The cover of the book shows a pile of suitcases all set for a big trip. This is the time to bring a suitcase to the class and have each child put in it what he or she would like to take on a trip. (Get items from other parts of the classroom: such as an item of clothing from the Dramatic Play Center or a toy from the Block Center). Does where you're going tell you what you would put in? What else would help you decide?

+ Telephone   Three entirely different types of telephones are illustrated in this book. Your class should already have two sets of toy phones for children to use in their dramatic play and in the Sound Center. Bring in a different kind of phone from home for the children to see and compare. Let them take turns playing the role of Mom and little girl, making and receiving a phone call from, say, Japan.

A Chair for My Mother (1982), by Vera B. Williams, New York: Greenwillow Books. Here is a story with action, excitement, and even a flashback to a year earlier. This elementary-school-age city girl Rosa has a mother who works as a waitress in the Blue Tile Diner. She is tired when she comes home, but the first thing she always does is to put all her tip money in a big glass jar. So does Grandma (who lives with them) with the change from grocery shopping. So does Rosa whenever she earns any money. They are saving to buy a big, fat soft armchair in red velvet with pink roses, because all of their old chairs burned up in a fire a year earlier.

The story then flashes back to the day of the fire with all its drama and danger. When they move to a new apartment building all the neighbors contribute items, but they have no soft chairs or sofa. At last the coin jar is full. They wrap the coins, take them to the bank, and all three of them go to the furniture store to buy their chair. In the happy ending, Rosa falls asleep in her mother's lap in the wonderful new chair, and mother reaches for the light cord to turn off the light.

+ Tell   This is a wonderful story that may be too long to read to many three- and four-year-olds. That is where storytelling has the advantage over story reading. As noted on page 12, storytelling: "allows the teller to tailor stories to children's attention span and interest." To prepare for telling, read the story over to decide which characters and plot incidents to feature. Because you will want to place the book in the Story Center for children to look at on their own, you may want to feature the incidents illustrated by the pictures on every other page of the book. Jot them down as follows:

1. Blue Tile Diner
2. empty coin jar
3. mother and grandmother in kitchen
4. mother and Rosa walking home
5. fire trucks
6. burned-out apartment
7. new neighbors bringing furniture
8. full jar of coins
9. mother and Rosa in bank
10. trying out new chairs in store
11. bringing home red chair in uncle's truck
12. mother and Rosa sitting together in new chair

Then try out your story following this outline. Tell the story to yourself more than once, aloud if you can. You could start with a traditional formula opening such as: "Once upon a time there was a little girl named Rosa. Rosa's mother worked as a waitress in the Blue Tile Diner. Every day when she came home she gave all the coins she got in tips to Rosa to count. Then they put them in a big glass jar...plink, plink, plink."

Some storytellers like to use props in their storytelling. A good prop for this tale can be a glass jar and a few coins to drop in as the story progresses. Telling the story by showing children the pictures in the book is not the same. You will want your children to create their own pictures in their mind's eye. Stimulating the imagination like this is one of the important goals of storytelling. Some tellers, however, like to end their stories by showing children the book that the story came from, in order to encourage children to look at the book. In that case you might end this story by showing children the picture of the big red chair with the pink roses.

+ Chair-making   If children enjoy this story they may want to make their own little red chairs for their dolls and people figures. You might want to invent a way to make such a chair, such as: 1)pushing blocks together in the form of a chair and covering them with cutout pieces of wallpaper samples; 2)covering pieces of styrofoam with wallpaper or colored construction paper and fastening them together into a chair; 3)covering a dollhouse chair with colored paper. Youngsters can have the experience of: tracing around a block or piece, and then trying to cut out the paper along the lines; as well as deciding which side of the wallpaper the paste should go on. (Preschoolers often put paste on the colored side).

+ Coin-toss   Bring in a large-mouthed jar and have the children toss pennies, toy money or chips into it. Let children stand as close as they want. Place the jar on a small shag rug to prevent coins that miss from rolling across the floor. Be sure to have plenty of coins or chips. Can anyone count the number of coins it takes to fill up the jar? The children can then help you put pennies, for example, into a paper coin roll, just as Rosa did. What can such a roll of coins be used for to help in the family? Will more coins be needed?

Tucking Mommy In *(1987), by Morag Loh, Donna Rawlins (illustrator), New York: Orchard Books.* This Asian Mommy is too tired to think at the end of the day. As she bathes her two daughters in preparation for bedtime, one of the girls, Sue, volunteers to tell the bedtime story so her Mommy won't have to think at all. Sue's story is so successful that Mommy falls asleep with her clothes on. The two girls awaken her, lead her to her bedroom, get her into her pajamas, tuck her into bed, and repeat the bedtime story one more time. When Daddy comes home and hears all about it, he offers to tell them their own bedtime story but by now they are both too sleepy; so Daddy tucks them in.

+ Read   Sensitive illustrations of the girls and their Mommy against a backdrop of fluffy pillows and puffy quilts make this a story to be seen as well as heard. Repeat it at naptime with the lights off. Read it slowly as your co-teacher goes around the room tucking in each child.

+ Bedtime Stories   Talk about the bedtime stories that your children especially like. Make up a bedtime story for naptime in your class. Have the children dictate the story as you write it on an experience chart or newsprint taped to an easel. Then you can read it over again at naptime. Children enjoy stories about their toys coming to life. Can they make up a story about the dolls in the Dramatic Play Center

AUTHORS
of **INTEREST**

VERA B. WILLIAMS grew up in New York City where she was encouraged to draw and tell stories at The Bronx House. She received a degree in graphic art from Black Mountain College in North Carolina, also learning to plant corn, make butter, and build a house. Later she moved to Canada where she and her husband helped establish a creative school. Her first children's book was written when she lived on a houseboat in Vancouver, British Columbia. (Hurst, 1990, 141)

or the figures of people in the Block Center? They may want to make up a series of stories for naptime.

 My Mama Needs Me *(1983), by Mildred Pitts Walter, Pat Cummings (Illustrator), New York: Lothrop, Lee & Shepard Books.* Jason, a young African-American boy, knows that his Mama needs him when she comes home from the hospital with a new baby sister. He would like to help her somehow, instead of playing with his friends, or feeding the ducks, or eating a neighbor's cookies, but his mother or the baby always seem to be sleeping. Finally when both are awake, he gets to help his mother give the baby a bath. But doesn't his mother need him for something else? Yes, Jason discovers happily: she needs him to give her a big hug. So he does, plus a second hug for good measure that also satisfies his need.

+ Read It is important for children to be close to the reader of this story in order to see the sensitive pastel illustrations in their double-page-style format, depicting the confused feelings of a young child when a new baby enters his world. It may help the young listener, too, to reconcile her own concerns about her mother and a new baby with the need to carry on her own life.

+ Do Things with a Baby Young children who have experienced new younger siblings coming into their lives as babies may realize that their mother needs help with the baby. What can they do? They may be allowed to help bathe the baby as Jason was. You can set up your Dramatic Play center with plastic pans for tubs for several children to bathe the baby dolls in the Center. You can show children the non-fiction picture book, *101 Things to do with a Baby,* by Jan Ormerod (1984), illustrating cartoon-fashion the many, many things you can do, including "dry him," "dress him," "brush his hair." Put out towels, clothes, and hair brushes next to the bath tubs in your Dramatic Play Center.

+ Invite a Mother and Her Baby Invite one of the mothers of your children to visit the class along with her baby. She can interact with the children in any way that she is comfortable. It will be too much to have all of the children take turns holding the baby, but the baby's brother or sister could demonstrate. Would the mother like to read the book, *My Mama Needs Me?* Inviting parents to participate in their children's classroom activities is another way of affirming that the program recognizes the children's families and that the families reciprocate that recognition.

Parents often complain that they have no real input in their children's early childhood programs; that they are only used for tasks like accompanying field trips or raising money. (Coleman, 1991) Here is the chance for a parent to make a difference in the life of the program and of that of her child.

Blueberries for Sal *(1948), by Robert McCloskey, New York: The Viking Press.* Little Sal and her mother and Little Bear and his mother inadvertently switch partners and get all mixed up while picking blueberries on Blueberry Hill in this blue-and-white, pen-and-ink classic of Robert McCloskey's. Children love the sound words, kaplink, kaplank, kaplunk! used for the blueberries plunking into the pail when Sal picks, and the munching, gulping, and hustling noises when Little Bear picks. The concern of the human mother and the bear mother for their misplaced offspring is only too real, as is their fear of one another.

+ Read   Here is another book where children enjoy being close to the reader to see the pictures of Little Sal and Little Bear as they get all mixed up with one another on Blueberry Hill. But the reader needs to use his or her best storytelling voice in order to make the sounds of berries and bears. The mother bear's words should be read in a deep, gruff voice, while Sal's mother speaks in a higher-pitched nervous mother-voice. Because of the repetition, the children will soon be repeating many of the words themselves after the first time through.

+ Tell   On the other hand, the repetition and folktale-like qualities of this story, just like those of *The Three Little Bears,* lend themselves to telling rather than reading this story, if you are so inclined. Children enjoy the story either way, so try it both ways if you want.

+ Feltboard   Any book with such well-defined episodes deserves to be converted into a feltboard activity. Buy an extra paperback copy of the book and cut out the following characters to be mounted as described on pp. 30–31: Sal, Mother, Mother Bear, Little Bear, the rock, the tree stump, the crow, and the quail. Children can move the characters around on the feltboard as you read or tell the story, or they can create their own story.

+ Blueberry Picking   Most berry picking occurs when many preschool programs are closed during July and August. You may want to send copies of the book home with the children for the summer, if any of them plan to pick berries. Blueberry pickers know how well this story describes the very real dilemma of losing your way in a large wild blueberry patch, and the very real danger of bears who love the berries as much as humans do.

+ Preserving Blueberries   Since canning, freezing, or making jam from picked fruit is not really feasible in the classroom, teachers may want to send home suggestions to be used by parents with their children during the summer. A simple way for children to help preserve berries for the winter is to place them in plastic sandwich bags to be frozen. How they enjoy nibbling frozen blueberries as a snack—especially if they have read *Blueberries for Sal!* Blueberries can also be purchased in

Convert this book into a feltboard activity with an extra paperback copy.

the supermarket during the summer season. If yours is a year-round program, take some of your children to the store to buy berries for the rest of the class.

• *Fathers*

Fathers love their children just as much as mothers do. Their role in bringing up children is just as important. Unfortunately, with the increase of single-parent families, it is often the father who is the missing parent. This makes it doubly important for teachers of young children to provide books and activities that feature fathers. Children need to know what fathers are like. They need to hear the deep male voice, the distinct male point of view. Vicarious experiences through books do not replace the real person, but it is a start. Through books like the following, actual fathers may even be brought into the early childhood program:

First Pink Light, by Eloise Greenfield; Moneta Barnett (ill.) 1976
Louie's Search, by Ezra Jack Keats, 1980
Dear Daddy... by Philippe Dupasquier, 1985
Daddy Makes the Best Spaghetti, by Anna Grossnickle Hines, 1986

 ***First Pink Light** (1976), by Eloise Greenfield; Moneta Barnett (ill), New York: Thomas Y. Crowell Co.* Little Tyree, an African-American boy, wants to stay up all night to greet his absent daddy when he finally gets home from a trip at the first pink light of dawn. His mother makes a deal with Tyree: he can stay up if he puts on his pajamas and waits in the big chair with his pillow and blanket. Tyree is asleep when his daddy finally comes and the big man carries him tenderly to bed.

+ Read   The sensitive charcoal illustrations washed with pink make this book one that children should look at as they sit close to the reader.

AUTHORS
of INTEREST

ROBERT McCLOSKEY'S books are based on his own experience and that of his family members, especially when they lived on an island in Penobscot Bay, Maine. He writes and draws from life. The ducks in his Caldecott Award book, *Make Way for Ducklings,* for instance, swam in his bathtub in his New York apartment. *Blueberries for Sal* is based on the experiences of his daughter Sal and his wife Peggy. (Hurst, 1990, 84)

+ Dramatic Play Pretending can occur in most of the centers of your classroom. Have a special time every month when fathers are featured. Read books about fathers, play in the Block Center with small figures of men. Have audio tapes featuring men's voices. Have men's hats in a large variety of kinds in the Dramatic Play Center, along with men's wallets, belts, shoes, suspenders, and ties.

+ Invite a Father Send an invitation to a different father to visit your classroom every week. Children can help create the invitations. Some of the fathers may want to read a story to the children when they visit. Other fathers could help children feed the fish or guinea pig, build a block building, run a computer program, or show children how to use the saw, pliers, or hammer in the Woodworking Center. Ask them what they would like to do with the children when they visit. Some might want to play the harmonica or another instrument to accompany singing or creative movement. For children with no father at home, their mother might arrange for another male family member to visit. Because of work, not all fathers will be able to visit. Could they come to a parent meeting held in the classroom at night?

 Louie's Search (1980), by Ezra Jack Keats, New York: Four Winds Press. Here is one of the books about *Louie,* an inner city boy you will meet as a friend in Chapter 4. This slightly older Louie sets out to find a father for himself and his single mother, but ends up being accused of stealing a music box that has fallen off the truck of "Barney's Wonderful Things." Barney's blustering about Louie to his mother Peg ends when the music box begins to play. Before the summer is up, Peg and Barney have a wonderful wedding with all their inner city friends in attendance.

+ Read Each one of Keats books should be read to children sitting close enough to see the illustrations. All of the pages are wonderful double-spread scenes of the inner city: men working, blustering Barney, the harbor, and the wedding celebration. The brief text is tucked away in the corner of every other page. Children can have fun finding the torn bits of paper Keats uses as collage in all of his books. Another Keats signature is his use of colorful wallpaper for his characters' clothing, their walls, or their curtains. Can your children find any in this book?

+ Music Boxes Many children have never seen or heard a music box. Try to find one or more so that the children can have the fascinating experience of winding up the box and listening to it play.

+ Paper Hats   In preparing to use a book such as this with the children, look through it yourself with an eye to discovering appealing activities your children can do on their own. Is there anything different or unusual you see in the illustrations of the characters or read in the storyline? The sharp eye will notice that creative Louie wears a paper bag hat and a wild-looking tie in order to call attention to himself during his search for a father. Your children might like to make their own paper hats for a walk around their neighborhood. Bring in a supply of paper grocery sacks of different sizes and have children choose one that fits. They can paint or color their hats any way they want, or perhaps paste collage items to the hats for a really off-beat effect.

+ Field Trip   Take a walk around the block with a small group of the children in their paper bag hats. Field trips are often more meaningful for the children when done in small groups. On another day take a different group. Does anyone notice them or make comments about the hats? Have children look to see what the people around them are doing. Take an instant-print camera along to record what the children see. After the trip read *Louie's Search* again, asking the children what the people were doing that Louie saw. You can make a list on a large chart. Then make a similar list for your own group. Was there any difference in what people were doing in the book and on the field trip? Ask the children why. Such observations, questions, and recollections help children develop thinking skills. Lists like this help pre-reading children understand what print is used for, an important learning tool in emergent literacy. The field trip itself is more meaningful to children if there is a follow-up activity like this that helps them to internalize the experience and then communicate what happened.

Dear Daddy... *(1985), by Philippe Dupasquier, New York: Viking Penguin, Inc.* This unique picture story features Sophie in England who writes to her daddy who is away at sea on a merchant ship. The bottom two-thirds of the double-page spreads shows the same home scene with Sophie's activities during the changing months of the year, while the top third shows corresponding pictures of what's happening at the same time with Sophie's Daddy on shipboard or in port at Hong Kong. The text at the very bottom of the pages is Sophie's letters to her father.

+ Read   Children will need to see the pictures in order to understand what is happening in the story, since the father's activities are shown only through the strip pictures at the top of the page rather than in words. This book is best read to one or two children sitting next to the reader. Give the children plenty of time to look at the pictures before turning the page. Let them comment on what they see. In this instance, the continuity of the story is not interrupted by the children's comments. Does any listener notice that the mailbox in front of Sophie's house is red (an English custom)?

+ Letter Writing   Children can write letters to their own fathers, brothers, uncles, or grandfathers after hearing this story. Although preschoolers cannot be expected to write in "conventional script," their own scribbles can serve as "personal script," a prewriting stage previously mentioned that all children go through. Children often tell you what these writing scribbles mean, or they may want you to write words in conventional script underneath. Some children may be at the point of printing words, and may want you to print out the words they have dictated on one page for them to copy onto their real letter. Other children may try to write their own words in "invented spelling." There are many ways for young children to "emerge" into writing just as they "emerge" into reading. The preschool program should give them every opportunity to pursue such writing activities, especially on their own in the Writing Center, without actually "teaching" formal writing. (Beaty, 1992, 154–155) Writing a real letter to someone who is away on a trip is an excellent means for motivating the emergence of writing. Writing addresses, and return addresses, buying stamps, and mailing letters are other good follow-up activities. When children receive letters in return, their excitement may stimulate a whole new direction for your curriculum.

 ***Daddy Makes the Best Spaghetti** (1986), by Anna Grossnickle Hines, New York: Clarion Books.* When Daddy picks up Corey at the day care center and stops at the grocery store on the way home, Corey always wants him to buy the makings for spaghetti because "Daddy makes the best spaghetti." This tender story of a boy and his Daddy plus Mommy, shows the father-type games he plays with his son: slinging him over his shoulder like a sack of potatoes at the store, dressing up as "Bathman" to fly Corey to the tub for a bath, or hiding in Corey's bedroom with his pajama bottoms as "ears." Both mother and father in this story share household tasks and loving care for their child.

+ Read   This small-format book is another one for reading to children sitting close, so that they might view the pictures of Daddy dressing up and pretending.

+ Dramatic Play   A good spin-off of this story is for children to dress up and pretend to be home-type super characters like bathman. What other home-heroes can your children create from the dressup clothes in the Dramatic Play Center? What about: Dishdiver, who swoops up the dishes and cleans them with one kick of his swim fins; or Mophead, who skates around the room mopping the floors with three shakes of her lucky locks, or Supersweeper, who sweeps floors with an invisible broom in each hand; or Bedmonster, who carries children (dolls) to bed and lulls them to sleep with a magic tap on their toes?
   Children quickly clue in to such ideas of pretending, and will excitedly carry them out even further than most adults. It is well known that TV superheroes are often the major focus of pretending for children, three to six, much to the dismay of many adults. So why not encourage them to create their own household heroes, as the Daddy did in this story? They will enjoy dressing up in wild outfits to project their heroes' super strengths such as flying with a cape, turning invisible with a sheet, or lifting hundreds of pounds with magic mittens.

+ Invite a Daddy to Cook   As you read this story listen to the children talk about their fathers and the things they cook at home. Would any of the fathers be willing to cook a dish or a meal for your class? Talk it over with the family. You may decide to have a spaghetti supper with the fathers cooking the spaghetti and children helping to prepare the salad.

• *Brothers and Sisters*

Sibling relationships are often ones of conflict for young children. If they are the youngest in the family, they are often at the mercy of an older brother or sister in the give-and-take, rough-and-tumble of children's play. If they are the older sibling with a new baby in the family, they frequently feel displaced in their parent's affection, and may take out these feelings on the baby. Such sibling rivalry is the norm rather than the exception in families.

Children's picture books can help young children resolve such feelings by exposing them to book characters who are experiencing similar problems. We humans may think that we alone are the only ones suffering from a particular problem. Yet most interpersonal conflicts are universal. For a child (or anyone) to realize that others are dealing with a similar problem is sometimes a great relief. Whether or not this is the case, such books can also give children insight into how others like themselves resolve sibling conflicts. Picture books that deal with sibling rivalry include:

A Lion for Lewis, by Rosemary Wells, 1982.
I'll Be the Horse If You'll Play With Me, by Martha Alexander, 1975
My Little Brother, by Debi Gliori, 1992
One of Three, by Angela Johnson; David Soman (ill.) 1991

 A Lion for Lewis (1982), *by Rosemary Wells, New York: The Dial Press.* Little Lewis has to play all the unwanted dressup roles up in the attic with older Sophie and George. He is the baby when they play mother and father; the sick person when they are doctor and nurse; and out of it altogether when they play prince and princess. Then Lewis finds a lion suit in a dark corner of the attic and becomes the star of the role play when he puts it on.

+ Read and Discuss   Here is another good book to read to your youngest children, since the character is a three-year-old they can identify with, the pictures are large, and the text is simple. Talk about Lewis's feelings when the older children give him an inferior role to play. How could Lewis have resolved the problem of the unwanted roles if he hadn't found the lion suit? Which way was better for all concerned?

+ Dramatic Play This story is a wonderful lead-in to dramatic play for your own children. Bring in the costumes and props for several different role-plays, and have them available after a small group of children have heard this story. For example, have a box filled with old time dress up clothes for mothers and fathers as in the story: silk shawls, lampshade hats, vests, a cane, a derby, etc. Another box (call it a "prop box") can be filled with doctor paraphernalia: long white shirts for jackets, stethoscope, eye examiner, fountain pen for shot needle, empty medicine bottle, bandages. For prince and princess dress up have a prop box filled with ladies' high heeled shoes, men's high lace-up boots, a wand, lamp shades for hats, table cloths for capes. Let the group choose one of the boxes for their play, while you read the story to a second group of children.

I'll Be the Horse If You'll Play With Me *(1975), by Martha Alexander, New York: The Dial Press.* This very small format book is one of a series by Martha Alexander on sibling conflict when new babies appear on the scene. Here the protagonist is little Bonnie who is pulling her older brother Oliver in the wagon. Instead of pulling Bonnie when it is his turn, Oliver goes off to play with Ira. Bonnie is not successful in her play with Rufus the dog, with Oliver again, with Willy, or with David, until the others push her off on a still younger toddler Scott. Bonnie is delighted to discover that he can pull her wagon, and will do it happily even with her in it.

+ Read   All of Alexander's little books lend themselves to one-on-one reading, or with not more than two listeners. The youngest preschoolers appreciate seeing a book where the littlest or youngest is the hero. The illustrations are simple people against a blank white background, and the text is a line at the bottom of the page.

+ Feltboard   Buy an extra paperback copy of any of Alexander's little books for easy conversion into a felt board activity. (See pp. 30–31) One cutout of each of the characters plus the wagon should be enough for your children to follow the storyline in the book or make up their own in the Sound Center.

My Little Brother *(1992), by Debi Gliori, Cambridge, Mass.: Candlewick Press.* "My little brother is a pest," says the preschool sister narrator of this book about her toddler brother, as she recounts all of the things he does that bother her. When she tries getting rid of him, nothing works. But when she discovers him missing from his crib one night and can't find him, she worries that one of her imaginative schemes has really taken effect. She finally finds him in the linen closet with her cat and five baby kittens.

+ Read   Clever illustrations make this a book to be looked at as it is read. Children will relish seeing the sister's whimsical attempts to get rid of her brother. The cardboard rocket she builds to send him to the moon doesn't work because he gets it wet. Large print text close to the picture it describes helps young children to understand that print tells the story too, just like the illustrations.

AUTHORS *of INTEREST*   ROSEMARY WELLS says that she learned to write for children by reading to her own children Victoria and Beezoo. Her friend and business partner Susan Jeffers is another children's picture book illustrator. (Hurst, 1990, 134)

+ Write Own Stories Talk with the children about big and little brothers and sisters, and how they feel about each other. What would they do if they were the big brother or sister? Where might they hide if they were the little one? Can they draw a picture of their idea? Can they make up a story about it? Read this book to a small group of children in the Writing Center and then help those who want to write their own story in personal script, invented spelling, or on a typewriter if you have one.

 One of Three (1991), *by Angela Johnson; David Soman, (illustrator), New York: Orchard Books.* The narrator of this story is the "me" in Eva, Nikki, and me, one of three African-American inner city sisters who do almost everything together. She is the littlest, however, and sometimes they leave her behind. Then she becomes "one of three" with Mama and Daddy at home.

+ Read Let children first hear the story read to individuals or a small group as they look at the colorful, realistic pictures of the sisters dressing up, playing hopscotch, and riding on the subway.

+ Tell Then tell the story to the children without using the book. Can they help you fill in any incident you might have left out?

> Dressing up
> Walking in the rain
> Playing hopscotch
> Waiting at the bakery
> Riding in the taxi
> Holding hands in the store
> Riding in the subway
> Getting a daisy from Mr. Lowen
> Walking down the street like stairsteps
> Being left behind
> Keeping Mama and Daddy company

+ Tell the Incidents in Order "What happens next?" is an important question that emergent readers need to know about. Have children who want to tell this simple story to see if they can remember what happens next. If they forget, let them look it up in the book and try again. Then have them make up their own stories about what they do with their own sisters or brothers.

• *Grandparents*

Grandparents are several generations removed from their grandchildren, and can often look back on this time with insight that most parents and siblings have not yet acquired. Thus, it is especially important that adults of "grandparent age" be in touch with young children. Grandparents need to be needed, and young children need to be loved. Yet too often in this day and age, the young and the old are widely separated. Grandparents may be living across the country or in a nursing home. Grandparents having grandchildren in a blended family may not be allowed to visit them because of the breakup of the parent's marriage or their own.

Children's picture books may not be able to correct the situation, but a few of the wonderfully sensitive books featuring old and young together may spark an interest that opens new lines of communication between young and old. Here are some:

Song and Dance Man, by Karen Ackerman; Stephen Gammel (ill.), 1988
Bigmama's, by Donald Crews, 1991
Wilfrid Gordon McDonald Partridge, by Mem Fox; Julie Vivas (ill.), 1984
Storm in the Night, by Mary Stolz; Pat Cummings (ill.), 1988
Abuela, by Arthur Dorros and Elisa Kleven (ill.), 1991

 ***Song and Dance Man** (1988), by Karen Ackerman; Stephen Gammel (illustrator), New York: Alfred A. Knopf.* When his three grandchildren come to visit, Grandpa leads them up the steep, wooden steps to the attic where he finds his old leather-trimmed trunk. Out of it come a bowler hat, a top hat, a gold-tipped cane, a vest with stripes, a banjo, and his shiny black tap shoes. He turns on an old lamp and aims it down like a spotlight; the children sit back on one of Grandma's woolen blankets; and the show begins. The attic is transformed into a vaudeville stage for the marvelous song and dance man. After the show is over the children tell their grandpa that they wish they could have seen him dance in the good old days, but he whispers as he envelopes them all in one big bear hug, that he wouldn't trade a million good old days for the days he spends with them.

+ Read   Children should see the exceptional award-winning art in this book. Be sure they are close to the reader to view the action from a by-gone era rendered in multi-hued crayon colors creating the lively grandfather and his entranced audience encircled by red, blue, yellow, and pink shadows. Children also need to be able to see the "old soft shoe," the bowler hat trick, the red hanky joke, and the twinkling tap shoes.

+ Invite a Grandparent   Most grandparents may not tap dance, but many can tell stories about what entertainment was like before television. Ask through your "family newsletter" if any grandparents would be willing to talk to a small group of children in your Story Center, telling them what kinds of things they enjoyed doing for fun when they were young. Grandparents can also be contacted through agencies like Foster Grandparents, Retired Senior Volunteer Program (RSVP), or a local senior citizens group. Make arrangements to bring a grandparent to your program at least once a month. They may want to read a book like this to a small group, and talk about it afterwards.

+ Invite a Tap Dancer   Invite to your program someone to demonstrate tap dancing. Perhaps an older sister of one of your children or a student from a tap dance school can come. Some of your children may take dance lessons themselves and could bring in their tap shoes to demonstrate.

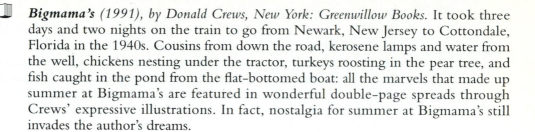

***Bigmama's** (1991), by Donald Crews, New York: Greenwillow Books.* It took three days and two nights on the train to go from Newark, New Jersey to Cottondale, Florida in the 1940s. Cousins from down the road, kerosene lamps and water from the well, chickens nesting under the tractor, turkeys roosting in the pear tree, and fish caught in the pond from the flat-bottomed boat: all the marvels that made up summer at Bigmama's are featured in wonderful double-page spreads through Crews' expressive illustrations. In fact, nostalgia for summer at Bigmama's still invades the author's dreams.

+ Read   Listeners must see the illustrations to appreciate the story of the children's exciting adventures at their grandmother's house before the coming of electricity to the rural neighborhood.

+ Tell Own Story   Can any of your children tell the story of their own visit to grandma's or grandpa's? Let them try it, one at a time. Ask them to tell:

1. what it looked like when they arrived;
2. who was there to greet them;
3. what they did first;
4. what they did next;
5. what else happened...

...just as Crews told in his story. Ask each teller these questions and jot down their answers on a newsprint pad. Then they can tell their story. Tape record each story and put it in the Sound Center to be played back and listened to on the head sets. Transcribe the story into a little book for each child. Work with a small group of no more than two or three children at a time, so that no one will have to wait too long for their turn. For those children who have not visited their grandparents, can they tell about another trip they have taken?

+ Dramatic Play   After reading this book be sure to have "trip props" available in the Dramatic Play Center. Have a small suitcase as well as gym bags, shoulder bags, purses, dress up clothes of all kinds, railroad or bus tickets, ticket punch, and play money. Children can make up their own pretend trips. Buses and trains can be made from chairs lined up one behind the other.

AUTHORS *of* **INTEREST**   **DONALD CREWS,** an African-American writer and illustrator from the New York City area, began as a freelance book-jacket designer, and later created wonderful wordless books such as *Freight Train* and *Truck* with designs and bold colors that completely fill each page. *Bigmama's* celebrates his own childhood summers at his grandmother's house in the Florida countryside of the 1940s. (Hurst, 1990, 38)

Wilfrid Gordon McDonald Partridge, *(1984) by Mem Fox; Julie Vivas (illustrator), Brooklyn, New York: Kane/Miller Book Publishers.* In this book little Wilfrid Gordon McDonald Partridge does not go to visit his grandma, but to the residents of the old people's home next door. Although he knows all of the residents, his favorite is 96-year-old Miss Nancy Alison Delacourt Cooper because she has four names just like him. When he finds out that Miss Nancy has lost her memory, he is determined to help her find it. He doesn't quite know what a memory is, but each resident he asks gives him a different definition. Thus, the collection of items he finally gives one by one to Miss Nancy (sea shells from his shoe box, a puppet on a string, the medal his grandfather gave him, his football as precious as gold, and a warm egg from under a hen), awakens her recollection to the lovely things she once experienced.

+ Read   The whimsical pictures of the old folks in their wicker chairs and Wilfrid Gordon on his skateboard are too good to miss, as is Wilfrid's basket full of memory treasures that he gives to Miss Nancy. Be sure your children follow these pictures as you read the story.

+ Storytelling Treasure Basket   Bring in your own basket of memory items and tell a brief story about each. Encourage the children to bring in an item for the basket to tell a story about. Make up funny stories about things the various items remind you of. Another time ask a child to carry the basket around the room and pick up several items. Then ask one of the children from a small group to choose one of the items and tell a funny story about it.

+ Invite a Grandparent   Invite a grandparent to choose an item from your basket and tell a story about what it reminds them of. Can they also add an item or two to your basket?

+ Visit a Nursing Home   Take a field trip with your children to a nearby nursing home or veterans hospital. You'll be amazed at how naturally and lovingly these youngsters and oldsters come together.

Storm in the Night *(1988), by Mary Stolz; Pat Cummings (illustrator), New York: Harper & Row, Publishers.* A thunder storm in the night engulfs the African-American boy Thomas, his white cat Ringo, and Grandfather in their living room as the lightning flashes and the lights go out. It is too early to go to bed, so there is "no help for it" but for Grandfather to tell Thomas a story of when he was a boy during a storm in the night. The three of them move out to the front porch and the story begins. While Thomas has declared that he isn't afraid of the storm, Grandfather's story recounts the time when he *was* very much afraid. The storm, meanwhile, roars and crashes around them.

+ Tell and Comment   Here is a wonderful story for a teller to use for demonstrating "sound imagery." Mary Stolz uses such imagery throughout the tale, describing thunder "like mountains blowing up," and Grandfather's voice "like a tuba," while Thomas' voice is "like a penny whistle." Grandfather's story is a simple one about a thunder storm that scares him so he runs in the house and dives under the bed

*Invite a grandparent
to your class to read
to the children.*

without remembering that he left his dog outside in the storm; and how he has to get up the courage to go out after him.

You, the teller, should prepare for this story by listing all of the sounds you want to make with your own voice. For example, when Thomas listens for sounds in the dark he hears:

1. Door creaking

2. Faucet leaking

3. Ringo scatching a post

4. Flames in the stove sputtering

5. Clock on the mantle chiming

6. Kitchen clock ticking

7. Church bells bonging

8. Car tires swishing

Out on the front porch he hears:

1. Rain whooping windily through the beech tree

2. Rain clattering on the tin roof

3. Swing creaking

4. Thunder booming

In addition to *telling* what Thomas hears, you can make the story very dramatic by *making* the actual sound with your voice, your hands, or your feet. For example, when you mention Ringo scratching a post, you can make the scratching noise with your voice or with your fingers actually scratching something, or both. Be sure to talk in a deep "tuba" voice when Grandfather speaks, and in a high squeaky "penny whistle" voice for Thomas. This is a story you can have a lot of fun with, and so can your children if you invite them to chime in with the sounds when you repeat the noises.

When you tell the story the second time, turn off the lights and have all the children cover their eyes with their hands. How does this make them feel during this storm story? What do they see in their minds' eye when they hear the story like this? Oral storytelling creates powerful images in the minds of listeners. That is why it is so important for children to have the experience of hearing stories without the book. Although seeing the pictures in the book has its own rewards, if you plan to *tell* the story, do it first, so that children can create their own images before seeing those in the book. Developing the imagination like this is how creativity itself is born.

How did you feel about *telling* the story first? Just as the children enjoy making their own images in their minds, most storytellers also enjoy the power of being in control of what happens in the story by focusing on the audience and their reactions rather than on the book. Children make the story their own by creating their own images in their minds' eye. You make the story your own by telling it in your own words and with your own sounds.

+ Read and Comment   This is also a book for reading aloud so that children can experience Pat Cummings' impressive night illustrations in blues, blacks, and glowing eyes. Can the children tell from the pictures whether Thomas or Ringo are afraid? How? Was Grandfather afraid? How did he lose his fear of the storm when he was young?

+ Listen for and Tape Record Sounds   What sounds can children hear in the classroom if they close their eyes and concentrate? You can tape record the sounds they identify: the aquarium bubbling, the door opening and closing, children walking and talking, the noise of a block building tumbling down, water coming from the faucet. Have children close their eyes and try to identify the sounds as you play them back. What other sounds would they like to tape record and later try to identify? What about playground sounds, traffic sounds, school bus sounds? They can keep the tape in the Sound Center to listen to on the head sets. Besides developing children's creativity and cognitive awareness, this activity is an excellent one for improving children's auditory discrimination.

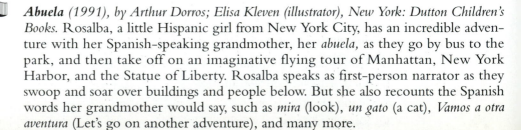

Abuela *(1991), by Arthur Dorros; Elisa Kleven (illustrator), New York: Dutton Children's Books.* Rosalba, a little Hispanic girl from New York City, has an incredible adventure with her Spanish-speaking grandmother, her *abuela,* as they go by bus to the park, and then take off on an imaginative flying tour of Manhattan, New York Harbor, and the Statue of Liberty. Rosalba speaks as first-person narrator as they swoop and soar over buildings and people below. But she also recounts the Spanish words her grandmother would say, such as *mira* (look), *un gato* (a cat), *Vamos a otra aventura* (Let's go on another adventure), and many more.

+ Read   Children should sit close as you read them this delightful story with its extraordinary bird's-eye views of the city illustrated in a Caribbean folk-art-style collage. The city and its people vibrate in a feast of colors, each window below radiant with flowers, curtains, windowpanes, and people like you've never seen before. Ask the children where they would like to land if they could fly above the city with Rosabla's grandmother. What do they think they would see there? Children especially enjoy looking for the tiny details in such pictures.

+ Spanish Speaking   Invite a Spanish speaking family member to come in and read the story—a grandmother would be wonderful! Perhaps such a person could then read a rhyme or sing a song in Spanish from her own background or from a book such as *Arroz con Leche: Popular Songs and Rhymes from Latin America*. If no family members speak Spanish, ask a student who is taking a course in Spanish to help out. Perhaps the Spanish teacher herself could make an appearance. Bring in a tape in Spanish and play it for the children. The public library can probably supply one. Find out if you can copy it for your Sound Center. What other languages do the grandmothers of your children speak? Can they visit the class and demonstrate?

• *Differently-Aligned Families*

Families come in all sorts of configurations these days. Single mothers or single fathers may raise their own children or have a blended family of their own plus adopted children. Children may alternate visiting or living between their separated parents. Remarried couples may have a realigned family with children from previous marriages. Adopted children in a family may be of different races or ethnic backgrounds altogether. Traditional families, in fact, with a mother and father and their own biological children are becoming fewer in number in American today.

How does this affect children? Most young children accept whatever situation they find themselves in. However it is composed, it is their family, they are a part of it, and it is a part of them. As you select picture books for young children, be particularly sensitive when choosing books that reflect these complex family situations. The books should have a positive, uplifting theme, not one of stress or blaming. Here are a few books containing examples of some of the differently-aligned families that children find themselves in today:

> *Through Moon and Stars and Night Skies,* by Ann Turner; James
> Graham Hale, illustrator, 1990
> *Black is brown is tan,* by Arnold Adoff; Emily McCully, illustrator, 1973
> *Sam Is My Half Brother,* by Lizi Boyd, 1990
> *My Dad is AWESOME,* by Nick Butterworth, 1989

 ***Through Moon and Stars and Night Skies** (1990), by Ann Turner; James Graham Hale (illustrator), New York: Harper Collins.* This tender tale tells a first-person story of how a little Southeast Asian boy comes to his family. "Let me tell the story this time, Momma. Let me tell how I came to you." Thus begins the tale of the small child who met his adopted family through photographs sent to him of his new poppa and momma, a red dog, a white house with a green tree, and a bed with a teddy-bear quilt—waiting for him. As he describes flying through night and moon and stars, he expresses his fears of all the new things. Only the pictures he clutches ease his anxiety. Then one by one he encounters each of the things in the photographs, and at last comes to feel not afraid anymore.

+ Read   Read this book to individuals and small groups. Let them look at the sensitive double-page illustrations. Most of the children may not be able to relate to traveling from a foreign country to meet their parents. But they can relate to being afraid of unknown things. What things make your children feel afraid or uneasy? What do their parents do to help them get over their fears? What things do the two parents in this story do that make their new child feel at home? Does anyone mention how the parents get down on their knees in the airport crowd to welcome their new son?

+ Photographs   Bring in an instant print camera and take pictures of each child in the group listening to the story as he or she holds an object that is meaningful. When the picture has developed ask the child what he would like to say about the picture that would make a new friend feel better. You can tape record each child's reply or write it down to be used in a personal book the child is making.

Black is brown is tan (1973), by Arnold Adoff; Emily McCully (illustrator) N.Y: Harper & Row. This children's classic is a prose poem of an interracial family with three children, a white father, and an African-American mother. They work and play together, eat and sing together, get hugged by granny white and grandma black, and reflect all the colors of the race.

+ Read   Read this quiet book to children sitting close. Simple, sensitive illustrations show the affection of parents and children toward one another as they read books, cook food, sing songs, and play together indoors and out.

+ Make a Scrap Book   Make a class family scrapbook from pictures that the children cut from magazines. They can cut out pictures of adult family members, children, and pets; food that the family group might like; activities they like to do together; places they like to go together. Children can tell the teacher what to label the various cutouts and what names to give the family members.

Sam Is My Half Brother (1990), by Lizi Boyd, New York: Viking Penguin. Hessie visits her father and stepmother every summer, but this year is different because there is a new baby, her half brother Sam. At first Sam's crying, sleeping, and eating bother Hessie. When she finally realizes that she can be the big sister who will teach him things, she cheers up. But why can't she remember being a baby? Her father shows her pictures of herself as a baby in a photo album. Hessie then makes a picture book for Sam so he will remember being a baby.

+ Read   Have children sit close to see the child-like illustrations in this book, especially of the book Hessie makes for Sam.

+ Make a Class Book   Have each child make a drawing of something he or she likes to do, and then write something about it on the same page. Fasten the children's pages together into a class book for visitors and the children themselves to look at. Be sure to accept scribbles in drawing and writing as worthy contributions.

***My Dad is AWESOME** (1989), by Nick Butterworth, Cambridge, Mass.: Candlestick Press.* The Dad in this simple story is strong, swift, agile, a talented musician, cook, singer, juggler, and altogether awesome according to the one of his six children who narrates the tale. The illustrations on every other page show the family consisting of a father, four white children, a black child, a baby, and a dog.

+ Read and Tell   After reading this story have children who want to, tell something one of their family members can do. Don't insist that it be a father, as some of your children may not have a father as part of their family.

+ Have an Awesome Day   Choose a day to be Awesome Day, once a week or once a month with a poster mounted on the wall. Write on the poster anything outstanding or unusual that someone has said or done that week. It can be from the children and teachers in your class, from the children's families, from something on television or in the newspapers. Ordinary happenings can be extraordinary if positive attention is focused on them. Some awesome happenings that one class recorded, for example, were: Melanie sang *Old MacDonald Had a Farm* for the first time; Maria's grandmother visited and read the book *Abuela* to us; Reggie S. wore a blue and yellow T-shirt his uncle brought him from the Bahamas.

So it is that stories about mothers, fathers, brothers, sisters, and grandparents can help children develop good feelings about themselves, as well as better interpersonal skills, cognitive skills and creativity. At the same time such books can involve families in their children's learning and development both at home and in school.

ACTIVITIES IN CHAPTER 3 TO PROMOTE CHILD DEVELOPMENT

Emotional Development

Child discussion *(My Mom Travels a Lot)*
Invite a mother and her baby *(My Mama Needs Me)*
Invite a father *(First Pink Light)*
Invite a grandparent *(Song and Dance Man)*
Feltboard *(Blueberries for Sal)*
Photographs *(Through Moon and Stars and Night Skies)*
Make a class book *(Sam Is My Half Brother)*
Have an Awesome Day *(My Dad is AWESOME)*

Social Development

Do things with a baby *(My Mama Needs Me)*
Dramatic play *(A Lion for Lewis)*
Feltboard *(I'll Be the Horse If You'll Play with Me)*
Make a scrapbook *(Black is brown is tan)*

Physical Development

Coin-toss *(A Chair for My Mother)*
Blueberry picking *(Blueberries for Sal)*
Invite a tap dancer *(Song and Dance Man)*
Listen for and tape record sounds *(Storm in the Night)*

Cognitive Development

Suitcase *(My Mom Travels a Lot)*
Preserving blueberries *(Blueberries for Sal)*
Field trip *(Louie's Search)*
Invite a daddy to cook *(Daddy Makes the Best Spaghetti)*

Language Development

Bedtime stories *(Tucking Mama In)*
Telephone *(My Mom Travels a Lot)*
Letter writing *(Dear Daddy)*
Write own stories *(My Little Brother)*
Tell incidents in order *(One of Three)*
Tell own story *(Bigmama's)*
Storytelling treasure basket *(Wilfrid Gordon McDonald Partridge)*
Invite a grandparent *(Wilfrid Gordon McDonald Partridge)*
Speak Spanish *(Abuela)*

Creative Development

Chair-making *(A Chair for My Mother)*
Dramatic play *(First Pink Light)*
Dramatic play *(Daddy Makes the Best Spaghetti)*
Dramatic play *(Bigmama's)*
Music boxes *(Louie's Search)*

REFERENCES CITED

Beaty, J.J. (1992), *Preschool Appropriate Practices*. Fort Worth, Tex.: Harcourt Brace Jovanovich.

Coleman, M. (1991), Planning for the Changing Nature of Family Life in Schools for Young Children. *Young Children* 46(4) 15–20.

Delacre, L. (1989), *Arroz Con Leche: Popular Songs and Rhymes from Latin America*. New York: Scholastic, Inc.

Greenberg, P. (1989), Parents as Partners in Young Children's Development and Education: A New American Fad? Why Does It Matter? *Young Children* 44(4) 61–75.

Leichter, H.P. (1984) Families as Environments for Literacy. H. Goelman, A. Oberg, and F. Smith, eds., *Awakening to Literacy,* Exeter, N.H.: Heinemann Educational Books.

Morrow, L.M. (1989) *Literacy Development in the Early Years: Helping Children Read and Write,* Englewood Cliffs, N.J.: Prentice Hall.

OTHER CHILDREN'S PICTURE BOOKS ABOUT *FAMILY FROLICS*

Barrett, J.D. and Cummings, P. (ill.) (1989), *Willie's Not the Hugging Kind.* New York: Harper Collins.

Berry, C. and Brusca, M.C. (ill.) (1990), *Mama Went Walking.* New York: Henry Holt and Co.

Caines, J. and Himler, R (1977) *Daddy,* N.Y.: Harper & Row.

Christiansen, C.B. and Trivas, I. (ill.) (1989), *My Mother's House, My Father's House.* New York: Viking Penguin.

Edelman, E and Watson, W. (1986) *I Love My Baby Sister (Most of the Time),* N.Y.: Viking Penguin.

Galloway, P. and Collins, H. (1984), *When You Were Little and I Was Big.* Toronto, Can.: Annick Press.

Gomi, T. (1979), *Coco Can't Wait!* New York: Viking Penguin.

Greenfield, E. and Steptoe, J. (ill.) (1974), *She Come Bringing Me That Little Baby Girl.* Philadelphia: J.B.Lippincott Co.

Griffith, H. (1987), *Granddaddy's Place.* New York: Greenwillow.

Hedderwick, M. (1986), *Katie Morag and the Two Grandmothers.* Boston: Little Brown & Co.

Hest, A. (1984), *The Crack-of-Dawn Walkers.* New York: Macmillan.

Hort, L. and Ransome, J.E. (1991), *How Many Stars in the Sky?* New York: Tambourine Books.

Isadora, R. (1991), *At the Crossroads.* New York: Greenwillow Books.

Johnson, A. and Soman,D. (ill.) (1989), *Tell Me a Story, Mama.* New York: Orchard Books.

Johnson, A. and Soman D. (ill.) (1990), *When I Am Old With You.* New York: Orchard Books.

Lewin, H. and Kopper, L. (ill.) (1981), *Jafta's Father.* Minn., MN: Carolrhoda Books, Inc.

Lewin, H. and Kopper, L. (ill.) (1981), *Jafta's Mother.* Minn., MN: Carolrhoda Books, Inc.

Lloyd, D. and Dale, P. (ill.) (1986), *The Stopwatch.* New York: Harper & Row, Publishers.

Martin, B. Jr., Archambault, J. (1987), *Knots on a Counting Rope.* New York: Holt.

Martin, B. Jr. and Archambault, J., and Rand, T. (ill.) (1986), *White Dynamite and Curly Kidd.* New York: Henry Holt and Co.

McCloskey, R. (1952), *One Morning in Maine.* New York: Viking Press

Miles, M. and Parnall, P. (1971), *Annie and the Old One.* Boston: Little Brown and Co.

Ormerod, J. (1982), *Moonlight.* New York: Viking Penguin. (wordless)

Ormerod, J. (1981), *Sunshine.* New York: Lothrop, Lee & Shepard Books. (wordless)

Pearson, S. (1987), *Happy Birthday, Grampie.* New York: Dial Books

Peterson, J.W. and Ray, D. K. (ill.) (1977), *I Have a Sister My Sister Is Deaf.* New York: Harper & Row, Publishers.

Quinlan, P. and Van Kampen, V. (1987), *My Dad Takes Care of Me.* Toronto, Canada: Annick Press.

Scott, A.H. and Coalson, G. (ill.) (1972), *On Mother's Lap.* New York: McGraw-Hill.

Sonneborn, R.A. and McCully, E.A. (ill.) (1970), *Friday Night Is Papa Night.* New York: Viking Penguin.

Wells, R. (1973), *Noisy Nora.* New York: Dial Books.

Williams, B. and Chorao, K. (ill.) (1975), *Kevin's Grandma.* New York: E.P. Dutton & Co., Inc.

Williams, V. B. (1990), *"More More More" Said the Baby.* New York: Greenwillow Books.

Zolotow, C. and Du Bois, W.P. (1972), *William's Doll.* New York: Harper & Row, Publishers.

FINDING FRIENDS

Action Chant

Looking here,	(turn right)
Looking there,	(turn left)
Looking almost everywhere,	(turn all around)
No fair!	(stamp foot)
In the house,	(turn right)
On the street,	(turn left)
Trying to find someone neat,	(turn all around)
Didn't meet!	(stamp foot)
Where to look,	(turn right)
In a book?	(turn left)
Is there someone overlooked?	(turn all around)
I'm hooked!	(jump)

Friendships in Early Childhood

How does a person find a friend? For many children in preschool and kindergarten this poses no problem. They are surrounded by peers with similar interests and needs. They are attracted to certain of these peers. If the attraction is mutual, a friendship is formed. For other children in the same classroom this process seems more difficult. They may try to play with a certain child, but be rejected. They may push their way into a play group, but be ignored.

Why does this happen? Researchers are looking for clues that indicate why certain children form friendships with ease and others do not. Popular children seem to interact with other children in appropriate ways: they call them by name; they touch them; they make eye contact with them. They also seem to stand back and assess what is going on in a play group before joining in, thus making a smooth and non-disruptive entry. (Buzzelli & File, 1989, 71)

On the other hand, children who are neglected by others seem to have poorer communication skills. They talk to no one in particular and use egocentric speech. ("I wanna play.") Children who are rejected often behave in inappropriate ways such as pushing their way into a play group, bossing the others around, or being unwilling to share. They also seem unable to realize the negative effect that their aggressive behavior has on the other children. (Buzzelli & File, 1989, 72)

What makes the difference? Why do some children seem to know almost intuitively how to behave and others do not? Much early childhood research focuses on two factors: maturity and experience. (Kemple, 1991, 49) To be successful in making friends children need to employ mature communication skills that involve another child and not just themselves. If they also have had experience playing with siblings and peers before entering preschool or kindergarten, they may have learned already what works and what does not.

Just as important is their trust in themselves. If they have developed a good feeling about themselves as worthy persons—the positive self-image as discussed in Chapter 2—then they are much more likely to feel self-confident about their dealings with others. It is a self-fulfilling prophecy: they expect to find friends at school, and they do.

❧ Who Is a Friend?

Preschoolers and kindergarten children often select friends for different reasons than do older children and adults. "A preschooler values friends for their abilities to meet her needs rather than for their personalities. The young child needs a friend to help build a block building, or play fire fighter, or push a wagon around. Because young children are so self-centered, early friendships like this are often one-sided and fluid." (Beaty, 1992, 195) A child may play with one friend one day and an entirely different friend the next day.

However, the more often a child interacts with the same child, the stronger the friendship becomes. Then there are children who go to extremes by playing only with one particular friend and no one else in the class. They may eventually need your help to expand their interactions to other children whether or not they choose the others to be friends.

❧ Are Friends Necessary?

It is extremely important for young children to learn how to interact success-fully with their peers. Finding a friend is one of the results of successful interactions. Child-adult interactions are not the same. They do not give children the same learning opportunities because adults are more powerful and more experienced than children's peers. Peers are equals. With them young children learn on their own how to get along with others and how to resolve conflicts. They learn through give-and-take to cooperate, negotiate, compromise, and contribute, as well as taking leader and follower roles.

Early childhood is the time to learn such skills. Young children who do not learn how to relate to peers are more likely to have adjustment difficulties in adolescence and adulthood, research has found. Later emotional and mental health problems may also be related to a child's poor relationships with peers in early childhood. (Kemple, 1991, 48) Thus, it is important for young children to find friends. If they do not know how, it is up to you to help them.

❧ Storytelling Can Help

Storytelling in all its forms—telling, reading, feltboard, or dramatics—is a powerful tool for reaching the minds and touching the hearts of the listeners. Stories form mental images that are often more meaningful than words: images that remain with the listeners long after the words have faded away. When those images are concerned with finding friends and forming friendships, young listeners can be affected, even transformed, in ways mere words can never hope to accomplish.

This chapter presents picture book storytelling featuring four aspects of the friendship theme:

Finding a friend
Playing together
Resolving conflicts
Moving away

• *Finding a Friend*

Can stories about children finding friends actually help in a real situation, you may wonder? Stories that are woven around universal themes of bravery and fear, love and hate, friends and enemies, seem to make a difference. They help children confront and reflect upon the problems of living. These universal problems are theirs as well, but to face them vicariously through the lives of storybook characters helps children face real life too. Charles A. Smith believes that "Stories transform children because they hold their attention and engage their hearts and minds. Children view life as a story, finding themselves starring in a comedy, a tragedy, or even occasionally an adventure. Each of them is at times a Raggedy Ann, a Little Tin Soldier, or an Ugly Duckling." (Smith, 1986, 47)

Four picture books that feature the theme of finding a friend include:

Will I Have a Friend?, by Miriam Cohen; Lillian Hoban (ill.), 1967.
The Shy Little Girl, by Phyllis Krasilovsky; Trina Schart Hyman (ill.), 1970.
Jessica, by Kevin Henkes, 1989.
Big Al, by Andrew Clements; Yoshi (ill.), 1988.

 Will I Have a Friend? *(1967), by Miriam Cohen; Lillian Hoban (illustrator), New York: Macmillan Publishing Co.* This original book in the series about Jim's experiences at school has already become a classic story of a child entering preschool for the first time. It is a children's favorite because of its realistic description of the first-day separation anxiety that many of them feel when a parent drops them off at school. When Pa takes Jim to nursery school for the first time, Jim wonders anxiously whether he will have a friend at school. The story explores Jim's first day activities as he warily watches other children painting, making puzzles, modeling clay, and eating a snack, all the time wondering where his friend is. Lillian Hoban's distinctive drawings of young children having fun in preschool fill whole pages, with the brief text tucked into a blank space on the classroom wall. They show a multiethnic group of children with a sensitive African-American teacher and a caring Pa, who escorts Jim to and from school. The simple plot reveals the first tentative steps of children making friends, just as they do in reality. It is a little toy truck that finally brings Jim together with Paul, just as in real life it is often materials and toys that are the connecting points between children.

+ Read   This book is more meaningful to children if it is read to one or two children at a time because the reader can then discuss its implications with the children listeners in a much more personal way. Children so strongly identify with the character and situation that *Will I Have a Friend?* really speaks to them personally. You can prepare for reading the story as described on page 19 in order to make the experience successful for both you and the children. A good way to begin is to show the children the book's cover, state the title, and say something like: "This is a story about Jim. What do you think he's doing in this picture? Why do you suppose he wonders whether he'll have a friend?" Your exact approach will depend upon the children's response to the cover picture.

As you read the story, have a child pick out Jim and his father on their way to school. Then continue reading the story, sometimes pointing out the characters yourself, sometimes letting your listeners pick them. Don't encourage too many interruptions once you have the children's attention. They want to hear the story all the way through. If they really like it, they will want it read again and again. Afterward if it seems appropriate you can discuss how they personally felt when they came to your class on the first day, or how they found a friend at school.

+ Feltboard   This particular story lends itself especially well to feltboard activities with the homemade feltboard characters you can cut from a third paperback copy of the book. (One copy for your Story Center, one for your Home-Lending Library, and a third for book extension activities like this). Do your cutting away from the children as mentioned previously, to avoid giving children the invitation to cut up books. You will want to cut out at least one of each of the important characters in the book as well as any items that help to tell the story. You need only one Jim, so select carefully in order to have the one that will best serve for the entire story. Because illustrations occur on both sides of a page, select with care before you begin cutting.

Nine characters and two objects can be cut out to tell this story effectively:

Pa bending over
Jim facing away from Pa
Teacher reading book with Jim at her feet
Paul kneeling
Paul standing with toy car in hand
Bill as rocket man
Anna–Maria pulling a wagon
Group of three children bumping tummies
Danny pretending to be a monkey
Lump of clay
Tray of juice

Although there are many more pictures than this in the book, it is better to select as few as possible in order not to confuse the children who will later be using them on their own to dramatize the story. For instance, it is not necessary to cut out the children lying down to take their naps. It is more effective to use the characters you already have and merely place them on their backs when nap time occurs in the story.

Mount your cutouts on cardboard or oaktag to give them rigidity as suggested on page 30. Light oaktag of the type used in file folders works well. Cut them out of the oaktag and then attach the felt, sandpaper, Velcro, or whatever material you use to stick the characters loosely to the feltboard. Some teachers protect their feltboard characters by covering their fronts with clear contact paper before the final cutout.

Feltboard cutouts can be used in a number of ways. Once the children are familiar with the story, you can introduce this activity by reading the story again, and asking various children to pick out the characters or objects being described and place them on the feltboard as they hear the action occurring. Another activity has the adult or a child *retelling* the story using the characters to illustrate the various incidents. Still another variation has the adult asking the children what comes next in the story, and having them select the proper character to put on the board.

Feltboard activities have a life of their own. If you store the characters in a marked envelope, children can use them independently to develop their own stories, and perhaps tape record them in the Sound Center. Who knows what friends Jim will find when your children take charge of the characters in *Will I Have a Friend?*

The Shy Little Girl *(1970), by Phyllis Krasilovsky; Trina Schart Hyman (illustrator), Boston: Houghton Mifflin Company.* Anne is the shy little girl in this story, who doesn't make friends easily and doesn't like herself very much. She doesn't speak loud enough for anyone to hear, or raise her hand in school because she knows she won't be called on. She does everything by herself although she wishes she had a friend. When Claudia the new girl comes to school, Anne finally finds a friend through picking dandelions and showing Claudia how to make chains with their stems.

+ Tell   Here is a story that is a good one for telling. After reading it to yourself, you will note that there is an order to the things the shy little girl can't do, much on the order of *Leo the Late Bloomer*, but for older children. You can jot down this order to help you remember the story:

Home: face—wrinkle
             voice—whisper
             clothes—stoop over
             house—no inviting
School: raise hand—never
             jump rope—no places
Alone: collect leaves
             slide on ice
             pick dandelions
             chase butterflies
             watch ants
Claudia comes (everything changes)

With this order in your mind (or in written notes) you can tell the shy little girl's story. If you remember pictures more easily than words, you can teach yourself the story by drawing simple sketches of the incidents (mnemonic cues) in the order they occur. One of the great storytellers of all time, Mark Twain, invented the technique of making sketches for remembering the order of the stories he told night after night on his humorous lecture tours across America. Once he had drawn his simple sketches he filed them away, since he could visualize them in his mind's eye as he delivered his stories. (Janssen & Beaty, 1988, 50) You try it.

For *The Shy Little Girl* you might make the following sketches:

1. frowning face

2. face with "voice balloon"

3. stick figure bent over

4. house

5. raised hand

6. stick flower

7. smiling face

For the change that occurs in Anne when Claudia comes, you can go back through these items telling how she changes her behavior for each item. Try learning a story first with word notes and then with sketches. Ask yourself which one works best for you in remembering a new story. Use that technique, then, whenever you want to add a new story to your repertoire.

+ Friendship Greeting Cards   Children can make a greeting card for a friend and send it through the personal mailboxes you will provide for each of the children. Young children need all kinds of experiences with print. Whether or not they can read or write, they can make their own personal greeting card for a friend with your help. Put out collage materials in the Writing Center along with double folded paper for the card, scissors, and paste. A collage "picture" can be pasted to the outside of the card, and the message written inside. Messages can be written by preliterate children in several ways as previously discussed:

1. They can dictate the message for you to write on the card.

2. They can copy their dictation onto the card that you have written on a separate paper.

3. They can scribble their own message in "personal script."

4. If they ask you, you can write their message in "conventional script" under their scribbled message.

An envelope for their card can be made by folding a sheet of blank paper crossways around the card and taping it together. Can your children print the name of their friend on the outside of the envelope? You may have to print out the name for them to copy. Did they sign the inside of the card with their own name? Young children are not always familiar with these conventions.

+ Mail Boxes Children enjoy receiving cards and letters. Be sure your Writing Center contains personal mail boxes for every child. Make them out of shoe boxes or cereal boxes covered with contact paper or poster paint. Ask the children to supply empty boxes of a certain kind or size. Because it is important to have them all the same size, you may have to supply some of the boxes yourself. Then have a mail-box painting day in the Art Center where each child covers a box with poster paint. Bring in a selection of commercial greeting cards for display in the Writing Center during the card-writing activity. This is another "whole language" experience where children use language for real situations such as communicating a friendship message to another child on a homemade greeting card.

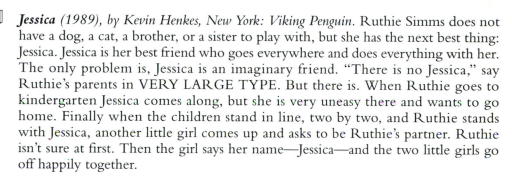 *Jessica (1989), by Kevin Henkes, New York: Viking Penguin.* Ruthie Simms does not have a dog, a cat, a brother, or a sister to play with, but she has the next best thing: Jessica. Jessica is her best friend who goes everywhere and does everything with her. The only problem is, Jessica is an imaginary friend. "There is no Jessica," say Ruthie's parents in VERY LARGE TYPE. But there is. When Ruthie goes to kindergarten Jessica comes along, but she is very uneasy there and wants to go home. Finally when the children stand in line, two by two, and Ruthie stands with Jessica, another little girl comes up and asks to be Ruthie's partner. Ruthie isn't sure at first. Then the girl says her name—Jessica—and the two little girls go off happily together.

+ Tell This simple story makes a fine tale for telling to the total group. You will be making eye contact with each of the children as you tell the story, thus including all of them in the experience. As a storyteller you can easily relate each of the things that Ruthie and Jessica do together, with occasional interruptions by Ruthie's parents who say: THERE IS NO JESSICA! But there is. Afterwards ask your listeners if they know any invisible friends. Some of them may want to tell about their own imaginary companions and what happened to them when they started school.

+ Name Cards This is also a story about names. The kindergarten teacher announces everyone's name, but Ruthie and Jessica are not listening. When you tell the story, be sure to stop and name each child in the class at this point. When you read the story later, point out the printed names of each child that are scattered around the white space on one of the pages. You may want to give each of your children a name card on which you have written his or her name in large bold letters. They can hold up their name cards during the story when you tell it aloud. Another time have them find their own name card before you tell the story. Some children will know only the first letter of their name. Others may recognize the whole name. Do you have more than one child with the same name?

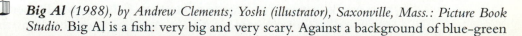 **Big Al** *(1988), by Andrew Clements; Yoshi (illustrator), Saxonville, Mass.: Picture Book Studio.* Big Al is a fish: very big and very scary. Against a background of blue-green

pages like the tropical sea itself, Big Al's story unfolds: he tries to find friends among the colorful smaller fish of the sea, but they are all afraid of him because of his looks. He disguises himself with seaweed; he puffs himself up; he buries himself in the sand; he even changes his colors to look like a passing school of fish, but nothing works. Not until he finally rescues the little fishes from a net is he finally accepted for his own friendly self.

+ Tell   Here is another story with an orderly sequence of incidents that are easily remembered and simply told. The teller may want to make sketches for remembering the five most important incidents as in *The Shy Little Girl:*

1. fish covered with seaweed
2. fish puffed up
3. fish covered with sand
4. fish with stripes
5. fish net

+ Read   After you tell this story to a large group of children, you should read it to a smaller group so they can enjoy the wonderful pictures of scary Al and his colorful friends.

+ Child Discussion   Have your children ever been afraid of someone or something that turned out later to be friendly? Large dogs are often frightening to small children, for instance. After reading this story you may want to talk about such fears.

• *Playing Together*

Just as your own children enjoy playing with friends, so do the storybook characters they will come to know through your picture book storytelling. This second aspect of friendship is represented here by five popular children's books:

Dreams, by Ezra Jack Keats, 1974
Louie, by Ezra Jack Keats, 1975
Anna Banana and Me, by Lenore Blegvad; Erik Blegvad (ill.), 1985
Harry and Willy and Carrothead, by Judith Caseley, 1991
The Extraordinary Ordinary Everything Room, by Rhea Tregebov; Helene
   Desputeaux, (illustrator), 1991

 ***Dreams** (1974), by Ezra Jack Keats, New York: Macmillan Publishing Co., Inc.* This and the following book are two in a series created by Ezra Jack Keats, better known perhaps for his earlier books featuring Peter and his friend Archie, both inner city African-American boys. These two books, on the other hand, feature several Hispanic kids from the same neighborhood. In *Dreams* Roberto leans out the window to show his next door African-American neighbor Amy the paper mouse he made in school. Amy wonders what the mouse can do. Roberto shakes his head and sets it on the windowsill. Later when everyone but Roberto is asleep and dreaming, he accidentally knocks the mouse off the windowsill where it tumbles down to the sidewalk making eerie shadows in the streetlight, and scaring off the dog that had cornered Archie's cat. Roberto can't wait to tell his friends about it, but by the time the others are awake, Roberto himself is dreaming.

+ Read   Children are charmed by Keats' characters whether or not they are from the inner city. It is important to have picture books showing multiracial characters like this, not only for your own children to identify with, but also to acquaint all children with the multiethnicity of American life. Read this book to one or two children at a time for a closeup view of the apartment windows and the swirling colors of Keats' marbleized paper sky as it turns from dark to dawn.

+ Paper Mouse   Once children have seen Roberto's mouse, they will want to make one of their own. The mouse is made from a large and a small cone of colored construction paper, plus cutout ears, nose, hands, feet, and tail that are taped or pasted to the cones. If you prepare patterns for the cones and appendages, the older children can trace around them and cut them out. Although threes and fours will find this difficult, many fives and sixes can have fun cutting and pasting. The cone patterns are a large (nine-inch) and a small (five-inch) flattened out teepee. Roll them to the size and shape desired and tape them shut in back. To make a more durable mouse, cover the construction paper with clear contact paper. Cut a hole near the wide end of the head cone and insert it onto the top of the body cone. Tape the hands, feet, and tail to the body, and the ears and nose to the head. Draw eyes and whiskers with a marker, and the mouse is finished. Children can use the mouse as a free-standing doll and later as a hand puppet. (see page 81.)

+ Shadow Making   Let the children try tumbling their paper mice off the window sill or a high shelf in your darkened room with someone shining a flashlight on them to make shadows.

AUTHORS
of INTEREST   EZRA JACK KEATS, a New York City author and artist, drew pictures from the time he was four years old. Most of his children's books feature the city and its wonderful multiracial mix of children. His Caldecott Award winning book *The Snowy Day* in 1962 introduced Peter, and was the first full-color picture book to feature a black child. His illustrations of swirling marbleized color, of cutouts, spatter paint, and of collages revolutionized children's book illustration. He saw beauty everywhere, in the city's crumbling walls, graffiti smeared fences, and broken sidewalks, as if through the eyes of the children he portrayed. His books are known throughout the world and have been translated into over 16 languages. (Hurst, 1990, 62)

+ Marbleized Paper   Have two children at a time fill a large cake tin half full of water. Drip oil based paint of three or four colors onto the water. (Water based paint does not float.) Let it swirl around just a little. Each child can place a piece of uncolored manila construction paper on top of the water one at a time and let it soak up the paint. Pull the papers off carefully and hang them up to dry. Are the two papers the same or different? Even when children are doing the same activity together, things sometimes turn out differently. How many different designs can they and others make? (Be sure children are wearing paint aprons to protect clothing from this non-soluble paint, and put plenty of old newspapers on the floor to protect it.)

 Louie (1975), by Ezra Jack Keats, New York: Greenwillow Books. Roberto's mouse has learned to do something else in this next book in the series. Roberto and Susie put on a puppet show for the neighborhood kids with the mouse as a puppet along with Susie's clown puppet Gussie. In the audience sits Louie, a boy who never talks. When the show begins an amazing thing happens. Louie stands up and says "hello" to Gussie and then starts talking to the puppet. After the show Louie is disappointed that he can't take Gussie home, and slumps off by himself to his lonely apartment where he dreams about feeding Gussie from a huge yellow ice cream cone. The kids later relent and slip a note under Louie's door directing him to a long green string that leads him to Gussie.

+ Read   All of Keats' books deserve to be read rather than told because of their outstanding illustrations. Children who have enjoyed the shadow activities in *Dreams* should be intrigued by Keats' use of light and shadow in the *Louie* puppet show. Young children often notice such details even before adults, since theirs is more a world of images than words. Some children, though, may notice the graffiti on the walls of buildings and fences that Keats created from collage: torn bits of newspaper and colored paper. He has used scraps of paper his readers sent him in creating his illustrations. (Hopkins, 1969)

+ Clown Puppet   Gussie is another paper-cone doll like the mouse. Use the same nine-inch teepee pattern you used for the mouse. Children can color or paint the cone the colors of Gussie's dress in the story, or use colored construction paper. For the puppet's head use a styrofoam ball colored green, with eyes, nose, and mouth painted or pasted on from paper cutouts. The arms can be rolled paper tubes inserted into the body cone, or flat paper cutouts like the mouse's. A separate hat can be pasted on. Cover all of the cutouts with clear contact paper for permanency. If making puppets like this is too complicated for your children, make several puppets on your own for use by the children when the story is read.

+ Puppet Show   The use children make of puppets depends on their age. Threes and fours find it hard to understand the concept of a puppet as a doll that acts. Instead, they tend to use hand puppets as an extension of themselves, often using puppets with movable mouths to "bite" another person. Most young children also find it difficult to sit still to watch a formal puppet show in a puppet theater. They are so intrigued with puppets they want to become involved with them by sticking

Make paper cone puppets of the mouse and Gussie for children to use for telling their own stories.

their hands through the front of the theater or going around back to see what's happening. Therefore you may want to use these paper puppets more informally with the youngest children. Have the mouse or Gussie tell their own story about Roberto or Louie while a child in the group holds it. Older children can put on a puppet show behind a blanket strung across a clothesline or behind a turned-up card table. The Keats book does not tell what the puppet play was about, only that the children laughed at the adventures of Gussie and the mouse. Fives and sixes can have fun making up their own silly adventures for their puppets.

 Anna Banana and Me (1985), *by Lenore Blegvad; Erik Blegvad, (illustrator), New York: Macmillan Publishing Co.* Here is another city story told from the point of view of the little boy narrator, about his adventures in the park with his friend Anna Banana. She is the leader of the adventures: crawling under the park bench, climbing up on a statue, swinging higher than the trees, finding a white "magic" feather. The boy is not as brave until he too finds a "magic" feather and a way out of his fears.

+ Read   This is also a story to read to the children so that they see the illustrations of the imaginative girl and the boy follower.

+ First-person Feather Stories   Be sure to bring a feather when you read *Anna Banana,* so that children who want can create their own first-person stories. Give your children storytellers the magic feather that makes them "brave" or "gigantic" or "lighter than a feather," and see where their imaginations will take them.

+ Tell Story to a Friend   Ask a child who has enjoyed *Anna Banana* to choose someone and tell him or her the story. Then it can be that child's turn to tell her own "feather" story. Some children may want to record their stories on tape in the Sound Center.

Harry and Willy and Carrothead *(1991), by Judith Caseley, New York: Greenwillow Books.* The three friends in this story meet when they first start school. Harry who was born without a hand has a prosthesis instead, but plays baseball almost as well as Willy. Carrothead, who wants to be called by his real name Oscar, tells the story in first-person narrative. The children are curious about Harry's prosthesis, but when he treats it like a normal hand, so do they.

+ Read   Children will enjoy sitting close to see the lighthearted pictures when you read this book to a small group. There are really few picture books for young children about children with handicapping conditions who make no fuss about it. The story is an important contribution toward children's learning to accept differences in others.

+ Puppet Names   A name is something people feel strongly about. Nicknames like "Carrothead" are often insulting to a person with red hair or some other identifying characteristic. How do your children feel about this? Put a puppet on each of your hands and have a conversation between them about their two funny names that neither of them likes. Speak in a different voice for each puppet. Then give a child a chance to operate one of the puppets while you play the role of the other one.

+ Glove and Mitten Pick-up   Have children try to pick up items scattered on the table first with a mitten on one hand and then with a glove on the same hand. Which works better? Ask the children about Harry's hand prosthesis. Does he use it like a mitten or like a glove? How do they think he learned to do this? Would practice using a mitten help them to pick up items as easily as they did with the glove?

The Extraordinary Ordinary Everything Room *(1991), by Rhea Tregebov, Helene Desputeaux (illustrator), Toronto, Canada: Second Story Press.* Are any of your children collectors? They will enjoy the story of Sasha, who seems like an ordinary kid, but is really "Sasha of the Everything Room." Sasha is a little boy who walks to and from daycare every morning and afternoon first with his mother and then his father, collecting everything on the way. Marbles, feathers, leaves, acorns, and magic wands all find their way into his Everything Room. One by one his multiethnic friends from daycare come to borrow extraordinary things from Sasha. Daniella wants a saxophone to play a sleepy song so her little brother will go to sleep, so Sasha finds her a giant one. Tai wants to eat a mountain of green jello, so Sasha helps him slurp and slog it out of the Everything Room. Talia wants the boring day fixed, so Sasha squeezes her into the Room where a whole circus is in progress.

+ Read   This is a book for the children to see close up, in addition to hearing the story. Illustrations of *everything* pour out of the room like the leaves, flowers, and acorns pouring from Sasha's pockets. What a wonderful friend to have! Do your children finally realize that Sasha's "everything" is really his imagination?

+ A Collecting Walk, a Collage, and a Story   Give pairs of children a paper sack and go on a collecting walk around the building or down the street. When you return give the pairs a backing paper and glue to mount their collection. Can the friends tell an imaginary story about their collage?

• *Resolving Conflicts*

Friendship is not always smooth. Even best friends sometimes have a falling out. Many young children are not prepared for conflicts with friends. For some it can be devastating. For others it is a dilemma they don't know how to deal with. Your picture book storytelling may help such children over the rough patches in their friendships. The following four books are popular examples of books that deal with conflicts between friends:

Best Friends, by Miriam Cohen; Lillian Hoban (ill.), 1971
Let's Be Enemies, by Janice May Udry; Maurice Sendak (ill.), 1961
The Hating Book, by Charlotte Zolotow; Ben Shecter (ill.), 1969
Best Friends for Frances, by Russell Hoban; Lillian Hoban (ill.), 1969

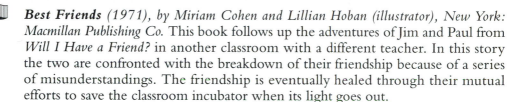

Best Friends (1971), by Miriam Cohen and Lillian Hoban (illustrator), New York: Macmillan Publishing Co. This book follows up the adventures of Jim and Paul from *Will I Have a Friend?* in another classroom with a different teacher. In this story the two are confronted with the breakdown of their friendship because of a series of misunderstandings. The friendship is eventually healed through their mutual efforts to save the classroom incubator when its light goes out.

+ Read   It is best to have read *Will I Have a Friend?* first to your children so that they have the background on how Jim and Paul first become friends. You yourself should read the book ahead of time in order to prepare yourself to deal with incubators. The book turns out to be a wonderful lead-in for a science project on incubating eggs.

+ Incubator   Although it is possible to construct your own incubator, many teachers rent one through a farm agency such as Cooperative Extension. If you prefer to construct your own, such an organization can usually supply the plans. Information on how to incubate eggs comes with the rented incubator. Be sure to arrange a place for your hatched chickens before you begin the project. The hatchlings should not be sent home with the children. It is also better not to identify an egg for each child as some will not hatch. You will need at least a dozen fertilized chicken or duck eggs, from the Cooperative Extension or a farm or agricultural station that sells them.

The incubation process is a long one, involving the turning of the eggs three times a day for nearly a month. Children can sign up for opportunities to turn the eggs, so they can learn that this is a cooperative effort. For teachers this means coming into the classroom over the weekend. Some teachers prefer to start the incubation just before a long winter or spring vacation, taking the incubator home during the holidays, and returning it to school in time for the children to watch the eggs hatch.

As soon as the eggs begin to hatch, remove the new chicks to another box with a lamp to keep them warm. The children can watch their wet feathers fluff out within hours. Any deformed chicks must be removed or the normal chicks will kill them. Once the chickens are hatched you should take them to the farm you had arranged with previously. It is important to arrange this ahead of time because many farmers will not accept incubator chicks. Nor is it appropriate for the children to take them home as pets. Either they die from being handled or they grow up very quickly into large unmanageable birds. With careful forethought and planning, this activity can be a successful one, just as it was for Jim and Paul in *Best Friends*.

Let's Be Enemies *(1961), by Janice May Udry; Maurice Sendak (illustrator), New York: Harper & Row, Publishers.* This tiny book is a classic tale of a little boy being upset with his best friend because he is too bossy, so "today he is my enemy." John walks over to his enemy James' house to inform him of this, all the while muttering about the different ways James bosses him around. Then he remembers all the neat things they did together, but still he is determined to become enemies. Every page shows a line drawing of the two kids in distinctive Sendak style with a line of text at the bottom. The boys have a very brief confrontation, but in the next breath are back to being friends.

+ Read   Try reading this very simple dialog in two different voices: one for the angry John, and the other for the puzzled James.

+ Child Discussion   Because the conflict is laid out in such simple childlike language and thought, this story is a good lead-in to talking about friends and enemies. What is a friend? What is an enemy? Can a friend be an enemy? Can an enemy become a friend? Did you ever feel this way about a friend of yours?

+ Overhead Transparencies   Any book with simple, clear illustrations like this can have its characters duplicated on overhead transparencies to be used in different ways. Purchase clear overhead transparency sheets and put them, one at a time, in the paper tray of a duplicating machine instead of white paper. Duplicate a picture from the book just as you normally duplicate other material. It will come out on the transparency sheet and can be used on an overhead projector. Copyright laws allow one copy to be made for educational use. For *Let's Be Enemies* make the following transparency sheets: one each of John as an enemy, James as an enemy, John as a friend, and James as a friend. As you project the image of John as an enemy on a screen or the wall, have your children speak for him. What does he say to James in anger? Project James' image and have children reply for him. Then project each of the characters as friends and have the children speak for each of them. For example, they can tell what kinds of things each character likes to play with the other, just as in the book, or they can make up their own games.

The Hating Book *(1969), Charlotte Zolotow; Ben Shecter (illustrator), New York: Harper & Row Publishers.* Girls can be enemies too. In this small book two girls who are a bit older have a falling out over a misunderstanding. The narrator girl's mother tells her to ask her friend why. But she won't. For page after page she recalls all the snubs her friend has committed. At last she confronts the friend and discovers that she had misunderstood a comment.

+ Read   Both boys and girls can gain from having this story and the previous one read to them. Whereas boys may identify with John, girls can identify with this narrator. Both can come to realize that conflict is common among friends, although it may be different for girls and boys.

AUTHORS
of **INTEREST**

CHARLOTTE ZOLOTOW wanted to write and illustrate books for children from as far back as she can remember. Her work as a children's book editor at Harper in New York City eventually brought her into contact with many people like herself. Since the 1940s she has written over 60 books for youngsters on themes as diverse as wanting a doll to having a son. (Hurst, 1990, 150)

+ Child Discussion   Have any of your children had such a misunderstanding as the narrator of this story? What did they do about it? Should you talk to someone you are angry with? What should you say? These are questions children may want to talk about.

+ Paper Masks   The cover of the book shows two girls with masks on confronting one another. Your children can play these two roles to settle such a misunderstanding after you have talked about the story. Prepare two paper masks ahead of time: one with a smiling face and one with a frowning face. Let two children volunteer to wear them and act out a misunderstanding. You can set the stage by stating something like: "You be Connie and you be Jennifer. Connie, what would you say to Jennifer if you heard that she had said you were too bossy?" Some young children have trouble wearing masks. Don't force the issue. This role-play should be entirely voluntary.

 Best Friends for Frances *(1969), Russell Hoban; Lillian Hoban, New York: Harper & Row Publishers.* This book from the popular Frances series features little badger Frances, her younger sister Gloria, and her friend Albert. It is a story for older children with a much longer text, but with many examples of conflicts among friends. Frances won't let Gloria play; Albert won't let Frances play; Frances and Gloria won't let Albert come on their outing. All is resolved in the end with everyone joining in a game of ball.

Prepare paper masks for children to use after hearing this story.

+ Read   All of the Frances books should be read aloud for the children to appreciate the humorous verses Frances sings as she proceeds through life.

+ Child Discussion   What do you do when someone won't let you play? Did Gloria do the right thing? Did Frances? Did Albert? What was it that made them all friends again? Can sisters be best friends? These are some of the questions your children can talk about if you read the book to individuals and small groups.

+ Picnic Hamper   Frances and Gloria go on an outing with a picnic hamper full of food. Your children can go on a pretend picnic by packing a picnic basket with food cutouts they make from magazines that you provide. Each child can contribute one item of food for him/herself and one for a friend. When they arrive at the pretend picnic site, the cutout items can be distributed to everyone along with crackers and juice that you have provided.

• *Moving Away*

In our mobile society families are frequently on the move. They move across town, across the state, across the country. Children respond to such moves in different ways depending on their ages and temperaments. If the move involves the separation of friends, children of any age feel badly. Four books that deal with such separation include:

The Trip, by Ezra Jack Keats, 1978
We Are Best Friends, by Aliki Brandenberg, 1982
Best Friends, by Steven Kellogg, 1986
The Leaving Morning, by Angela Johnson and David Soman (ill.), 1992

The Trip *(1978), Ezra Jack Keats, New York: Greenwillow Books.* A third book in the series about Louie and his inner city friends has Louie moving to a new neighborhood where he doesn't know anybody: not the kids nor the dogs nor the cats. But Louie, the nonverbal boy with great imagination, makes up his own world from a shoebox. He cuts out the back of the box and part of the cover, makes a hole in the front, and pastes all kinds of cutout buildings inside the box. Then he covers the back of the box and the cover with colored cellophane, hangs his little red airplane from the top, puts on the cover, and looks through the hole. "Wow!" He has created a peep show neighborhood of his own. As he looks through the hole he pretends to be flying over an imaginary city in his red airplane, and is soon lost in a dream fantasy back in his old neighborhood with his friends dressed in Halloween costumes.

Shouts of "trick or treat" from real children wake Louie from his dream. He puts on his homemade Halloween costume and joins them as a large yellow ice cream cone.

+ Read   Children who enjoyed Louie's experiences in *Louie* will want to hear more about him in this book. The pictures of strange creatures in paper costumes:

a giant mouse, a flowerpot, a witch, and a green–checkered midget should excite them, especially when they turn out to be Louie's old friends Roberto, Amy, Archie, and Archie's cat all dressed up for Halloween. When Louie takes them for an imaginary plane ride through the city, will your listeners notice that real children are looking out of their windows to watch them? You can tell them that the man in one window is Keats himself and that the children are his friends.

+ Peep Show   Keats gives directions on how to make a shoebox peep show on the last page of the book. Older children can do much of this on their own. Preschoolers will need help; or you may want to make the peep show yourself and bring it in after reading the story. If you have an extra paperback copy of *The Trip* you can cut out the costumed Halloween characters from the story. If they are too large to fit in your box, merely bend and crease them at the bottom to fit, and tape them to the floor. Look through the peephole you have made before the final pasting to make sure the larger figures are in back and not blocking the others. You can line the inside walls of the box with street scenes from the story as well. Don't forget to dangle Louie's red airplane and the moon from the cover of the box.

   Your peep show is an another item you will want to keep in the Story Center when the Keats books are there. If children make their own peep show, let them take it home along with a copy of *The Trip*.

+ Peep Show Stories   What can a child do with a peep show? She can look through the hole and imagine her own world full of fantastic adventures. She can make up stories for the characters in her world and tell them to the tape recorder in the Sound Center if she wants. Her stories can even be transcribed into a book of her own.

+ Halloween Costumes   Children can create Halloween costumes for themselves similar to those of Louie and his friends. Large pieces of oaktag or colored poster board are cut, painted, and taped together to represent the mouse, the flowerpot, and the ice cream cone. An umbrella over the top of the cone becomes the ice cream. Children can also use the *Louie* costumes to dramatize the story.

We Are Best Friends *(1982), by Aliki Brandenberg, New York: Greenwillow Books.* Robert and Peter are best friends until Peter moves away. Not only is Robert lonely, but he is so upset that he will not play with the other children. Nor will he accept at first a new boy, Will, who is looking for a friend. Then Robert receives a hand-printed letter from Peter telling how Peter also did not like his new house or his new school at first, but that things are better now that he has found a new friend Alex. Robert draws a "picture-letter" to Peter saying "if you were here this is what we'd be doing." Robert finds that Will likes frogs and tadpoles, just like Peter. By the time he writes his second letter to Peter, he and Will have become friends.

+ Read   Children need to be up close to see the pictures in this book as the teacher reads the words, for they tell two different stories. The text "There was nothing to do. There was no one to play with" accompanies a picture showing an active playground full of busy children. Peter's letter in wriggly crayoned letters, and Robert's with drawings surrounding the written words, are important for children to see.

+ Letter Writing The book itself may stimulate children to want to "write a letter." Preliterate children can do this with your help just as they did for the friendship greeting cards. In addition to their message, they will learn from Robert's letters about including a greeting and closing in their letters. Children can draw from a hat the names of the other children in the class and write them each a letter to be placed in their classroom mailboxes. They can use their own scribbled "personal script," your printed transcriptions of their words, or just drawings. The excitement of receiving a letter from someone may keep this activity going for many days in the Writing Center.

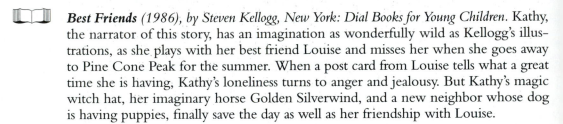

Best Friends *(1986), by Steven Kellogg, New York: Dial Books for Young Children.* Kathy, the narrator of this story, has an imagination as wonderfully wild as Kellogg's illustrations, as she plays with her best friend Louise and misses her when she goes away to Pine Cone Peak for the summer. When a post card from Louise tells what a great time she is having, Kathy's loneliness turns to anger and jealousy. But Kathy's magic witch hat, her imaginary horse Golden Silverwind, and a new neighbor whose dog is having puppies, finally save the day as well as her friendship with Louise.

+ Read Kellogg's stories are truly in touch with modern children's feelings. Your listeners will want to be close to you and the book as you take your time reading this story so that they can savor the illustrations. The pretend stallion Golden Silverwind, the haunted neighborhood that was not scary as long as the girls were together, and the volcanic eruption that blasted Pine Cone Peak into pebbles are just too exciting for them to miss.

+ Post Cards Bring in a number of picture post cards for your children to see. Would they like to "write" a post card, like Louise did, to someone in the class just as they did the letters for *We Are Best Friends?* Have a post card day in which children can cut out pictures from magazines and paste them to the front of post cards you have provided (cut out your own). Then help them to "write" a message to the child whose name they have drawn from a hat. Again, they can scribble in "personal script," copy from dictation, or use your transcriptions for their messages. Fill the Writing Center with picture post cards during this activity. Perhaps parents will donate some.

The Leaving Morning *(1992), by Angela Johnson; David Soman (illustrator), New York: Orchard Books.* Angela Johnson again looks at inner city African-American children as she did in *One of Three.* Here a little brother and bigger sister are moving with their mama and daddy away from their apartment where they know everybody. The brother narrates the story on "the leaving morning" after they have said good-bye to their friends, the grocer, everybody in their building, and especially their cousins. They press their faces against the hall window as they wait for the movers, and leave cold lip marks on the window. The movers give the little boy a moving hat and Miss Mattie upstairs gives him a kiss on the head. His daddy says they'll soon be in a place they'll love. So the little boy leaves lip marks on the front window of their apartment as they say goodbye on the leaving morning.

+ Read   David Soman's wonderfully expressive illustrations make this a book children must see closeup as the teacher reads it to one or two at a time. Each picture is a double-page spread in the style of the 1990s, that draws the reader into the world of the picture book characters.

+ Finding Friends in a New Place by Sharing a Toy   How do you find a friend in a new place? Read this book to four or five children at a time and then talk to them about it. Sometimes you find a friend as Jim did in *Will I Have a Friend?* by sharing a toy. Ask your children what kind of toy they would share with a new friend. Have each child in the group look around the room for such a toy and bring it back to the Story Center to share with the other listeners. How would they go about sharing it? Ask them to pretend they are meeting a new friend and would like to share the toy with them.

Friendship activities can take place throughout the school year. When your children seem concerned with finding a friend, playing together with friends, resolving conflicts with friends, or dealing with separation from friends, you can provide picture books and storytelling activities that can be meaningful to them.

ACTIVITIES IN CHAPTER 4 TO PROMOTE CHILD DEVELOPMENT

Emotional

Child discussion *(Big Al) (The Hating Book)*
Paper masks (The Hating Book)
Puppet names (Harry and Willy and Carrothead)

Social

Feltboard *(Will I Have a Friend?)*
Child discussion *(Let's Be Enemies)*; *(Best Friends for Frances)*
Overhead transparencies *(Let's Be Enemies)*
Finding friends in a new place by sharing a toy *(The Leaving Morning)*

Physical

Glove and mitten pick-up *(Harry and Willy and Carrothead)*

Cognitive

Shadow making *(Dreams)*
Incubator *(Best Friends)*
Collecting walk *(The Extraordinary Ordinary Everything Room)*

Language

Home lending-library *(Will I Have a Friend?)*
Friendship greeting card *(The Shy Little Girl)*
Name cards *(Jessica)*
Puppet show *(Louie)*
Peep show *(The Trip)*
Letter writing *(We Are Best Friends)*
Post cards *(Best Friends)*

Creative

Paper mouse *(Dreams)*
Marbleized paper *(Dreams)*
Clown puppet *(Louie)*
First-person feather stories *(Anna Banana and Me)*
Collage and story *(The Extraordinary Ordinary Everything Room)*
Picnic hamper *(Best Friends for Frances)*
Peep show stories *(The Trip)*
Halloween costumes *(The Trip)*

REFERENCES CITED

Beaty, J.J. (1992), *Preschool Appropriate Practices*. Fort Worth,Tex.: Harcourt Brace Jovanovich.

Beaty, J.J. (1992), *Skills for Preschool Teachers,* New York: Merrill Macmillan.

Buzzelli, C.A. and File, N. (1989) "Building Trust in Friends," *Young Children* 44(3) 70–75.

Janssen, D.H. and Beaty, J.J. (1988), *Storytelling Mark Twain Style*. Elmira, N.Y.: McGraw Bookstore, Elmira College.

Hopkins, L.B. (1969), *Books Are By People*. New York: Citation Books.

Hurst, C. (1990), *Once Upon a Time...An Encyclopedia for Successfully Using Literature with Young Children*. Allen, Tex.: DLM.

Kemple, K.M. (1991), "Preschool Children's Peer Acceptance and Social Interaction," *Young Children* 46(5) 47–54.

Smith, C.A. (1986), "Nurturing Kindness Through Storytelling," *Young Children* 41(6) 46–51.

OTHER CHILDREN'S PICTURE BOOKS ABOUT *FINDING FRIENDS*

Asare, M. (1986), *Cat in Search of a Friend*. Brooklyn,N.Y.: Kane/Miller.

Blaustein, M.(1990), *Make Friends, Zachary!* New York: Harper & Row.

Carle, E. (1971), *Do You Want to Be My Friend?* New York: Thomas Y. Crowell Co. (wordless)

Escudie, R. and Wensell, U. (ill.) (1988) *Paul and Sebastian*. Brooklyn, N.Y.: Kane/Miller.

Greenfield, E. and Barnett, M. (ill.) (1975), *Me & Neesie*. New York: Thomas Y. Crowell.

Heine, H. (1986), *Friends*. New York: Macmillan.

Hughes, S.(1983), *Alfie Gives a Hand*. New York: Lothrop, Lee & Shepard.

Komaiko, L. (1988), *Earl's Too Cool for Me*. New York: Harper Collins.

Knowles, S. and Clement, R.(1988), *Edward the Emu*. New York: Harper Collins.

Lester, H. and Munsinger, L. (ill.) (1988), *Tacky the Penguin*. Boston: Houghton Mifflin.

Lionni, L.(1969), *Alexander and the Wind-Up Mouse*. New York: Pantheon.

Lionni, L. (1970), *Fish is Fish*. New York: Pantheon Books.

Lionni, L. (1964), *Tico and the Golden Wings*. New York: Pantheon.

Lyon, G.E. and Rosenberry, V. (ill.) (1989), *Together*. New York: Orchard Books.

Mahy, M. and Smith, W. (ill.) (1990), *Making Friends*. New York: Macmillan.

Marshall, J. (1978), *George and Martha One Fine Day*. Boston: Houghton Mifflin Co.

Mayer, Mercer and Mayer, Marianna. (1971), *A Boy, a Dog, A Frog and a Friend*. New York: Dial Books. (wordless)

Polacco, P. (1992), *Chicken Sunday*. New York: Philomel Books.

Riggio, A. (1990), *Gert and Frieda*. New York: Atheneum.

Russo, M. (1992), *Alex Is My Friend*. New York: Greenwillow Books.

Trivas, I. (1992), *Annie...Anya: A Month in Moscow*. New York: Orchard Books.

Waber, B. (1988), *Ira Says Goodbye*. Boston: Houghton Mifflin Co.

Waber, B. (1972), *Ira Sleeps Over*. Boston: Houghton Mifflin Co.

Winthrop, E. (1989), *The Best Friends Club*. New York: Lothrop.

PET TALES

FROGS   *Action Chant*

Frogs are fun
If you can catch 'em;
Jump too quick   *(jump)*
For me to snatch 'em;
Swim too fast   *("swim" with arms)*
For me to follow;
Dive too deep   *("dive" with arms)*
For me to wallow;
Frogs are fun
But best to look   *(open hands like book)*
In the pages
Of a book!   *(clap)*

✀ Animals in Children's Lives

Whether or not young children have pets of their own, they seem to be drawn to animals, especially small animals. Perhaps they are captivated by the way little animals romp and play and cavort around completely uninhibited. Or they may feel an instinctive bond with animals because they are little like themselves. One of the first words infants often say is "doggie," whether or not they have a pet dog. This word is then generalized by the infants to include all little animals, even kitties and toy teddy bears.

When Sylvia Ashton-Warner, the noted New Zealand reading specialist, spent a year teaching young American children in Colorado, using her "key vocabulary" method, she was surprised to find that one of the first reading words to emerge naturally for many of her youngsters was "dogs."

These dogs are obviously genuine key words and I've never seen this score before. Dogs in this town are just like people, are treated like people and act like people, even to attending their own school, and all but talk the language... For my own interest, I compare the surfacing of five words:

Own name	2
helicopter	3
Daddy	7
Mommy	8
dogs	15

which no doubt would impress the dogs.
(Ashton-Warner, 1972,96)

There are other explanations for young children's captivation with animals. Animals seem to satisfy some of children's deep-seated needs:

1. The need to love and be loved unconditionally
2. The need to care for something smaller than yourself
3. The tactile need to touch something soft or cuddly
4. The need for a friend or companion that follows you or comes when you call

All humans have this instinctive need for love, both to give love and to receive it. Although human caregivers may well satisfy this need for many young children, some adults are not as openly affectionate as others. With an animal pet, the child can hold it close, pet it, and shower it with love and affection in an open and unembarrassed way that is not always possible with another human. Furthermore, the animal pet usually returns this affection in like measure, much to the child's delight.

Because young children find themselves to be little and helpless in the world of adult giants around them, they are often drawn intuitively to small animals in a similar plight. Here it is the child who can be protector and caregiver of someone little and helpless: in other words, to be in charge. It is not only therapeutic for young children to be in this position, but also invaluable for them try on an adult role in a meaningful way. Children learn a lot from trying on roles, pretending to be someone else. So when, as in this case, the situation is real, the learning experience is more powerful.

Then there is the need for a close friend or companion. Animal pets can satisfy that yearning in ways no brother, sister, or playmate is able to. Animals can provide the warmth and comfort of a companion who enjoys being close, but is not demanding, intrusive, or judgmental.

❧ Animals in Picture Books

Animal stories have long been favorites of young children. The animal characters themselves are often one of three different types:

1. *Animals as humans who talk, think, act, and often live like humans.* Folktale animals from the "talking-beast tales" such as Aesop's fables or "The Three Bears" fall into this category.
2. *Animals who display both human and animal characteristics.* Peter in "The Tale of Peter Rabbit" is able to talk, cry, and feel like a human, but also sneaks into the farmer's vegetable garden to nibble lettuce like a real rabbit.
3. *Animals who behave as animals and do not have the ability to talk or act like a person.* These true animal characters are often found in stories about pets.

Children relish all three types of animal stories, but young children especially enjoy books from the first two categories where they can identify with the animal characters as if they were humans. Because three- to six-year-old children are in the "pretending" stage of their development, they take great joy in pretending to be the animal characters of their favorite books.

Claudia Lewis in her book *Writing for Young Children,* tells how simple it is for children to pretend to be animals:

Identification with animals is phenomenally easy for him anyway, as anyone knows who has watched a child turning himself into a baby kitten or a spirited horse as he plays. The border line between the human baby and the animal baby seems almost nonexistent to the three- or four-year-old, for his play purposes—and that is to say, for his reliving and integrating of experience. Furthermore, rabbits, bears, and billy goats are without skin color; they do not lose their teeth at six, or freckle in the sun; red hair, blond hair, black hair, are unknown. Any child can slip into their ample fur and play the part. (Lewis, 1954, 124–125)

Another important reason children respond so well to animal characters like these is that the youngsters can undergo the vicarious thrill of being scared, or being heroic, or being loyal—in fact, a whole range of feelings they might not otherwise experience. A child often sees him- or herself in the actions of the storybook animal characters, but there is just enough distance between them for the child to feel safe. (Oppenhein, Brenner, & Boegehold, 1986, 110)

Picture books with animals as principal characters that act as humans are discussed throughout this text. For example, in Chapter 1 the alligator family acts just like people in *Keep Your Mouth Closed, Dear,* and the little llama in *Is Your Mama a Llama?* talks to the other animals as if he were a person. In Chapter 2 the little girl pig in *I Like Me!* is dressed, stands on two feet, and takes on the same emotional characteristics as a human. Big Al, the ugly fish in *Big Al,* finds friends just as a human child would.

This chapter, on the other hand, looks at books featuring animals as pets. This is the third type of animal story mentioned above. These animals act as animals that are the pets of child or adult characters. They can be found in books that are discussed under the categories of:

Pets in general
Cats
Dogs

Pets in General

Children's great affinity for animals shows itself early. Toddlers want to cuddle kittens or puppies, and must be warned not to squeeze too hard. Stuffed animal toys become "security blankets" for some youngsters, and are clung to and carried everywhere. Children with no pets often beg for one with such persistence that they finally wear down their parents and get one. Some children seem to attract animals naturally and are followed home by dogs or cats with little effort on their part. And all children love to have their pets recognized by others at a pet show.

Picture books included here under PETS IN GENERAL are:

Can I Keep Him?, by Steven Kellogg, 1971
Pet Show, by Ezra Jack Keats, 1972
A Bicycle for Rosaura, by Daniel Barbot; Morella Fuenmayor (ill.), 1990
To Bathe a Boa, by C. Imbior Kudrna, 1986

AUTHORS
of **INTEREST**

STEVEN KELLOGG is one of the favorite authors and illustrators of picture books featuring children and their animal pets. Growing up in Darien, Connecticut, he made up and illustrated stories to entertain his younger sisters. Animals were favorite characters, and he ended up trying to draw every animal and bird in the encyclopedia, covering the walls of his bedroom with their pictures. His special dog favorites are Great Danes, and he actually had a dog called Pinkerton. (Hurst, 1990, 68)

 Can I Keep Him? (1971), by Steven Kellogg, New York: The Dial Press. The story of little Arnold who wants a pet and a mother who doesn't is the typical Kellogg dilemma dramatized through increasingly exaggerated conditions. Arnold starts in a conservative way by wanting to keep the dog he has found, and then the kitten, but when his mother rejects these animals because dogs bark too much, and grandma is allergic to cat fur, Arnold ups the ante with imaginative requests. He wants to keep a shy fawn, a little bear, a tiger cub, a python snake, and finally a dinosaur. His mother rejects all these demands one by one with typical but hilarious housekeeping reasons such as: the python's skin will clog the vacuum cleaner. Finally lonely Arnold finds a real little boy, Ralph, and wants to keep him too, but the mother suggests they go outside and play, and no more questions about animals. Arnold doesn't need to ask on the last page, because Ralph is only too happy to ask the mother himself about keeping the real pigeon they have found!

+ Read   Introduce this book through reading to individuals or a small group. They need to sit close in order to see Kellogg's meticulous drawings of Arnold's imaginary animal finds. Also give your listeners a chance to examine the hilarious details that illustrate the mother's rejection of each animal. When she rejects the bear because of its disagreeable odor they will probably note the family members holding their noses, but do they also see the flowers in a vase wilting and falling off because of the terrible smell?

+ Tell with Toy Animals   Once children are familiar with the story, you can have a great deal of fun telling the tale over again to the total group with toy animals you pull out of a bag or box. Give the child in your story the name of a different child from your class each time you tell it. Pull out the animals from your bag one by one without looking, and pretend your child character has found each in some unlikely place, and wants to keep him. Children enjoy repetition in a story, so always have your child character ask: "Can I keep him?" Have your mother character reject each of these requests with some outrageous reason. Once your children have got into the swing of the story, let them help to make up the reasons for rejecting each animal. ("No. No parrots because they squawk so loud no one could hear the TV!") At the end, you might pull one more secret toy animal out of your pocket that the mother finally agrees to keep.

+ **Have Children Tell in Pairs**   Children love to become involved in this story if you have made it fun and funny. Once they understand the sequence and reasoning behind it, they enjoy being the tellers themselves. Two children can tell the story together, with one telling about the animal she wants to keep and the other taking the part of the mother who rejects the request. Even the youngest of them can pull a toy animal out of a box or bag and tell why she wants to keep it, while her partner can make up some silly reason why she can't.

+ **Keep a Classroom Pet**   It is important after reading this book to talk with children about pets in the home. Many homes cannot accommodate pets because of size or space, or because they are apartments. Many parents cannot care for pets because they work all day or because this is not one of their priorities. A classroom, on the other hand, can usually keep a small pet such as a guinea pig, rabbit, gerbil, tropical fish, or a small wild pet. Your youngsters can be involved in caring for the animal by feeding it and helping to clean its cage or tank. The ultimate responsibility for classroom animals is yours, of course. Children can learn a great deal about the needs of animal pets, their reproduction, and even dealing with the death of a pet. The book *Pets in a Jar: Collecting and Caring for Small Wild Animals* (Simon, 1975) helps teachers set up live collections of everything from tadpoles and toads to brine shrimp and butterflies.

***Pet Show!** (1972), by Ezra Jack Keats, New York: The Macmillan Co.* The inner city Manhattan kids hear about the pet show in the park, and each of them decides to bring his pet. Keat's original African-American character Peter will bring his dog, Willie. Roberto of paper mouse fame plans to bring his real mouse. Archie, Peter's friend, plans to bring the cat that followed him home, but can't find him. He looks everywhere. Finally, the show commences. Everyone gets a prize for something. As the last prize is awarded Archie appears with a paper bag. In the bag is a jar. In the jar is his pet, a germ! Its name is Al. The judges award Al a prize for the quietest pet in the show! Just then the cat shows up with an old woman, and the judges give the surprised woman a prize for the cat with the longest whiskers.

+ **Read**   Once again it is imperative to read this book to individuals or a small group. They need to see Keats' marvelous illustrations of the children and scenes of inner city life. The simple text of a few lines on each page, inserted onto the vibrant colors of city "wallscapes" and graffiti, excites the listeners just as it did the participants in Keats' *Pet Show!*

+ **Have a Pet Show**   Have your own pet show in the classroom. Do not have children bring real pets (many do not have them), but instead give children an opportunity to cut out the picture of a pet from magazines you have provided. Toy catalogs, mail order catalogs, and magazines featuring animals will give the children an array of pets to choose from. Have them paste the picture of their animal on a backing paper. They can name their pet if they wish. Some will surely be as creative as Archie, rejecting the commonplace and making up their own. Be ready with a list of prizes to award for the noisiest, quietest, friendliest, busiest, longest, biggest, smallest, softest, etc. Stick-on stars can be the prizes for everyone.

A Bicycle for Rosaura *(1991), by Daniel Barbot; Morella Fuenmayor; illustrator; Brooklyn, N.Y.: Kane/Miller.* Señora Amelia had a houseful of pets: a dog, a kitten, a talking parrot, a turtle, twin canaries, and a hen named Rosaura. When she asks Rosaura what she wants for her birthday, the hen tells her "a bicycle" because she wants to be the first hen to have one. Amelia has no luck finding such an item. But when a strange man comes to town who makes rollerskates for dogs and eyeglasses for cats, Amelia asks him to make a bicycle for Rosaura. He takes the proper measurements, works out a design, and finally completes the little bicycle in time for the hen's birthday party. If you should visit Señora Amelia's town in Venezuela you can see the little hen riding her bike, but watch out, warns the narrator, the strange man forgot the brakes!

+ Read   Colorful scenes of a Venezuelan town and Señora Amelia's house fill every other page of this lighthearted fantasy. Your children should enjoy experiencing a picture book from another culture. Have them note details of things that are the same and those that are different from their town.

+ Pet Rides   Your youngsters can give their pets a ride too. Have them ride their cutout paper pets (from the Pet Show activity) or stuffed animals in a little wagon, the wooden or metal vehicles you may have, or the trikes and wagons on the playground. They can even have a Pet Parade.

To Bathe a Boa *(1986), by C. Imbior Kudrna, Minneapolis, Minn.: Carolrhoda Books, Inc.* How would you bathe a pet boa constrictor who does not want to take a bath? The little boy narrator of this tale tells the story of his predicament in rhymes tucked into each large double-page picture of the house built just for a boa. The wily snake uses all his tricks and then some, like a dog trying to avoid a bath. In the end it is the boy who gets the bath and his pet who scrubs him!

+ Read   The absurdity of the tale is reflected in the fantastic house with its snakey wall paper, scaley bathtub fixtures, a twining snake lamp, and a doghouse built to contain a snake's slither. Ask the children what other unusual items they see in the house. What other tricks might the snake play to avoid its bath? For children who might be afraid of snakes, does this lighthearted story make them feel any better?

+ Baths for Pets   Is the bath for a pet different from a bath for a person? Why take a bath? Does a pet snake really need a bath? Have a bath-day for the animal toys in your classroom—rubber or plastic ducks, pigs, cows, horses, dogs, etc. Bring in scrub brushes and sponges of different sizes, liquid soap, and plastic pans for bath tubs.

ஃ Cats

A home without a cat—and a well-fed, well-petted and properly revered cat—may be a perfect home, perhaps, but how can it prove title? (Twain, 1894)

This quote by Mark Twain, says it all for many people, children and adults alike. Cats, you will find, are one of your children's most popular pets, (dogs, of course, are the other). Twain, in his day, may have started the trend, for not only did he stock his home with a multitude of cats with names like *Blatherskite, Soapy Sal, Motley, Sour Mash,* and *Buffalo Bill,* but he also did storytelling on the lecture platform that included wonderfully funny tales about the cat tribe, (Beaty, 1984). A recent picture book *A Cat Tale* (Mark Twain, illustrated by Charles Blackman, 1987) is intended for older readers, but could be adapted for youngsters. Most of his written cat tales, however, are buried in his longer books rather than published in separate picture books ("Peter and the Pain-killer" in *The Adventures of Tom Sawyer;* "The Cat and the Elephant" in *The Innocents Abroad;* "Tom Quartz, the Goldmine Cat" in *Roughing It,* for example). A few oral cat tales still go the rounds in Twain locations such as his boyhood home in Hannibal, Missouri or his summer retreat in Elmira, New York.

Hand Gestures. This textbook author's husband, Dale H. Janssen, a Mark Twain look-alike, picked up such an oral tale in Hannibal depicting the mischievous young Sam Clemens (Mark Twain), called "Cats in Hat Boxes." He told the tale in many school appearances using hand gestures to make his points:

Cats in Hat Boxes

As a young boy in Hannibal, Missouri, I remember seeing this group of ladies come there for a meeting. Rather fashionable ladies wearing fancy clothes and carrying their hats in hat boxes. They had to check into a hotel where they were going to stay for the night. When the ladies left that evening to go to their meeting, each one would take her fancy hat out of her hat box and put the lid back on the box. Well, in the meantime, some of the boys in Hannibal thought they would play a trick on these ladies. They found a gunny sack and went around town gathering up stray cats. Then they sneaked into the hotel and in each one of the hat boxes they put a cat. Very softly they put the lid back on the box. That little kitty cat was probably very comfortable, and curled up and had a snooze. The boys then went back over the hill just a little way to see what would happen when the ladies came back. Each of the ladies, as you can imagine, would come into her room, light her candle or her kerosene lamp, remove her hat, raise up the lid on her hat box, and OUT WOULD JUMP THIS KITTY CAT! Probably MEOWed, and the lady screamed. Then in the next room a light would go on and another scream. You could see the lights coming on in one room after the other, and hear the screams. First thing you know, there was a cat fight in the hall. Then the dogs in the street heard the cats in the hall, and they started barking. And the next thing you know, there was a dog and cat fight. One of the darndest commotions you ever heard! Lasted all night. Next day it was written up in the St. Louis papers. Some folks thought that this young boy Sam Clemens might have had something to do with it, but I really don't remember that. I think it was all just a story people liked to tell. (Janssen, 1988)

+ Tell with Hand Gestures   An oral story like this can be made into your own story by reading it over, and then telling it silently to yourself several times until

"*. . . gathering up stray cats.*"

"*. . . very softly put the lid back on the box.*"

"*. . . out would jump this kitty cat!*"

you get it right. This particular story is very effective if told to the total group using hand gestures all the way through. You should decide which gestures to use to make the story most dramatic. You might decide on the following:

1. *carrying their hats in hat boxes:* hold imaginary hat box in front of you by the string as you say these words.

2. *take her fancy hat out of her hat box and put the lid back on the box:* take lid off imaginary box with two hands; put lid down; take out imaginary hat; put hat on head; put lid back on box.

3. *gathering up stray cats:* bend over and scoop up an imaginary cat; put it in imaginary gunny sack.

4. *sneaked into the hotel:* bend over and tiptoe

5. *put a cat in one of the hat boxes and put the lid back on the box:* pick up imaginary cat with one hand; put it in imaginary box; put lid back on box with other hand.

6. *curled up and had a snooze:* put hands together and lay head on them

7. *light her candle:* scratch imaginary match on something; pick up imaginary candle and light it; shake out match.

8. *remove her hat, raise up the lid:* take off imaginary hat with one hand; take off imaginary lid with other.

9. *out would jump this kitty cat:* raise both hands and jump back.

10. *one of the darndest commotions:* cover ears with hands

11. *the St. Louis papers:* open imaginary paper.

As you note, the entire story can be dramatized with hand gestures. Your audience, in the meantime, is creating visual images of the story in their mind's eye. After you finish the story, ask the children what they saw. Do different children see different images? Oral storytelling like this is one of the most effective ways to stimulate such creative imagery in children, and Mark Twain's stories give them an indelible glimpse of people who lived at an earlier time.

Some storytellers feel it necessary afterwards to discuss the ethics of this particular story. You can ask the children what they thought about this trick, whether or not it was a good trick to play, and why or why not.

Props. Another time you might decide to use props in telling this story. You can use a single prop such as a real hat box, or several props such as a hat box, a hat, and a stuffed cat toy. Then your gestures will consist of manipulating these props rather than imaginary objects. Children generally like both methods of telling this story. Professional storytellers, however, often prefer not to use props—or at least, not more than one prop—because they feel it distracts from the story. If your goal is to help children create their own imagery, then you will probably limit your props. But if your goal at another time is to have fun with the children, then you may want to pop a hat and a cat in and out of a real hat box. Try it and see.

Other CAT picture books you may want to use with children include:

Cloudy, Deborah King, 1989
Charlie Anderson, by Barbara Abercrombie; Mark Graham, illustrator, 1990
The Tenth Good Thing About Barney, by Judith Viorst, 1971
Lucky Russell, by Brad Sneed, 1992

Cloudy *(1989), by Deborah King, New York: Philomel Books.* This lovely book illustrated in the soft grays of clouds, rain, and dust, tells the first-person story of Cloudy, the author's cat who comes and goes silently and secretly.

+ Read   Once again, children should sit close to the book to appreciate the subtle gray colors of Cloudy and her world. Can they see her in a murky puddle or a shadowy stable?

+ Tell a First-Person Story   Can your children speak for their own pets and tell a first-person story from the pet's point-of-view? Try it and see. ("I am Jennifer's new kitten, Inky. I love to chase yarn balls and hide in paper bags.")

Charlie Anderson *(1990), by Barbara Abercrombie; Mark Graham (illustrator), New York: Margaret K. McElderry Books.* Charlie is a gray striped cat that stays at the house where Elizabeth and Sarah live. He comes in at suppertime, sleeps at the foot of Elizabeth's bed, and leaves for the woods in the morning when the girls go to school. Anderson is a gray striped cat that lives in the house with a man and a woman on the other side of the woods. He stays in the house all day and prowls the woods every night. Elizabeth and Sarah visit their father and stepmother in the city every weekend. They wish they could take Charlie with them, but their mother says he is a country cat. Then one day Charlie does not come in at suppertime.

The girls eventually find him in the house on the other side of the woods where he is known as Anderson. Charlie has two houses, just like they do, and two families that love him: lucky cat, Charlie Anderson!

+ Read   The lovely illustrations of the cat and the background done in soft fuzzy grays contrasted with the red of the girls' nightgowns and the yellow of their raincoats, make this a book to be read to only a few children at a time, close up. Contemporary children can identify with a pet that has two families and two houses to visit. They especially like the feeling of love and concern expressed by all the humans, and the fact that everyone accepts the situation and doesn't try to keep the cat for themselves alone.

+ Sharing Things You Like   What are some of the things in the classroom that children like that they can share? Sitting on the teacher's lap at storytime? Sitting next to the teacher at lunchtime? Holding and petting the class guinea pig? Reading a favorite storybook? A turn at the computer? Listening with a head set to a story tape on the cassette recorder? Riding the tricycle? Using the eggbeater in the water table? Talk about the things that the children mention. Ask them about sharing and how they are willing to do it.

+ Sharing a Cat Toy   Bring in a stuffed toy cat or kitten for the children to share and play with. Ask them to set up their own rules for sharing and taking turns.

The Tenth Good Thing About Barney *(1971), by Judith Viorst, New York: Atheneum.* "My cat Barney died last Friday. I was very sad," begins this small serious book by an author who often probes the emotional dilemmas of childhood in her thoughtful books for young children. Mother, father, and sister help the boy bury his beloved pet in the back yard, while he tells ten good things about Barney at their funeral. However, he can only think of nine things to say. Afterwards, the boy and his sister get into an argument about whether Barney is in heaven or in the ground. Father helps them think about both possibilities. Then the boy helps his father in the garden planting flower seeds. The little brown seeds in the boy's hand seem unlikely things to turn into flowers, the boy remarks. But his father tells him that the ground changes things. Barney will change, too. He'll become a part of the ground. It is then that the boy discovers the tenth good thing about Barney: he will help to grow flowers, "a pretty nice job for a cat."

+ Read and Discuss   Death is a difficult subject to deal with even for adults. The death of a beloved pet can be just as heart-wrenching for both children and adults. This thoughtful little book describes one family's response. Although a book cannot truly prepare a person for the emotional experience of a real death, reading it to children after the death of a pet may relieve sorrow by helping children to talk about the pet.

Lucky Russell *(1992), by Brad Sneed, New York: G.P. Putnam's Sons.* Russel, the farm kitten, doesn't want to be the little girl's pet, but instead wants an important job on the farm. He tries to help the farmer to catch mice like his mother, to help the

AUTHORS
of **INTEREST**

JUDITH VIORST is another author who has always wanted to write. She wrote poems since age eight and sent them to be published, but they never were until very much later. Her children's books are often about the feelings or actions of her own children, Nicholas, Anthony, and Alexander. Another of her classics is *Alexander and the Terrible, Horrible, No Good, Very Bad Day.* (Atheneum, 1972).
(Hurst, 1990, 131)

horses plow, to help the chickens lay eggs, to help the cows give milk, to help the guard dog protect the farm, to make wool for the farmer's clothes, to get as fat as the pig, and to eat grass like the goat—all to no avail. Then the farmer comes over to his little girl's picnic under a tree and pets the kitten, saying, "you, little fella, are the luckiest critter on the farm," which makes Russell feel important at last.

+ Tell   Because this story is long for your youngest children, but follows a definite pattern just as folktales do, it lends itself well to telling aloud. The art, however, is too good for the children to miss with its kitten's eye perspective of the different animals. In this case you can tell the story but show the pictures as you go along. This will also help you remember the incidents in the order they occur. Glance at each animal as you turn the page, but keep your eyes on your audience. You can speak for the kitten in a high or squeaky voice, and respond for each farmyard animal in a different voice.

+ Children Tell the Story   After you have retold the story several times to different small groups of children, suggest to a small group that they tell the story themselves using figures of animals from the Block Center. One child can be the teller for the entire story or each child in the group can hold a different animal and contribute to the story when it is that animal's turn to speak.

+ Children Write and Illustrate the Story   If the children's telling of this story goes well, ask each child to write his or her part of the story. They can draw a picture of their animal (scribbles are fine) and write the words that their animal says in their own personal script. Afterwards their contributions can be bound together to make a book about Lucky Russell.

✺ Dogs

Dogs are also very impressive to young children as mentioned earlier. Those who have dogs as pets and those who do not will enjoy hearing stories from books such as:

Pinkerton, Behave!, by Steven Kellogg, 1979
Harry, the Dirty Dog, by Gene Zion, 1956

Trouble with Trolls, by Jan Brett, 1992
A Boy, A Dog and a Frog, by Mercer Mayer, 1967

Pinkerton, Behave! *(1979), by Steven Kellogg, New York: Dial.* Here is the first book in the hilarious Pinkerton series about the Great Dane who behaves according to his own off-beat rules. When the little girl's mother tries to teach their new pet the basics of dog commands, she gets quite a surprise. At the command "Come!" Pinkerton jumps through the window. For "Fetch!" he tears the newspaper to shreds, and for "Get the burglar!" he stands up and licks a dummy burglar's face. At the obedience school Pinkerton teaches the other dogs his rules, leaving the place in shambles. But when a real burglar breaks into their house, the little girl saves the day by shouting the wrong commands for the right actions. In the end even mother catches on, telling Pinkerton "I'm a burglar!" for his face-licking response.

+ Read   Best of all, children love Kellogg's exaggerated illustrations in this large-format book. The simple one-line text at the top each page does not interfere in the detailed full-page drawings of Pinkerton's antics.

+ Play Follow-the-Directions Game   Obviously Pinkerton's problem involves not following directions accurately. After reading this book is the time to play a follow-the-directions game. Individual children in your small listening group can be given a single direction to follow. When everyone has had a turn, start over with two directions at a time. Then three directions. Can anyone follow four directions at a time (such as "Go across the room. Turn off the light switch near the door. Go over to the Block Center. Bring me the red truck on the shelf.")?

Harry the Dirty Dog *(1956), by Gene Zion; Margaret Bloy Graham (illustrator), New York: Harper & Row.* This classic picture book is another first in a series, introducing Harry the little white dog with the black spots who hates to take a bath. One day when he hears the water running, he buries the scrub brush in the back yard and runs away. His adventures in the city make him so dirty that his family doesn't recognize him when he finally returns home. Only when he digs up his brush and carries it up to the bathtub, do they finally give him the bath that transforms him back to his old self.

+ Read   Children want to see the pictures of Harry and his adventures that turn him into a black dog with white spots, so read the book to individuals or a small group. How do they feel about taking a bath? Some of your children may identify closely with Harry because they also resist taking a bath. Is there some toy, game or material that makes them feel better about it (bubble bath or a toy boat, for instance)?

+ Play Hide-the-Scrub-Brush   What else can you do with a picture book besides read it? To decide what activities you and your children can enjoy and learn from, take another look at each of the books you read, to see what experiences it contains that can be converted to classroom activities. In this book the idea of hiding a scrub brush presents interesting possibilities. One child can hide an actual scrub brush while the other children put their hands over their eyes. To make it possible to find the brush in a well-stocked classroom, tell the child to hide it on the floor behind something. The hider can say "hot" or "cold" when the seekers get close or far from the brush. The finder can be the next hider.

+ Make a Where-Did-Harry-Go? Board Game   This story also makes an excellent board game to promote counting skills and one to one correspondence. Most of your children should be able to count to six, and this game will give them practice moving a marker for a certain number of spaces (up to six) on a game board that you create. The board can be a sheet of colored posterboard twenty-two by twenty-eight inches. Cut out an extra paperback copy of *Harry the Dirty Dog* to show the following episodes on your board:

1. Harry walking past market
2. Harry looking at locomotive
3. Harry coming out of concrete pipe
4. Harry sliding down coal chute
5. Harry watching man on ladder
6. Harry walking past restaurant
7. Harry performing tricks
8. Harry with scrub brush in mouth
9. Harry in tub
10. Harry sleeping on pillow

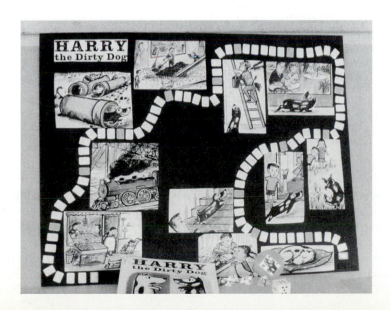

Harry's adventures make an excellent board game as cutouts with a counting trail around them.

Paste these pictures around the posterboard in some sort of sequence, leaving room for a path to wind its way around the pictures. The board should be a dark color so that the path will show up readily. To make the path that the players will follow, use white self-adhesive blank labels (squares or circles). Stick these to the board in a winding stepping-stone trail. Color in one label near each of the pictures. If the player lands on this colored label, he must answer the question: "Where is Harry now?" This can be a lot of fun for the players, not a win or lose game.

Markers can be a cutout picture of Harry's head pasted onto something like a bottle top. Make four markers if you want four players at a time. For the youngest children, you can call out the number of spaces to be moved. Older children like to shake dice and count the dots to see how many spaces to move. Pairs of dice are difficult for most preschoolers to use, but you can try one die with them. To make a one-inch hollow cardboard cube to be used as the die, cut out six one-inch squares and tape them into a cube. Mark dice dots from one to six on the six sides of the cube.

A player throws the die, counts the dots that show on the top side, and moves his marker that number of spaces. The object of the game is to move each Harry-marker all the way around the board to the end where Harry is asleep on his pillow. Do not make a fuss if children miss a space or two, or if someone says he has "won." Children can learn to take turns and wait for a turn. Let each of the players finish the game. Store the die and markers in a plastic margarine cup with a picture of Harry pasted on it.

 ***Trouble with Trolls** (1992), by Jan Brett, New York: G.P.Putnam.* What do you do when someone wants to take your dog to be their pet? Little girl Treva has this trouble with trolls who try to steal her dog Tuffi as she is climbing up Mount Baldy to ski. First one and then another troll comes out of the woods or the rocks to grab the hapless German shepard. Treva manages to trick each troll on the way up the mountain by trading off an article of her ski clothing: her beautiful blue mittens, her lovely red leather pom-pom hat, her green knit sweater, her leather boots with the blue tassels, and finally almost her skis. She tells the trolls that she can fly with the skis but will first need her mittens, then her hat, then her sweater, and finally her boots in order to do it. She asks the trolls to push her off the top of Mount Baldy so she can show them how she flies. The dimwitted trolls ask her to hold Tuffi so they can push, and off she goes skiing down Mount Baldy with everything intact including Tuffi.

+ Read   Jan Brett writes and illustrates books to be savored by children sitting close to the reader. Scandinavian snow scenes with gnarly pine trees and lichen-etched rocks stretch above the underground world of the trolls as Treva proceeds up the mountain. Do your listeners catch what is going on in the troll's cave on every page under Treva's feet? Your listeners will appreciate the trolls' squeals, growls, bellows, and roars each time they are outwitted by Treva, if you change your voice for each encounter.

+ Dramatize the Story   Bring in your own winter mittens, hat, sweater, boots, and skis, and re-enact the role of Treva on her hike up Mount Baldy. Children can take turns being the trolls who capture the dog each time, but then give him up for an article of your clothing. A child can also take the role of Tuffi as you tramp around the classroom on your imaginary climb. If the drama goes well, the children will want it repeated over and over. Let one of them be Treva another time.

+ Ski with Blocks   Have your children ever skied? They really enjoy skiing around the room on two long blocks from the Block Center.

Wordless Books

A Boy, A Dog and a Frog (1967), by Mercer Mayer, New York: The Dial Press. Here is still another classic that introduces a series of small-format wordless books with the same three characters: a boy, a dog, and a frog. The little boy, equipped with boots, bucket, and net, and accompanied by his dog, attempts to catch a frog that he spies on a lily pad in a nearby pond. Each page shows his vain attempts to sneak up and net the frog, first falling in the pond and then netting the dog instead. He gives up in disgust and goes home. The frog who enjoys the game, follows their muddy footprints back to their house, up the stairs, and into their bathtub where he lands on the dog's head as the story ends.

+ Tell   There are no words to read in a wordless book, so you must tell the story by "reading" the pictures. Young prereaders respond in different ways to wordless books. Many know that the printed text in a book has a great deal to do with the story. They may be upset with a book without a text, and consider it to be for babies. Others will like the many pictures of the frog's antics to avoid capture, as well as the whimsical expressions on his face. Some children will enjoy participating in the story by answering your questions as you go along, for example "What do you think the boy is saying now?"

Can young children tell the story on their own by looking at the pictures in a wordless book like this? Will this help them to tell their own stories, and later to read stories with understanding? This is what many teachers expect. Research has unexpectedly found, however, that young children through kindergarten and early elementary grades tend to describe the pictures in wordless books separately rather than telling a connected story. They *need adult help* to connect what is happening from one picture to the next. In the words of Hough, Nurss and Wood:

> If we do so, wordless books help children predict story events using an internalized concept of story and thus foster language comprehension. If not, wordless books assume the same role as single pictures; that is, they foster vocabulary development but not the development of story sense and prediction needed for success in beginning reading. (1987)

Wordless books like this one can be highly successful with young children, however, if you spend time talking about them. After you have "read" the story and left it in the story center for the children to look at, go through it again with a small group, asking them to describe what happens to the main character on page after page. (Raines and Isbell, 1988) Then let one of them volunteer to "read" the story. They may even want to name the characters or rename the story. With your help such books are an invaluable aid in helping children develop a "story sense."

+ Make a Footprint Trail   Another appropriate activity is the making of a footprint trail just as the boy and dog did in the story. In warm weather children can make footprints on the sidewalk outside by stepping in a pan of water and then walking. Have one child make "giant steps" or walk on tip-toe and let the others play follow-the-leader. Children also enjoy making paint footprints on paper to be displayed with their names on the classroom walls. What about making a doll footprint trail? Dip a doll's foot in water soluble paint and make a zig-zag footprint trail across paper. Children can cut out house, tree, and street pictures from old magazines, paste them here and there on a large sheet of newsprint, and make a doll footprint trail from one picture to another. Can they then tell a story about their picture? If children show interest in the concept of making footprints, read them the simple story of the little girl and mother who identify footprints in the snow from *Whose Footprints?* (Coxe, 1990)

+ Do an Action Chant   The action chant at the beginning of the chapter is a good one for the total group to do together after experiencing this story. They may want to make up their own body actions. There is a second ending to this chant. Ask the children which ending they like best:

Frogs are fun
If you can catch 'em;
Jump too quick
For me to snatch 'em;
Swim too fast
For me to follow;
Dive too deep
For me to wallow;
Frogs are fun
But sort of soggy;
Leave them for
Some other froggy!

Stories about pets like this and the others mentioned in this chapter help children to identify with a live creature that is smaller than they are, that may need their help and protection, and that can offer them affection or devotion. Some of their favorite books are often about pets that they have or wish they had. This strong interest may lead them to make up their own oral stories about animal pets. And a love for telling stories like this can lead later to a love for reading.

ACTIVITIES IN CHAPTER 5 TO PROMOTE CHILD DEVELOPMENT

Emotional Development

Have a pet show *(Pet Show)*
Keep a classroom pet *(Can I Keep Him?)*
Read and discuss *(The Tenth Good Thing About Barney)*

Social Development

Share things you like *(Charlie Anderson)*
Share a toy cat *(Charlie Anderson)*

Physical Development

Play hide-the-scrub-brush *(Harry the Dirty Dog)*
Ski with blocks *(Trouble with Trolls)*
Make a footprint trail *(A Boy, a Dog and a Frog)*
Pet rides *(A Bicycle for Rosaura)*
Baths for pets *(To Bathe a Boa)*

Cognitive Development

Tell with toy animal *(Can I Keep Him?)*
Children tell in pairs *(Can I Keep Him?)*
Play follow directions game *(Pinkerton, Behave)*
Play where-did-Harry-go? game *(Harry the Dirty Dog)*
Make a footprint trail game *(A Boy, a Dog and a Frog)*

Language Development

Do an action chant *(A Boy, a Dog and a Frog)*
Tell first-person story *(Cloudy)*
Tell the story *(Lucky Russell)*
Write and illustrate the story *(Lucky Russell)*

Creative Development

Write and illustrate the story *(Lucky Russell)*
Dramatize the story *(Trouble with Trolls)*

REFERENCES CITED

Ashton-Warner, S. (1972), Spearpoint, *"Teacher" in America.* New York: Alfred A. Knopf.

Beaty, J.J. (1984), "Cats at Quarry Farm," *Mark Twain Society Bulletin* 7(2) 1–6.

Burke, E.M. (1990), *Literature for the Young Child.* Boston: Allyn and Bacon.

Coxe, M. (1990), *Whose Footprints?* New York: Thomas Y. Crowell.

Hurst, C.O. (1990), *Once Upon a Time…An Encyclopedia for Successfully Using Literature with Young Children.* Allen, Tex.: DLM.

Hough, R.A., Nurss, J.R., and Wood, D. (1987), *"Tell Me a Story: Making Opportunities for Elaborated Language in Early Childhood Classrooms,"* Young Children 43(1) 6–12.

Janssen, D.H. and Beaty, J.J. (1988), *Storytelling Mark Twain Style.* Elmira, N.Y.: McGraw Book Store, Elmira College.

Lewis, C. (1954), *Writing for Children.* New York: Penguin Books.

Oppenheim, J., Brenner, B. and Boegehold, B.D. (1986), *Choosing Books for Kids.* New York: Ballantine Books.

Raines, S.C. and Isbell, R. (1988), *"Tuck Talking About Wordless Books Into Your Classroom,"* Young Children, 43(6) 24–25.

Simon, S. (1975), *Pets in a Jar: Collecting and Caring for Small Wild Animals,* New York: Puffin Books.

Twain, M. (1894), *The Tragedy of Pudd'nhead Wilson.* New York: American Publishing Co.

Twain, M. and Blackman, C.(ill.) (1987), *A Cat-Tale. Sydney,* Australia: P.C.I.

OTHER CHILDREN'S PICTURE BOOKS ABOUT PET TALES

Alexander, M. (1969), *Blackboard Bear.* New York: Dial Books.

Brown, R. (1986), *Our Cat Flossie.* New York: Dutton.

Cohen, C.L. and Begay, S. (1988), *The Mud Pony.* New York: Scholastic, Inc.

Dragonwagon, C. and Tafuri, N. (ill.) (1984), *Coconut.* New York: Harper & Row.

Eisler, C.and Ivory, L.A.(ill.) (1988), *Cats Know Best.* New York: Dial.

Goble, P. (1978), *The Girl Who Loved Wild Horses.* Scarsdale,N.Y.: Bradbury Press.

Hazen, B.S. and Cruz, R. (ill.) (1974), *The Gorilla Did It.* New York: Macmillan Publishing Co.

Keats, E.J. (1970), *Hi, Cat!* New York: Collier Books.

Kellogg, S. (1981), *A Rose for Pinkerton.* New York: Dial Books.

Kellogg, S. (1987), *Prehistoric Pinkerton.* New York: Dial Books.

Kellogg, S. (1982), *Tallyho, Pinkerton.* New York: Dial Books.

Livermore, E. (1973) *Find the Cat.* Boston: Houghton Mifflin Co.

Mathers, P. (1985), *Maria Theresa.* New York: Harper Collins.

Mayer, M. (1974), *The Great Cat Chase.* New York: Four Winds Press.

Noble, T.H. and Kellogg, S. (ill.) (1980), *The Day Jimmy's Boa Ate the Wash.* New York: Dial Books.

O'Neill, C. (1987), *Mrs. Dunphy's Dog.* New York: Viking Penguin.

Ross, T. (1989), *I Want a Cat.* New York: Farrar Straus Giroux.

Sutton, E. and Dodd, L. (ill.) (1973), *My Cat Likes to Hide in Boxes*. New York: Viking Penguin.

Schweitzer, B. B. and Williams, G.(ill.) (1963), *Amigo*. New York: Collier.

Ungerer, T. (1958), *Crictor*. New York: Scholastic.

DINOSAUR, DRAGON, AND MONSTER TALES

Action Chant

I have a little dragon;

I lead him by a string;   *(walk in place, one arm out)*

Sometimes he's breathing fire;   *(blow out breath)*

I've even heard him sing!   *(sing la-la-la)*

They say he's most unusual;

They want to take a look;   *(turn head side-to-side)*

But I keep him well hidden

In the pages of my book!   *(clap hands together)*

Dinosaurs, Dragons, and Monsters in Children's Lives

Most people know that children love dinosaurs these days. There are dinosaur cartoons, dinosaur videos, dinosaurs books, stuffed dinosaur animals, dinosaur computer programs, and school dinosaur projects. Gigantic robotic dinosaurs travel the science museum circuit, bringing in hundreds of admirers. Children collect miniature dinosaurs or build their own out of papier mâché. Have you ever wondered why? And why now?

After all, information about dinosaurs has been available to children for some time. The Flintstones TV cartoon series of the 1960s that showed their pet Dino, never elicited such excitement. Is it all just a fad? Hardly.

Dinosaurs, dragons, and monsters are more than they seem to be in the lives of young children. They represent in a powerfully symbolic way something very big and overpowering: FEAR. They are the dark unknown: the unspeakable thing waiting to spring out of the corners of life to do something terrible. They symbolize *fear.* They need to be controlled. They need to be overcome.

But fear has been with children forever, you may argue. Yes, it has. Yet consider the real, not imaginary, fears that children of the '90s must face daily: child abuse (physical, mental, and sexual), violence on the streets and in the home, loss of a parent through divorce or separation, homelessness (if not themselves, then others they see on the streets), the damage of drugs, deadly diseases such as AIDS, unemployment and poverty, of racism, and the damage of pollution in the environment.

The list could go on. We all know it. But young children are affected out of proportion to the rest of society because they are little and helpless. Even children not directly affected by any of these curses know people who are. In addition, all children learn the lesson of "stranger danger." All of them witness the violence on TV. Yes, the fears of today's young children are, indeed, monstrous.

Surely, you may say, this has nothing to do with children's interest in dinosaurs. But before you dismiss the notion, think again. Who were those dragons in the folktales of yore? They also symbolized the dark unknown—a negative force—evil. They tried to capture innocent young maidens, you may remember, the symbol of purity—goodness. What were those knights really doing, who slew the dragons? In the words of the noted mythologist Dr. Joseph Campbell: "...the slaying of the dragon is doing away with fears." (Campbell, 1988)

✿ Dinosaurs, Dragons, and Monsters in Picture Books

Look now at the fictional picture books about dinosaurs, and you will have to agree that their principal theme is about children's control of them. Dinosaurs, after all, are gigantic and fearsome. If a little child can control such a beast, what else could he or she be afraid of?

Children's books about dragons are the same. They show children conquering or controlling these creatures too: the ancient symbols of fear. And books about monsters? More obviously than the rest, these creatures do represent children's persistent fears, and some are quite scary, indeed.

✿ Controlling or Overcoming Fear

That naming your fear is the first step toward overcoming it is an old adage. Children's fears, often though, go nameless. Something scary is there—in the dark. Dreams are sometimes terrifying. The unknown is frightening. What is going to happen? What will I do if something bad happens?

If this terrible, unknown fear comes out in the open, a person can somehow deal with it. Picture books about dinosaurs, dragons, and monsters are based on this premise. Obviously children do not realize that these creatures in picture books are symbols for their inner fears. That is a sophisticated adult notion. But they certainly realize that these awesome creatures are scary. Thus it is quite satisfying to see that such fearsome beasts can be controlled by children, as happens in the books. The underlying message is: you can control your fears.

How does it happen? How are these creatures conquered or controlled? A glance at a representative sampling of current fictional picture books featuring dinosaurs, dragons, and monsters, shows almost as many methods as there are books:

Controlling the Creature in a Picture Book

1. Laugh at it; make it laugh. *(How to Get Rid of Bad Dreams)*
2. Name it something friendly and be nice to it. *(The Mysterious Tadpole)*
3. Expose it for something harmless. *(Jim Meets the Thing)*
4. Reason it away. *(Patrick's Dinosaurs)*
5. Erase it. *(The Scribble Monster)*
6. Become king of it. *(Where the Wild Things Are)*
7. Tame it with a magic trick. *(Where the Wild Things Are)*
8. Make it grow small. *(The Monster That Grew Small)*
9. Talk to it in a friendly way. *(The Reluctant Dragon)*
10. Play with it. *(Beware the Dragons)*
11. Have a barbecue picnic with it. *(The Knight and the Dragon)*

12. Befriend it when it's little. *(Amanda's Dinosaur)*
13. Play music to it. *(Abiyoyo)*
14. Make it friendly-looking and friendly-acting. *(The Dinosaurs Who Lived in My Backyard)*
15. Make funny rhymes about it. *(Count-A-Saurus)*
16. Scare it away with a flashlight. *(There's a Monster Under My Bed)*
17. Build a trap for it. *(Maybe a Monster* by Alexander)
18. Make a monster wall. *(Maybe a Monster* by Creighton)
19. Put it to work. *(If the Dinosaurs Came Back)*
20. Get a kitten. *(Go Away Monsters, Lickety Split)*

Whereas the previous chapter discussed pet story books as being therapeutic because they show young children in control of a small animal who is devoted to them, this chapter talks about therapeutically valuable books that show children overcoming fears by subduing huge creatures. Common categories through which these creatures are made submissive in picture books seem to be: humor, friendliness, magic, physical manipulation, and labor. The books in this chapter are discussed within these categories under the principal topics of:

Dinosaurs
Dragons
Monsters

Dinosaurs

Inappropriate Books. Children are definitely attracted to dinosaurs. The number of dinosaur books on the market today reflects this interest. You need to review them carefully. Whenever a new fad becomes commercial, the market is soon flooded with books featuring the popular topic. Some of the books dashed off on the spur of the moment may be of poor quality. Happily, they usually fade away after a year or so. But in the meantime they may:

1. give erroneous information.
2. appeal to adult sensibilities rather than to children's.
3. feature inferior art or writing.
4. have inappropriate incidents or endings.

Appropriate Books. Good books, on the other hand, stay around for awhile. Some of the better dinosaur books for young children include:

Patrick's Dinosaurs, by Carol Carrick; Donald Carrick (ill.), 1983
What Happened to Patrick's Dinosaurs?, by Carol Carrick; Donald Carrick (ill.), 1986
The Dinosaur Who Lived In My Backyard, by B.G.Hennessy; Susan Davis (ill.), 1988
Amanda's Dinosaur, by Wendy Orr; Gillian Campbell (ill.) 1988

Patrick's Dinosaurs (1983), by Carol Carrick; Donald Carrick (illustrator), New York: Clarion Books. Preschooler Patrick learns about dinosaurs from his older brother Hank who goes to school already. When they visit the zoo together, Hank tells Patrick about the brontosaurus that weighs as much as ten elephants, the huge diplodocus that can stay submerged under water, the stegosauruses that are bigger than the city buses and the tyrannosaurus that is up to the second floor of their house. Trouble is, Patrick conjures up these creatures in all their terror at the zoo, in the street, and at their house, until he practically scares himself to death. Only when Hank assures him that dinosaurs have been gone for sixty million years, does Patrick give a sigh of relief—as the ugly face of the tyrannosaur staring in their second story window finally disappears.

+ Read and Discuss   Children need to be close to the reader to see the full-page illustrations of realistic dinosaurs in browns and pinks and greens stalking the city streets. Although they are the figments of Patrick's vivid imagination, they are very real-looking. Afterwards, talk with your children about dinosaurs, and what is real or imaginary. Do any of them ever make up huge imaginary creatures in their minds?

+ Play a Computer Game   Use dinosaur programs in your Computer Center when books about dinosaurs are being read in the Story Center. The coloring program *Dinosaurs Are Forever* (1988) and the matching program *Dinosaurs* (1984) can be used by young computer users to good advantage at this time. (Beaty, 1992)

What Happened to Patrick's Dinosaurs? (1986), by Carol Carrick; Donald Carrick (illustrator) New York: Clarion Books. The follow-up book is even better because Patrick is in complete control of the situation this time. When he and his brother discuss what happened to the real dinosaurs, his brother tells what scientists think, but Patrick has his own ideas. His is a wondrous story about dinosaurs and people being friends in ancient times when dinosaurs did all the work for people, building houses, cars, and airplanes, and even putting on shows. In the end the dinosaurs get tired of doing all the work so they build themselves a space ship and leave the earth, never to return.

+ Read and Discuss   The realistic full-page drawings illustrate Patrick's fascinating story, so your listeners will need to sit close enough to see them. Could Patrick's story be true? Ask your listeners what they think.

+ Child Storytelling   Have children volunteers tell their own story of what happened to the dinosaurs. This may help you to discover which of your children are highly imaginative, a quality that needs cultivating in order to promote creativity.

AUTHORS
of INTEREST

CAROL AND DONALD CARRICK from Martha's Vineyard, Massachusetts, have often used their own children Christopher and Paul in their books. Carol is the writer and Donald the illustrator, using charcoal washed with watercolor.

The Dinosaur Who Lived In My Backyard *(1988), by B.G.Hennessy; Susan Davis (illustrator), New York: Puffin Books.* Here is a first-person story about a little boy who imagines what it would be like for the dinosaur who once lived in his backyard. He imagines his birth, his growth (with feet so big that one wouldn't even fit in the sandbox), and the hundreds of pounds of vegetables he had to eat every day. The boy only wishes that he still lived there, and is saving his lima beans, just in case.

+ Read and Discuss   These colorful illustrations portray a happy dinosaur who gambols about the street and yard, with only one dinosaur fight being shown. Let children sit close to see them.

+ Children Tell Their Own Stories   This time, have a child "read" the book to another child or a small group, telling her own story about the pictures as she turns the pages.

+ Sandbox Play   Put sand in your empty water table or into a large flat plastic tub on another classroom table. Cut out the dinosaur, the characters, and the scenes from an extra copy of this book and mount them on cardboard. Then cover them with clear self-adhesive vinyl. Stand them up in the sand of the sandbox and let the children play with them. You might also add the miniature dinosaurs from the Block Center, as well. Children who play creatively with miniature toys like this develop a positive feeling of being in charge that helps to counterbalance the fact that they are controlled by the adults in their world.

Amanda's Dinosaur *(1988), by Wendy Orr; Gillian Campbell, illustrator, New York: Scholastic, Inc.* Girls are interested in dinosaurs, too. In this book Amanda, who lives on a farm in Australia with her mother and father, cows, chickens, kangaroos, possums, wallabies, parrots and peacocks, wants a dinosaur. When she learns that dinosaurs hatch from eggs, she looks in an old log and finds a dinosaur egg. A little green baby dinosaur finally emerges. Under Amanda's care, the animal grows to enormous size. When a fox tries to invade the hen house, Amanda riding her dinosaur gives it the chase of its life.

+ Read and Discuss   This is a very realistic-looking and -sounding story. Your listeners will enjoy the colorful pictures of the Australian domestic animals and exotic wildlife. The dinosaur's appearance does not seem out of place in such a setting. Is it real? This is the question you should discuss with the children after reading this story.

+ Hatch Eggs in an Incubator   This is another book that can motivate your children to become involved in an egg-hatching activity. Amanda watches the dinosaur egg carefully, asking her mother questions about its readiness to hatch. Directions for hatching eggs in a classroom incubator are given on p. 83. Another book to read during this activity is the gorgeously-illustrated *Chickens Aren't the Only Ones* (Heller, 1981) that presents rhyming non-fiction information about creatures who lay eggs. It includes a colorful double-page spread of dinosaurs, as well as a number of the other birds, reptiles, and mammals shown in Amanda's story.

After hearing dinosaur stories children can hatch eggs in an incubator.

🔯 Dragons

Dragons are not as popular as dinosaurs with younger children, therefore fewer picture books about them exist. But the popular game *Dungeons and Dragons* played by older youngsters has begun an interest in these mythical beasts. Two books that might appeal to children of preschool and kindergarten age are:

The Knight and the Dragon, by Tomie de Paola, 1980
Beware the Dragons!, by Sarah Wilson, 1985

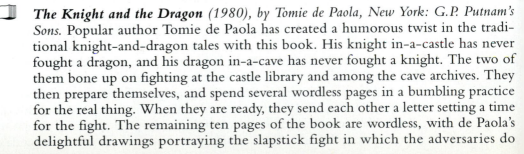

***The Knight and the Dragon** (1980), by Tomie de Paola, New York: G.P. Putnam's Sons.* Popular author Tomie de Paola has created a humorous twist in the traditional knight-and-dragon tales with this book. His knight in-a-castle has never fought a dragon, and his dragon in-a-cave has never fought a knight. The two of them bone up on fighting at the castle library and among the cave archives. They then prepare themselves, and spend several wordless pages in a bumbling practice for the real thing. When they are ready, they send each other a letter setting a time for the fight. The remaining ten pages of the book are wordless, with de Paola's delightful drawings portraying the slapstick fight in which the adversaries do themselves in without touching one another. The castle librarian/damsel comes along, picks up the pieces, and lends them each a new book on building a barbecue and outdoor cooking. This time they finally get it right and set up the "K & D Bar–B–Q" that grills shish-ka-bob hamburgers for the entire castle community. (Your children will applaud!)

+ Read   Read the words and the pictures of this book with a small group of children looking on.

+ Children "Read"   Have children "read" the wordless pictures, telling the story as they turn the pages. One child can "read" for the knight, one for the dragon, and one for the librarian.

+ Dramatize with Overhead Transparency Costumes   This particular story is an excellent one to dramatize since the pictures are so dramatic and funny. To make a costume for the three main characters, have the children choose their favorite picture of the knight, the dragon, and the damsel. Make a photocopy of each picture on an overhead transparency sheet instead of regular copy paper. Project each transparency onto newsprint or some other large sheet of paper the size of a child, and trace around the picture. (An adult may need to help preschoolers do the tracing). Cut out the traced picture, have the children color or paint it, and finally tape it onto a plastic trash bag costume with holes cut out for head and arms.

To dramatize the story, you will need the three characters described, a narrator, and three sound-effects children (for the dragon's fiery breath, the knight's galloping horse, and the crashes.) The only speaking part is the narrator's. An adult may want to do the narration the first time through. Let the children characters use their creative talents to act out the characters' roles and make the sound effects. Each time you dramatize this story, let different children take the parts.

 Beware the Dragons! *(1985), by Sarah Wilson, New York: Harper & Row.* This modern fantasy is about brave little Matilda who rows her boat across Spooner Bay despite the dragons that are sometimes as thick as gnats. It is a long story for your youngest children, but may keep their interest with Tildy's comical expressions, such as "Great Crying Cuttlefish!" and "Shivering Shark Tails!" Matilda discovers that the dragons come there only to play, not to eat people, so she gets them balls and kites and rafts from the general store, and proves to the townsfolks that they are harmless.

+ Read with Expression   Read this story to individuals or small groups with as much expression as you can put in your voice. There is a great deal of good dialog in the story, and children enjoy hearing it done in different tones. Try having Tildy speak in a high and squeaky voice, her mother lower and strict-sounding, the dragons deep and grumbly, and Mr. Scott shaky-sounding.

+ Tell with Expression   This long story can be told successfully, too. Read it over to yourself several times until the plot is familiar. Jot down the incidents in the order they happen if this helps you to remember the story.

1. Tildy prepares to row across Spooner Bay.
2. Tildy stops rowing to eat her lunch.
3. A storm strikes.
4. Tildy gets stuck on a dragon-bump.
5. The dragons toss her up in the air.
6. Tildy scolds the dragons.
7. They say they're lonely and just want to play.
8. Tildy escorts the dragons back to Spooner Bay.
9. She gets them beach toys from the general store.
10. The townsfolk watch the dragons play and agree to let them stay.
11. Tildy is a hero.

Be sure to speak in Tildy's voice and the voice of the dragons at the appropriate times. Use some of Tildy's exclamations if you want: "Great Crying Cuttlefish!" or "Shivering Shark Tails!" or "Leaping Lobsters!" Take a bow at the end. You can hold young children's attention better by telling than reading a long story.

+ Dragon Mitten Puppets   With an extra paperback copy of this book, cut out the dragon pictures you like best and tape them onto mittens to be used as hand puppets. If you prefer not to cut up the book, place onionskin paper over a picture, trace around it, cut it out, color it, and tape it onto a mitten. When all the children have dragon mitten puppets, let them have fun catching inflated balls just as the dragons did in the story. Make a Tildy puppet too, and have the children take turns telling their own versions of this tale.

Monsters

Monsters, on the other hand, are populating more and more books for young children. Twenty years ago, Maurice Sendak's award-winning *Where the Wild Things Are* was one of the few monster books on the market. Today there are dozens. As with dinosaur books, you need to look them over carefully to make sure they are appropriate for your children. Some are more scary than they need to be, or feature more violence. Keep in mind that the idea is to tame the monster, to control the fear it represents. If the stories fail to do this, think twice about using them. Books featuring the monster theme discussed here include:

Jim Meets The Thing, by Miriam Cohen; Lillian Hoban (ill.), 1981
The Beast in the Bathtub, by Kathleen Stevens; Ray Bowler (ill.), 1978
There's a Monster Under My Bed, by James Howe; David Rose (ill.), 1986
Where the Wild Things Are, by Maurice Sendak, 1963
The Mysterious Tadpole, by Steven Kellogg, 1977

Jim Meets The Thing (1981), *by Miriam Cohen; Lillian Hoban (illustrator), New York: Greenwillow Books.* Little Jim, previously seen in Cohen's *Will I Have a Friend?* and *Best Friends,* is frightened by "The Thing," a monster from a television show. He has bad dreams about it all night. The next day the children at school are all talking and laughing about it. Jim tells them not to talk about it, but they make fun of him. Out on the playground the others play Super Heroes, but Jim walks away, embarrassed because he is afraid. Then Danny, the loudest of all, finds a praying mantis insect crawling on his jacket. All of them are scared of it except Jim who quietly takes the mantis off the jacket and sets it free in the corner of the playground. Then the others begin to confess other fears about TV heroes. They end up calling Jim "Mantis Man."

+ Read and Discuss   Here is a book everyone should hear. Read it to smaller groups or to the whole group this time. Ask the children about the TV Super Heroes they like, and those they are scared of. It is important for children to know that everyone is afraid of something at one time or another.

+ Dress Up and Play Super Heroes   Children will role-play the Super Heroes from TV whether or not you encourage it. They can learn what are good and bad traits from such play, if you talk it over with them. How should a good Super Hero act? How does a bad Super Hero behave? Should they act this way in the classroom? Bring in some clothes props to encourage Super Hero play from this book: Gravity Girl, Web Man, Captain Mighty, and Mantis Man. What should the actions of each of these Super Heroes be? The children will be delighted to realize that they can make up their own Super Heroes and control their actions. Children get great satisfaction out of pretending to be someone bigger and stronger than themselves. (Johnston, 1987, 15–17)

The Beast in the Bathtub (1980), *by Kathleen Stevens; Ray Bowler (illustrator), New York: Harper and Row.* Lewis tells his folks that he can't take a bath because there's a beast in the bathtub, but his folks won't listen. So Lewis takes his bath, anyway, in between the front claws of a huge green hippo-looking beast. Lewis and the beast have a water fight, sneak downstairs for a snack, have a pillow fight, spill all the marbles, say their prayers, and finally settle down to sleep. When Mother kisses him goodnight, Lewis admits that there isn't a beast in the bathtub. (No, because it's now under the bed!)

+ Read and Discuss   Children will want to see these pictures, too, of the huge blubbery but friendly-looking beast. Ask them how this beast would act in their bathroom. How would it help them get dressed? Eat lunch with them? Go for a ride in their wagon? Come to school with them?

+ Make Monster Puzzles   This book with its slick pages and colorful illustrations filling every other page, is especially well-suited for making puzzles. Each illustrated page from an extra paperback copy of the book can be a separate puzzle. Mount them on different colored poster boards, and cut them into puzzle pieces. For the youngest children, they are best cut into four large pieces. Older children can usually put together six-piece puzzles. Keep the pieces of each page-puzzle in a separate color-coded envelope, the color of the puzzle's backing cardboard.

There's a Monster Under My Bed (1986), *by James Howe; David Rose (illustrator), New York: Macmillan Publishing Co.* Nighttime is scary for many children. There is something lurking there in the dark. They are afraid to close their eyes and go to sleep. This little book is told in first-person by Simon as he lays in bed thinking about a monster being under his bed...or maybe two, or three, or four.... He is too old for a night–light like his little brother Alex, but then he finds that Mom left him a flashlight, just in case. When he uses it to check for monsters he actually finds something under his bed: his little brother Alex!

+ Read and Discuss   Each double-page illustration shows Simon in bed, along with a different number and kind of imaginative monsters under the bed. Besides being a story, this is a monster-counting book. Ask children to comment on the monsters Simon imagines. Did any of them ever imagine there were monsters under their beds? What did they imagine them to be like? What did they do to overcome their fears?

An even more popular book with the same theme is *There's a Nightmare in My Closet* (Mayer, 1968). In this book the little boy in bed confronts the rather horrible looking nightmare in his closet by shooting it with his popgun. The monster is so afraid, the boy lets it get into bed with him. When they are both asleep another nightmare comes out of the closet. It is difficult to recommend this book for a classroom because most programs for young children do not allow playing with toy guns. In addition, the message seems to be that even if you conquer one nightmare another one is still lurking in the closet.

+ Make a Monster-in-the-Shoebox Game   Have each youngster trace a monster onto a piece of colored construction paper. You can provide the cardboard monster pattern to be traced. Make it a jolly monster, something like a snowman with horns. The children can name their monsters and put smiles on their faces . Be sure each one is a different color. To play the game, put the monsters in a shoebox, cover the box, and give each child a turn to draw out a monster. He or she must first guess what color monster they think they will get. Then without looking, they should reach in a hand and draw out a monster. If they have guessed the right color, they keep the monster till the next round. If not, they pass the monster box on to the next person. Play until all the monsters have been drawn out. If the children have named their monsters, then they can also try to guess by name as well as color.

Where the Wild Things Are (1963), *by Maurice Sendak, New York: Harper and Row.* Here is surely the "king" of all the monster books. It is a classic of its kind, winner of many awards, and translated into more than half a dozen languages. It is the story of little Max who wears his wolf suit one night and makes mischief until his mother sends him to bed without any supper. Max's imagination and dreams turn his bedroom into a forest with an ocean and boat to take him to the place where the wild things are. Although the five huge monsters roar at him, he tames them with the magic trick of "staring into all their yellow eyes without blinking once." So they make him king of all the wild things. Together they have a "wild rumpus" dance in the woods for six wordless pages, until Max becomes lonely and sails back into his bedroom, where his supper awaits him.

+ Read and Discuss   This book reads like the classic that it is, with the poetic rhythm that all good prose should have. It was certainly written to be read aloud, as you will discover the first time you read it. Yes, a few children may be frightened by the pictures of the monsters, but it is mostly adults that are unnerved by them. Most children relish the idea that little Max can tame the beasts, and become one of them in their wild rumpus. Ask your children what they would do if they were Max. You may be interested to note that the first pictures in the book start out small with a great deal of white around them, but that as the fantasy grows, so do the illustrations, eventually covering all of the double-page spreads.

+ Have a Wild Rumpus Dance in Overhead Transparency Costumes   To make the costumes, photocopy pictures of Max and the Wild Things onto overhead transparency paper; then project each one onto newsprint; trace around it; cut it out; color it; tape it to plastic trash bag costumes as you did for *The Knight and the Dragon*. Make several costumes of each monster so that each of the children has one. To have a "wild rumpus" dance, put on a record or tape of weird music or music with a strong beat that children can move to. Children enjoy creative movement once they feel free to move. The dance does not have to be wild. If the music is solemn and plodding, the children will be, too.

 The Mysterious Tadpole *(1977), by Steven Kellogg, New York: The Dial Press.* This is the kind of story older children would invent for themselves if Kellogg hadn't thought of it. Louis's Uncle McAllister in Scotland sends him a birthday gift every year. This particular year the gift is a tadpole. His teacher encourages Louis to bring it to school so the children can watch it develop into a frog. Instead, the mysterious tadpole, who loves cheeseburgers, eventually develops into the Loch Ness Monster. What a time Louis has as the monster outgrows every watery space he finds for it, scaring everybody along the way. Improbable adventures grow as quickly as Alphonse, as the monster is called. But they end happily a year later with a swimming pool and plenty of cheeseburgers for Alphonse, and a new present for Louis from his uncle: a large egg-shaped stone with a crack that suddenly develops in it.

AUTHORS
of INTEREST

MAURICE SENDAK began writing early when he was nine. He lived in Brooklyn and watched from his window while children played on the sidewalk. His books often reflect his own memories and fears of childhood. This best-known of children's book authors and illustrators received the Caldecott Medal for *Where the Wild Things Are* and the Hans Christian Andersen Illustrator's Medal in recognition for the entire body of his works. He often includes his dogs in his books. (Hurst, 1990, 106)

+ Read   Let children sit close as you read this story in order to see the details in Kellogg's typically boisterous illustrations, and to follow the action of the story.

+ Play Cheeseburger Beanbag   Children can feed the hungry monster and at the same time improve their eye-hand coordination with a beanbag game. Draw a large freehand outline of the monster's head on a sheet of green construction paper. Add an eye with eyelashes, orange dots, and a large open mouth. Paste your monster on a cardboard carton and cut out the mouth hole.

To make the cheeseburger beanbags, trace around a cup and cut out four-inch circles from a brown supermarket bag. Cut out four and a half-inch circles from orange felt or orange construction paper. Staple or stitch together two brown disks with one orange disk in between. Keep your staples close together. Leave an opening for filling the beanbag with rice, macaroni or beans. Then staple or sew it shut. Make at least four beanbags. Let children stand in front of the carton monster and try to throw cheeseburger beanbags into his mouth.

+ Raise Tadpoles   Pond tadpoles will not develop into a Loch Ness Monster, but nevertheless their transformation from swimming, fish-like beings, into frogs with legs is just as remarkable. To keep tadpoles in your classroom you will need a gallon jar, three-quarters filled with pond water and some pond plants. One jar like this can support five or six tadpoles. Keep the water at room temperature. Tadpoles eat pond plants, but also a bit of lettuce or spinach. Once they have turned into frogs you may want to let them go, as it is more difficult to provide them with small live moving food necessary for their survival. (Simon, 1975)

Tried and tested books like the ones discussed in this chapter are the best kind to use with young children to help them deal with this touchy emotional topic: fear. As mentioned previously, a few of the most sensitive children may be frightened by

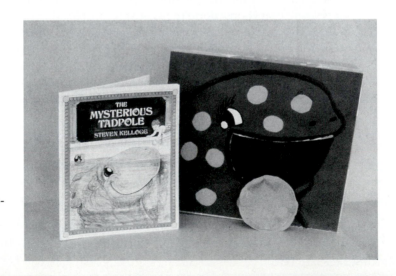

Children can play "cheeseburger bean-bag" after hearing this story about a monster who loves cheeseburgers.

pictures of monsters, no matter how friendly they seem. These children may also be the ones who are terrified by their own dreams. It is not so much children's books that frighten such children, but the fear within the children themselves, and their sensitive reaction to it. Books such as these, if treated lightheartedly, may be a liberating agent, helping such children to overcome their fears.

ACTIVITIES IN CHAPTER 6 TO PROMOTE CHILD DEVELOPMENT

Emotional Development

Dramatize with overhead transparency costumes *(The Knight and the Dragon)*
Dress up and play super heroes *(Jim Meets The Thing)*
Make a monster-in-the-shoebox game *(There's a Monster Under My Bed)*

Social Development

Dragon mitten puppets *(Beware the Dragons!)*

Physical Development

Dragon mitten puppets *(Beware the Dragons!)*
Play cheeseburger beanbag *(The Mysterious Tadpole)*

Cognitive Development

Play a computer game *(Patrick's Dinosaurs)*
Hatch eggs in an incubator *(Amanda's Dinosaur)*
Make monster puzzles *(The Beast in the Bathtub)*
Have a wild rumpus dance *(Where the Wild Things Are)*
Keep live tadpoles *(The Mysterious Tadpole)*

Language Development

Child tells a story *(What Happened to Patrick's Dinosaurs?)*
Child tells a story *(The Dinosaur Who Lived In My Backyard)*
Child "reads" wordless story *(The Knight and the Dragon)*

Creative Development

Have a wild rumpus dance *(Where the Wild Things Are)*
Have sandbox play *(The Dinosaur Who Lived In My Backyard)*
Dramatize with overhead transparency costumes *(The Knight and the Dragon)*

REFERENCES CITED

Beaty, J.J. (1992), *Preschool Appropriate Practices*. Ft.Worth,Tex.: Harcourt Brace Jovanovich.

Campbell, J. and Moyers, B. (1988), "The Hero's Adventure," *The Power of Myth Series* (Video 1), National Public Television.

Heller, R. (1981), *Chickens Aren't the Only Ones*. New York: Grosset and Dunlap.

Hurst, C.O. (1990), *Once Upon a Time… An Encyclopedia for Successfully Using Literature with Young Children*. Allen, Tex.: DLM.

Johnston, J.M. (1987), "Harnessing the Power of Superheroes: An Alternative View," *Day Care and Early Education* 15(1) 15–17.

Simon, S. (1975), *Pets in a Jar: Collecting and Caring for Small Wild Animals*. New York: Puffin Books.

COMPUTER SOFTWARE

Dinosaurs (1984), Advanced Ideas, Inc., Berkeley, CA.

Dinosaurs Are Forever (1988), Polarware, Inc., Batavia, Illinois

OTHER PICTURE BOOKS ABOUT *DINOSAUR, DRAGON, AND MONSTER TALES*

Blumenthal, N. and Kaufman, R.J. (1989), *Count-A-Saurus*. New York: Four Winds Press.

Cooney, N.E. and Chambliss, M. (ill.) (1990), *Go Away Monsters, Lickety Split*. New York: Putnam.

Garrison, C. and Goode, D. (ill.)(1978), *The Dream Eater*. New York: Alladin Books.

Goode, D. (1988), *I Hear a Noise*. New York: Dutton.

Gordon, S. and Cushman, D. (ill.) (1988), *The Jolly Monsters*. Mahwah, N.J.: Troll Associates.

Grant, J. and Schwarz, J.K. (1987), *The Monster That Grew Small*. New York: Lothrop, Lee and Shepard.

Graham, K. Richardson, I.M. and Ekman, M. (ill.) (1988), *The Reluctant Dragon*. Mahwah, N.J.: Troll Associates.

Haley, G.E. (1977), *Go Away, Stay Away*. New York: Charles Scribner's.

Haley, G.E. (1988) *Jack and the Fire Dragon*. New York: Crown.

Hutchins, P. (1985), *The Very Worst Monster*. New York: Greenwillow.

Kellogg, S. (1973), *The Island of the Skog*. New York: Dial Books.

Kellogg, S. (1983), *Ralph's Secret Weapon*. New York: Dial Books.

Mayer, M. (1968), *There's a Nightmare in My Closet*. New York: Dial.

McQueen, J.T. and Brown, M. (1986), *A World Full of Monsters*. New York: Harper & Row Publishers.

Mosel, A. and Lent, Blair. (ill.) (1972), *The Funny Little Woman*. New York: E.P.Dutton.

Most, B. (1978), *If the Dinosaurs Came Back,* San Diego: Harcourt Brace.

Most, B. (1987), *Dinosaur Cousins?* San Diego: Harcourt Brace Jovanovich.

Munch, R. (1980), *The Paper Bag Princess*. Toronto, Canada: Annick.

Oram, H; Kitamura, S., illustrator, (1990), *A Boy Wants a Dinosaur,* N.Y: Farrar Straus Giroux.

Ross, T. (1984), *I'm Coming to Get You*. New York: Dial Books.

Rovetch, L. (1989), *Trigwater Did It*. New York: Viking Penguin.

Seeger, P. and Hays, M. (ill.) (1986), *Abiyoyo*. New York: Macmillan.

Schwartz, H. (1989), *How I Captured a Dinosaur*. New York: Orchard.

Viorst, J. and Chorao, K. (1973), *My Mama Says There Aren't Any Zombies, Ghosts, Vampires, Creatures, Demons, Monsters, Fiends, Goblins, or Things*. New York: Alladin Books.

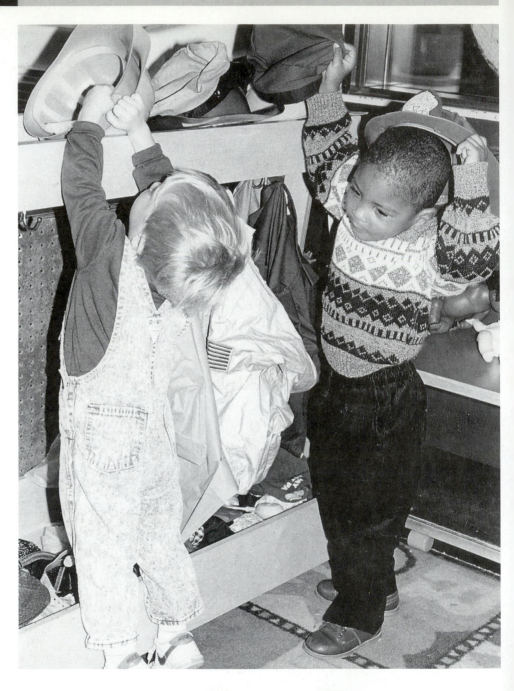

FOLKTALES TO TELL OUT LOUD

POOF!   *Action Chant*

I can be a princess	*("strut" in place)*
In a castle tall;	
Poof!	*(clap)*
I can be a handsome prince	
Climbing up the wall;	*("climb" in place)*
Poof!	*(clap)*
I can be a wicked witch	*(scrunch up face and fingers)*
With power over all;	
Poof!	*(clap)*
Oh no, I'd rather be...	
ME!	*(arms out, feet apart)*
Poof!	*(clap)*

Folktales and Fairy Tales to Tell Out Loud

The picture books in this chapter are treated somewhat differently from the others because they are very different: all of them contain stories that can be told out loud, and all of them are fantasies. These stories come out of an oral tradition that makes them eminently suitable for retelling orally and for dramatizing. They follow a prescribed pattern that is easy to remember. They contain a repetition of action and dialog that is hard to forget. And they end "happily ever after."

Young children love to hear these stories told over and over. The excitement of the chase, the drama of the quest, and the satisfaction of the happy ending are gripping and engrossing. Furthermore, even young children can understand the characters and their motives in fairy tales better than characters in most other stories. No explanation is necessary. Folktale characters are one-dimensional. They are types rather than well-rounded people. They are purposely either all good or all bad. The villains are wicked and the heroes or heroines are wonderful through and through. As Bosma notes in her *Fairy Tales, Fables, Legends, and Myths: Using Folk Literature in Your Classroom:*

> Folktale characters are drawn very clearly and generally depicted as symbols of good or evil, wisdom or foolishness, power or weakness. This polarization of characters fits into the children's expectations, which have been developing since age two, through both realistic and fanciful stories... this stock characterization helps the child comprehend the differences between reality and fantasy more readily than is possible when figures are drawn true to life. (Bosma, 1987, 3)

Having stereotyped characters makes it so much easier for inexperienced youngsters to do the thing that all listeners do: identify with a character. In addition, it makes it possible for the same child to identify with *different* characters at different times: the good sister and the bad sister, the handsome prince and the ugly troll, the wicked stepmother and the beautiful princess, the fairy godmother and the witch.

Why would they want to do that? Why would a little girl take on the role of the stepmother one day and the prince the next? Because young children are experimenting with life. They are trying to make sense of life and of themselves. Who are they? How should they act? Why do they feel the way they do about people and about the things that happen? What is it like to be a father? A stepmother? What is a lie? What happens to you if you tell a lie? These kinds of questions are constantly being processed deep within young children from the time they first recognize themselves as persons. Children work out these problems by pretending—and fairy tales are structured pretending.

By identifying with fairy tale characters, children make subconscious comparisons between themselves and the characters. These tales touch something deep within the children. It is satisfying for them to learn from the tales that they are not alone with their feelings, that others also are faced with the same problems:

Sibling rivalry
Fear of the unknown
Jealousy
The threat of rejection
The need to be loved by parents
What happens when you do something wrong
How to get what you want
How to survive in a bad situation

These are the universal dilemmas presented by folktales and fairy stories. Yes, you may answer, but aren't these characters the stereotypes that we are trying to remove from children's literature (such as females as passive, males as winners, stepmothers as wicked, and old women as witches)? You are perfectly right. When such stereotyped characters appear in current fiction or realistic stories, we have every reason to object. But in literary fantasies where pretending takes place, it is different.

As Mary B. Howarth found as a teacher of young children:

Some fairy tales do show girls as passive, boys as strong, and old women as witches. But in acting out the stories I've found that boys and girls enact both male and female roles, according to their individual needs. (Howarth, 1989, 63)

Nevertheless, you may counter, who wants to hear stepmothers described as "wicked"? We understand that such tales as *Cinderella* came from centuries ago when many women died in childbirth, and their husbands quickly remarried for survival purposes. Such stepmothers who found themselves in an unloved and secondary position, often treated their stepchildren badly. Yet the many stepmothers of today in realigned families, who have brought with them children of a previous marriage, certainly do not want any of their children to hear stories in which stepmothers are considered wicked. Nor should they in realistic stories.

Yet how is it that tales like *Cinderella* with its wicked stepmother have survived and prospered over the centuries? Clare Cherry in her well known book *Creative Play for the Developing Child* puts it this way:

Actually, these stories have developed through the ages, though in ever-changing forms, because they *are* important to both storyteller and listener. These stories have survived while thousand of others have gotten lost along the way. Those which have survived parallel, in their sequence of events, symbolic sequences of events that are universal in the lives of all people. They are all concerned with overcoming threatening situations and they generally have happy endings. The symbolism finds its universalism in the fact that children's thought processes, and thus human thought processes, all develop in the same way. (Cherry, 1976, 227)

The Importance of Fairy Tales in Children's Lives

Child psychologist Bruno Bettelheim made us all aware some years ago of the value and importance of fairy tales for children in his book, *The Uses of Enchantment: The Meaning and Importance of Fairy Tales* (Bettelheim, 1976). Not only do fairy tales entertain, he told us, but they also speak to something deep within the child that helps him to understand more about who he is, and why he feels the way he does.

Bettelheim's profound insights presented in this now-classic book changed the way many teachers viewed these tales: from totally negative to extremely positive. Suddenly they understood that it was permissible for characters to be stereotyped, for violence to be described and dealt with, and for the tales themselves to be unrealistic and fanciful. That was always the point with these tales. They were supposed to be removed from reality so that the *deep truths they taught about life* could more readily be internalized. Mary B. Howarth, parent, nursery school teacher, and later college instructor of fairy tale courses, was one of those people who felt she had been let down by the fairy tales of her youth:

> For example, I didn't marry a Prince, though it's true I thought my husband was perfect when I married him. Because of my disillusionment, I wasn't going to mislead my children with 'and they lived happily ever after' fantasies. I was going to be honest, truthful, and nonsexist in my nurturing. (Howarth, 1989, 58)

After she read Bettelheim, Howarth decided to explore fairy tales with her three- to five-year-old nursery school children. She was overwhelmed by the intentness with which the children approached the tales—they wanted them over and over and over. She eventually decided that "the reason fairy tales are so engrossing is that they speak to the basic questions children ask themselves. As one child put it, 'They think about what I think about.'" (Howarth, 1989, 58) Howarth also understood why adults do not want to expose children to fairy tales:

> In order to solve life's problems one must not only take risks, one must confront the worst that might happen. Children, like the rest of us, ruminate and worry about these worst things. Fairy tales confront them. This is the chief reason many adults have trouble with fairy tales. They think they can protect children from the hard realities of life. That is the real myth and the children know it. (Howarth, 1989, 61)

Stepmothers in today's realigned families may still have their doubts about the worth of fairy tales like *Cinderella*. Their point is well taken. But perhaps they need to think about the therapeutic value of such tales for children who are experiencing a traumatic separation and recombining of family members. Joseph Campbell, the dean of folklore and myths from all cultures and time periods comments in his acclaimed book *Myths To Live By:*

> In cases, for example, of a second marriage, where a second family comes along, a child of the first may feel and actually find itself excluded, thrown away, or left behind. The old fairy tale theme of the wicked stepmother and stepsisters is relevant here. What such an excluded one will be striving for in his inward lonely journey will be the finding or the fashioning of a center—not a family center, but a world center—of which he will be the pivotal being. (Campbell, 1972, 227)

In the final analysis it is the children who will show us whether or not such tales are worthwhile. If young children respond to them with deep emotion when they are told or read, if they want them repeated again and again, and if they want to re-enact the character roles during dramatic play, then we need to take fairy tales seriously. In our confused and bewildering world, it may even be that folk- and fairy tales are society's safety valve for children.

Something children learn quite vividly from these tales is that there are consequences to the actions that the characters perform. Good is rewarded and bad is punished. This is not to say that the youngest children actually understand "the moral of the story." Instead, children learn intuitively that there are great differences between people, and that you can choose the way you yourself want to be. As Bettelheim points out:

> A child's choices are based, not so much on right versus wrong, as on who arouses his sympathy and and who his antipathy. The more simple and straightforward a good character, the easier it is for a child to identify with it and to reject the bad other. The child identifies with the good hero not because of his goodness, but because the hero's condition makes a deep positive appeal to him. The question for the child is not "Do I want to be good?" but "Who do I want to be like?" The child decides this on the basis of projecting himself wholeheartedly into one character. If this fairy-tale character is a very good person, then the child decides that he wants to be good, too. (Bettelheim, 1976, 10)

We teachers and parents of young children always knew this, didn't we: that children learn best from someone who models the proper behavior? So let's bring fairy tales back into children's lives to give them good models—vivid models—to emulate! Other cultures do it. Fairy tales have long been used in homes and classrooms in Japan, China, India, Egypt, Lebanon, Germany, Poland, and Russia (to name only a few), to teach children proper behavior. Foreign visitors to American preschools and foreign students in children's literature courses are always surprised and puzzled that our books for young children do not include very many folk- or fairy tales. Let's get back on track with fairy tales for little folks, now that we understand what they are about and why we should.

❧ Why Convert Folktales in Books to Oral Tales?

Turning a story that is written in a book into a tale that you tell orally seems unnecessarily difficult for many teachers. Can't I just read it, you may ask? Yes, but then you miss the important point. The point is that oral telling forces the children listeners to depend upon their own mind's eye, their own imaginations, rather than on pictures from a book, to make up the imagery of the story. Thus, the characters in the story become the children's very own rather than the artist's who illustrated the book. If fairy tales are to have their full impact on children, we want this to happen.

Oral telling also forces the teller to look out at the audience rather than down at a book while presenting a story. By doing this, you make real contact with your audience. You depend upon them for your cues: who is with you and who is not; should you shout or whisper or cajole your audience to let them experience the character's predicament? Should you repeat a line of the story to emphasize a point? Should you take a long pause to build up suspense? Should you end the story sooner rather than later? Your eye contact with the audience will tell you. In the meantime, you will find that you, like the children, have made the characters and the story your own rather than an author's. It is satisfying, indeed, for the teachers and parents willing to take the time and trouble to learn these tales well enough to tell them orally. It is also well worth it.

How to Convert Folktales in Books to Oral Tales

Your first tale to convert should be a simple one you already know and like. Find a good picture book version of the tale and read it over to yourself. Then follow these simple guidelines mentioned in Chapter 1 to prepare for the telling:

Guidelines for Converting Written to Oral Stories

1. Read the story through noting characters, dialog, and plot.
2. Decide which characters to include and how to speak for them.
3. Decide how to begin the story to catch the children's attention.
4. Decide on three to five incidents of the story to dramatize with your voice.
5. Decide how to end the story to satisfy the children. (Beaty, 1992, 139)

These guidelines seem to be saying that you can change the story somewhat, if you want. Yes, that is the case. You should always make the story your own. You will want to tell it in a way that is comfortable for you. Folktales are usually already pared down enough so that there is little extraneous material for you to omit. You will probably want to stick close to the storyline. However, if the ending seems too abrupt or too violent, you may want to alter it.

How much leeway do you have? It all depends. You will want to keep the story as true to the original as possible, since you will be adding the picture book to your Story Center shelves for children to look at and "read" to themselves. Children also will want to hear the story repeated aloud the same way many times, so it is best to tell it as close to the book version as possible. Take, for example, the story *The Turnip*. This is an old Russian folktale translated into English in several different versions. The one considered here is Janina Domanska's simple cumulative story published by The Macmillan Company in 1969. Following the conversion guidelines, you should:

1. *Read the story through, noting characters, dialog, plot.*

It is a story about a grandfather and grandmother who plant a turnip, water it every day, and watch it grow into an enormous turnip. When they try to pull it up, the turnip does not move, so they ask for help from the people and animals around them. One by one they add a new puller to the line until at last a magpie flies down to help, and the turnip comes out of the ground so suddenly they all fall down.

2. *Decide which characters to include and how to speak for them.*

Grandfather	Patrick, the gander	A magpie
Grandmother	The other geese	
Micky, their grandson	The rooster	
Ringo, the dog	The hen	
Ulysses, the cat	Samson, the pig	

The only characters who speak are the grandfather, the grandmother, and the magpie. After each character is added to the pulling line, the grandfather says: "Now all together! One...two...three...PULL!" Then words are repeated in a cumulative manner about who is pulling whom from the end of the line up, as each new character is added: the magpie pulls Samson the pig, the pig pulls the hen, the hen pulls the rooster, the rooster pulls the geese, the geese pull the gander, the gander pulls Ulysses the cat, the cat pulls Ringo the dog, the dog pulls Grandmother, Grandmother pulls Grandfather, and Grandfather pulls the turnip. In some versions of the story the huge vegetable is called "the great, big, enormous turnip." In others it is called "that stubborn turnip." Here the repeated words also describe the pulling: "And they pulled and they puffed, and they pulled and they pulled. But the turnip did not move." Make your voice sound more tired and exhausted as you use these words each time.

3. *Decide how to begin the story to catch the children's attention.*

Many folktales and fairy stories begin with a formula opening that starts, "Once upon a time...." Or, as they say in the islands of the Bahamas: "Once was a time, a very good time, monkey chew tobacco and he spit white lime." (Hedrick, 1975) Formulas like these are used by old-time storytellers in every culture to let their audience know that an old-time story is about to begin. You can make up your own formula or use "Once upon a time..."

First, however, you may want to call your audience to attention with a signal. In the Bahamas the storyteller calls out, "Bunday!" until everyone quiets down. You may want to create your own special signal for storytelling time such as a tinkling bell, the clicking of maracas, or the shaking of a tambourine. Some tellers turn off the lights and light a candle at the start; then blow it out at the finish, asking the children to make a wish. Have your own invitation to storytime be something fun or funny for your youngsters, so that they will await the telling of the tale with great anticipation and respond with glee.

4. *Decide on three to five incidents of the story to dramatize with your voice.*

In this story the incidents are already determined by the particular animals who join the pulling line. You can make noises for each animal as it takes hold of the one in front to pull, if you want. Make Grandfather's voice low and Grandmother's high. Have the magpie bird sound squeaky or screechy.

5. *Decide how to end the story to satisfy the children.*

However you do it, be sure to end the story the same way every time. Your youngsters will expect this of you. In the book this story ends with the turnip coming out of the ground suddenly, everyone falling down, the magpie flying away to his tall tree, and screaming, "Oh, my! Look what I have done." Perhaps you can think of another ending, such as "That stubborn turnip finally came out!"

Then storytellers often tack on a formula ending such as, "And they all lived happily ever after," to let the audience know that the story is really finished. Or as they say in the Bahamas: "E-bo ben', my story en'." (Crowley, 1966)

Your telling of this story will not be at an end, however, if the children liked it. They will demand that you repeat it over and over. Please do so. Young children have a need to hear things they like more than once. Furthermore, they seem to have a different feeling about stories "told" as opposed to stories "read" to them. They want to hear the "told" tales again and again. They seem to know that such stories are more personal. They see you making eye contact with them. They hear your voice being grumpy or squeaky or whispery. They feel the emotion of the story as Grandfather gets more upset with that stubborn turnip. It is such great fun for them! "Tell it again, Teacher!"

❧ Dramatizing Folktales Through Story Re-enactment

Children have no trouble creating images in their mind's eye when you tell such stories aloud. They can see what the characters look like. They even know how they feel. But they can actually step into the shoes of the characters if you take this process one step further through classroom dramatics. Such story re-enactment really brings fairy tale characters to life for young children. They not only hear you describe the characters and their dilemmas, but they actually try on these roles themselves. They can find out for themselves what it is like to be the biggest Billy Goat, the baby bear, the good witch Strega Nona, or the magpie who thought that he pulled out the turnip all by himself. Best of all, children ages three to six, great pretenders that they are, *love* doing it!

Dramatizing folktales through story re-enactment is somewhat different from the regular dramatic play that the children are used to doing in the Dramatic Play Center. It is more structured than spontaneous dramatic play because the children will be following a prescribed storyline, and because you are involved in order to set the drama in motion and to keep it going. But it is less structured than a traditional play where children are chosen to take each role and must learn their lines.

Folktale story re-enactment is for the children themselves. They like pretending to be a character, not once, but again and again. They enjoy trying out different roles, once they are at ease with the process. They even relish being the audience. And that's who the audience should be in these classroom dramas: the children themselves. These are not plays for an outside audience. They are not being rehearsed until everyone learns his lines. Instead, they are another more personal form of storytelling, where the children become the listeners, the characters, and the creators of the story all at once. It is the *process* of being involved in these re-enactments that is most important for children, not the *product* of a polished performance put on for someone else. Guidelines you can follow to convert an oral story into a dramatic story re-enactment are as follows:

Guidelines for Creating a Story Re-enactment

1. Choose a folk story you and the children already know.

2. Inform the children about the characters in the play and ask them who would like to play each role.

3. Allow as many children as want to play each role at the same time.

4. Play any role yourself not selected by the children.

5. Everyone else in the classroom should be the audience.

6. Use the minimum of costumes and props; none if possible.

7. Take the role of the narrator yourself until children become very familiar with story re-enactment.

8. When the play is finished have everyone applaud each character in turn, and also the audience.

9. Perform the drama as many times as the children want, selecting characters each time.

1. *Choose a folk story you and the children already know.*

The folktale *The Turnip,* already described, is a good one to start with because it is so simple. First of all, though, you must already have told it orally enough times that the children know it by heart and love it.

2. *Inform the children about the characters in the play, and ask them who would like to play each role.*

Ask the total group of children if they would like to put on a play about the story *The Turnip.* If they agree, tell them that the first thing to do before putting on a play is to choose the characters. Ask them if they remember who the characters are in this story. Then write down each character they remember on an experience chart, chalkboard, newsprint or other surface, leaving space to write several children's names under each character. If they have omitted any character, add that name to the chart yourself.

Next ask who would like to be "Grandfather." Write down the names of all the children who want this role. It is perfectly all right to have more than one child play the role at the same time. Then ask who would like to play each of the other characters, and list their names after each character. Your teaching assistant can also choose a role.

3. *Play any role yourself not selected by the children.*

Tell the children you will play the role of any of the characters that haven't been chosen. Write your name on the chart after each role you will play.

4. *Everyone else in the classroom should be the audience.*

Anyone who did not choose to be a character can be the audience. Write down their names, as well. Shy children or children who hesitate to try something new may want to sit out this experience at first. That is perfectly acceptable. Tell the children that it is just as important to have a good audience as it is to have good actors.

5. *Use the minimum of costumes and props; none if possible.*

For the first time you and the children perform the story re-enactment, it is best not to use props. Let children's pretending and imagination have full sway at first. Later, simple costumes (hats and animal noses) can be introduced, if it seems appropriate.

6. *Take the role of the narrator yourself until children become very familiar with story re-enactment.*

When you are ready to begin, have the audience sit facing the classroom area where the acting will take place. Have the actors stand to one side, ready to come to the front when it is their turn. You can motion to them, if they forget to take their places. Then start telling the story just as you have in the past; only this time, when a character is mentioned, the child or children playing that role should come out in front and speak or act for that character. Give each of the "Grandfathers" a chance to act out the lines you say, for instance: "Grandfather planted a turnip in his garden." Then "Grandmother" will come on when you say: "Grandmother watered the turnip every day." Let all the "grandmothers" act their parts and say their lines when the time comes. Eventually, after the children have re-enacted this story a number of times, they may not need a teacher/narrator.

7. *When the play is finished have everyone applaud each character in turn, and also the audience.*

After the play is finished ask the children to applaud for each character. Have everyone, even the actors, applaud each other. You should take applause for your role, too. The audience should also stand and be applauded. This helps children to realize: 1) that the play has ended; 2) that everyone is important in a play; and 3) that applause is a personal "thank you" for the performance.

8. *Perform the drama as many times as the children want, selecting characters each time.*

Children will want to do the play over again...many times. Ishee and Goldhaber tell how their children performed *The Three Bears* twenty-seven times in four days! (Ishee & Goldhaber, 1990, 74) Unlike traditional drama, these repeat performances have nothing to do with practicing lines until they become perfect. It is the *process* itself that is important to the children. Often children play different roles for each repeat performance. Ishee and Goldhaber say this about repeat performances:

> This is the most important part. Many repetitions help children. For many children it is necessary to watch a play numerous times before making that first gesture of pretense within the play. For others, repetition allows an opportunity to elaborate and expand on the story as presented, to take on a variety of roles, and to assume major responsibility for a role. (Ishee & Goldhaber, 1990, 74)

❀ Levels of Child Interaction in Classroom Story Re-enactment

Whenever young children encounter a new object, game, or activity in their environment, this author has found that they tend to teach themselves how it works by spontaneously interacting with it in a progression of three levels, the first being what we call the *manipulation* level, then the *mastery* level, and finally the *meaning* level: we call this "the three M's."(Beaty, 1992, 23–26)

Manipulation is the first level, where children explore an object or activity, trying it out in different ways to find out how it works or what you can do with it. In using a paint brush for the first time, for instance, children often wrap their entire hand around it and paint by covering a paper with paint swished or scribbled every which way.

During *mastery* children are able to use their fingers in holding the brush and can control it well enough to direct the paint where they want it on the paper: often up and down in lines repeated over and over. The tendency to repeat an action spontaneously marks this level of interaction. It is almost as if the child is practicing.

Finally at the *meaning* level, children apply their own meaning—their own creativeness—to the interaction. With paints they begin to make representations such as people and houses.

What has this to do with story re-enactment? Imagine our surprise to find that children in this new activity seem to progress through these same three levels of interaction as they became actors and interpreters of these stories. By observing to determine at which level children are interacting, teachers can offer appropriate support (and patience) to help children progress to the next level. The following are examples of some actions children may display while progressing through these levels:

Manipulation Level
Child actor stands by another actor who is "center stage" but doesn't "act"
Child actor copies gestures of another actor but doesn't speak
Child actor mouths dialog of other actors without saying words out loud himself
Child actor wanders around "stage" switching roles and copying the gesture of various actors

Mastery Level
Child actor keeps own role and doesn't switch
Child actor says lines and makes gestures appropriate to role
Child actor repeats role over and over

Meaning Level
Child actor adds new dialog and/or gestures
Child actor varies the plot (such as has bird fly off with the turnip)
Child acts as narrator [older children usually]

✲ Picture Books for Converting to Oral Tales and Story Re-enactment

The following are examples of good books to use for telling folk- and fairy tales to your youngsters, as well as for presenting as story re-enactments. Keep the books on the shelves of your Story Center while the stories are being told or enacted. Children enjoy looking through them to see an artist's version of the tale.

The Three Billy Goats Gruff, by Paul Galdone, 1973
Goldilocks and the Three Bears, by Jan Brett, 1987
The Gingerbread Man, by Ed Arno, 1967
Hattie and the Fox, by Mem Fox; Patricia Mullins (ill.), 1986
Jack and the Beanstalk, by Matt Faulkner, 1986
Red Riding Hood, by James Marshall, 1987
Strega Nona, by Tomie de Paola, 1975
Zomo the Rabbit, by Gerald McDermott, 1992

The Three Billy Goats Gruff *(1973), by Paul Galdone, New York: Clarion Books.* Paul Galdone is well known for his dramatically illustrated versions of traditional folktales. This book is no exception. The three billy goats practically leap from its pages. Drawn in pen-and-ink and color wash, their horns sweep back from their heads with zest (except for the tiniest goat with only nubbins on his head) as they challenge the ugly troll yet one more time. Most striking are Galdone's troll's-eye-view illustrations looking up at the goats from under the bridge. The text is traditional. Once your children have heard you tell the story, they will soon be able to "read the pictures" word for word.

What will children learn from this tale? That there are dangers under bridges? That a big brother is a good thing to have? Maybe. But don't forget, as they take the roles of different characters, they also experience what it is like to be each of the different characters, including the troll.

+ Tell Many children may have already heard this story read aloud, as it is one of the most popular tales. Your telling of it will be something different and exciting for them (and for you?). Because it is a simple formula tale with elements of three (goats,

*Children can re-
enact "The Three
Billy Goats Gruff"
by using steps for
the bridge.*

times across the bridge), and simple dialog, you should have no trouble remembering it. You will want to repeat these elements of the story the same way each time.
This helps your children to learn it. Concentrate, then, on your voice tones and
your gestures. Have a different voice for each of the three goats, and still another
voice for the troll. Try it by yourself with a tape recorder to hear how you sound.

Your gestures can be simple, as well. Many tellers use different foot gestures for
each of the billy goats as he crosses the bridge: from tiptoeing to tramping. Others
make a particular gesture for the troll each time he speaks or is mentioned (for
instance hands on hips, face scrunched up).

This tale ends with a traditional Scandinavian formula ending that you may
want to use:

> So snip, snap, snout,
> This tale's told out.

+ Dramatize Through Story Re-enactment   Your only prop will probably be the
bridge (and even this is unnecessary). It is fun to have something for the children
to tiptoe or tromp across. If you have a "rocking boat" in the room, turn it upside-
down so that it becomes steps. This makes a fine bridge. Some teachers use low
tables with chairs or large hollow-block steps at either end. Boards can be balanced

across low blocks, as well. Have your children choose who they will represent as described on p. 136. You may end up being the troll in the beginning, but as children become more used to the method, the fun, and the excitement of story re-enactment, you may soon have more trolls than you know what to do with!

Goldilocks and the Three Bears (1987), *by Jan Brett, New York: Dodd, Mead & Company.* There are several versions of this popular story on the market today, many of which are good for classroom use. This particular book is exceptional in that the pages burst with Jan Brett's outstanding "folk" illustrations. The bear's fairy tale house in the woods, richly furnished with bear-motif wood-carver's furniture, animal bric-a-brac, and stunning "bear-ceramic" porridge bowls, is something no little goldilocks girl could ever resist. Bears and girl alike are garbed in colorfully embroidered Ukrainian folk costumes, and the borders of each page add carved and painted details to the action of the story in typical Brett fashion. (Hurst, 1990, 23)

This text goes back to traditional versions of the story, calling the bears: the "great, huge bear," the "middle-sized bear," and the "little, small, wee bear," rather than Papa, Mama, and Baby Bear. It uses the words: "has been at my porridge" instead of "eating my porridge." Children accept these words or any you decide to use in your oral telling as long as you are consistent.

As Bettelheim points out, this story is "a cautionary tale warning us to respect others' property and privacy." (Bettelheim, 1976, 216) It is also a tale of "the well-integrated family represented by the bears, and the outsider in search of himself," represented by Goldilocks. Your children, too, are trying to find out where they fit in their family; thus, a character like Goldilocks is someone they can identify with. Finally, the story can be considered one about a new child coming into the family, with the sibling jealousy on the part of the youngest child toward the newcomer. In that case, your youngsters can also empathize with the little bear whose place Goldilocks takes.

+ Tell   As with *The Three Billy Goats Gruff,* this story follows a formula with three things happening: trying porridge, trying chairs, and trying beds with Goldilocks and then again with the three bears. It is easy to remember and to tell. You will need to develop four different voice tones to represent the four characters. Your gestures should follow your word descriptions of the action.

AUTHORS
of **INTEREST**

JAN BRETT spent hours as a child reading and drawing. She knew she wanted to be an illustrator. Her art is decorative, influenced by her study of embroidery and porcelain at the Museum of Fine Arts in Boston. The illustrations of many of Brett's books have borders like *The Three Bears* with drawings that sometimes tell the story differently from the main illustrations. Her settings are usually Scandinavian or Ukrainian. (Hurst, 1990, 23)

+ Dramatize Through Story Re-enactment   The story can be dramatized without props, but some teachers and children like to use three different sizes of chairs. The chairs can serve as beds, too, with children pretending to sleep by putting their heads down on their hands.

The Gingerbread Man (1967), by Ed Arno, New York: Scholastic, Inc. This is a cumulative tale like *The Turnip*, making it easy to remember, tell, and dramatize. This story has the gingerbread man hopping out of the oven, running away, and being chased by a progressively longer line of people: a little boy, an old man, an old woman, three farmers, a bear, and a wolf, only to be caught and eaten by a clever fox who lures him close by telling him that he can't hear what he is saying. Each time he passes someone new, the gingerbread man calls out:

> "Run, run
> As fast as you can.
> You can't catch me.
> I'm the gingerbread man!"

Then he tells who he has run away from. This is another cautionary tale telling children several things: 1)not to brag about your abilities to others; 2)not to believe everything a stranger may tell you, and 3)not to listen to a stranger who is trying to lure you close, or something bad may happen.

+ Tell   The repetition helps keep this story interesting as the gingerbread man tries to outrun everyone he meets. Use a different voice tone for each of the people and animals, as well as that of the gingerbread man. Make up gestures for each of them, too, and then repeat the gestures each time you mention a character.

+ Dramatize Through Story Re-enactment   This story is also best done without props, except for one at the beginning of the story. A cardboard carton with a door in one end can serve as the oven. Then the gingerbread man can pop out of the oven to begin his merry romp. Children soon learn to dramatize their parts with voice tones and gestures through your modeling in telling the story.

At some point it is fun for all to bake real gingerbread man cookies. Then everyone can be the clever fox!

Hattie and the Fox (1986), by Mem Fox; Patricia Mullins, (illustrator), New York: Macmillan Publishing Co. Hattie the big black hen discovers a fox in the bushes little by little: first a nose, then two eyes, then two ears, then two legs, then a body, and finally a tail. After each of her discoveries, each of the barnyard animals says the same thing: Good grief! (goose), Well, well! (pig) Who cares? (sheep) So what? (horse) and What next? (cow). It isn't till the fox leaps out of the bushes and the hen flies up in the tree that the animals change their tune.

+ Tell   This simple formula tale makes an excellent one for telling. It is easy to remember what each animal repeats in order after each sighting by the hen. You will

During the re-enactment of "The Gingerbread Man," have a child charac-ter pop out of a cardboard box oven.

be repeating the animal litany six times before the end, so that your listeners should know it almost by heart. Use hand gestures for each animal and different voice tones. Next time through assign parts and let individual children say the animals' lines. On the final run-through have everyone say the words in unison.

+ Dramatize Through Story Re-enactment   Story re-enactment is different from the audience participation while you were telling the story, because the char-acters stand up in front of an audience when they say their lines. Write down the names of the animal characters in the order of their appearance: fox, hen, goose, pig, sheep, horse, and cow. Then ask the children who would like to play each role. Again, let as many as want play each part (even if that means you will have no audi-ence). Have them speak differently and gesture (except for the fox who is in hiding). When the time is right the fox can jump out and the hen can fly away. Because it is so simple and dramatic, children tend to love this story in both its told and acted forms. They will also enjoy looking at the illustrations in the picture book left in the Story Center.

 ***Jack and the Beanstalk** (1986), by Matt Faulkner, New York: Scholastic, Inc.* The "Jack" in this favorite story represents the English "everyman" just as "Hans" does in German and "Ivan" in Russian. There are many so-called "Jack tales,"

and this is one. The story begins with Jack foolishly selling his poor mother's only possession, their cow Milky White who no longer gives milk, for a handful of beans instead of for money. But then the story grows into a suspenseful fairy tale with a giant and his rich possessions, which Jack steals one by one: first a bag of gold, then a hen that lays golden eggs, and finally a golden harp that sings. The giant's wife helps Jack by hiding him in the oven so her husband won't eat him.

+ Tell   In telling this tale you will need to create different voices for Jack, his mother, the old man with the beans, the giant's wife, the giant, and the harp. Children love the repetition as the giant's wife repeats her lines to Jack and to her husband each time Jack climbs the beanstalk to visit their castle. They especially love the giant's refrain:

> Fe, fi, fo, fum,
> I smell the blood of an Englishman,
> Be he alive or be he dead,
> I'll grind his bones to make my bread.

If the last line is too gruesome for you, make up your own.

Your gestures can include Jack climbing the beanstalk, walking to the giant's castle, hiding in the oven, the giant tromping into the room, Jack running back to the beanstalk and climbing down again. Can you make the motions of climbing in place? Try it. On the final climb Jack cuts down the beanstalk and the giant crashes down—"and that was the end of the giant."

Isn't this particular story too scary for children this young, you may wonder? Mary Howarth who uses folk and fairy tales to help young children understand their lives, believes that it is the TV, stage play, or video versions of fairy tales like *Jack and the Beanstalk* and *Hansel and Gretel* that frightens young children:

> There is a tremendous difference between hearing a story that your mind interprets and illustrates, and watching as real children are left alone in a deep forest on a hypnotizing screen. In the first instance, your mind censors and interprets to meet your own needs and experience. In the second, nothing is left to the individual imagination. The children cannot get away from the realistic, adult images set before them.
> (Howarth, 1989, 62–63)

Talk to your children about being scared while listening to a story or watching it dramatized. Suggest that they can hold the hand of the person next to them or come and stand close to the teacher if they are watching a play.

+ Dramatize Through Story Re-enactment   If children ask to have you tell this story over and over, you will know it is also a favorite and should be converted into a dramatization. Sign up the children to play the different roles. You should play any role left over as well as being narrator. Once again it is not necessary to use props. Your children's imagination will make them in their mind's eye.

Howarth has found that a play like this provides her children a safe place to explore feelings they have been inhibited from expressing:

In fairy tales, stepparents, witches, trolls, and wolves do all the "bad" things people aren't supposed to do, but do. From the tales the children learn the results of these negative acts for both themselves and others; they don't make the bad things go away but do give each child an opportunity to examine with others how these dark sides make them feel and what their possible consequences might be. (Howarth, 1989, 62)

She has found that girls and boys treat a particular role or character differently. The role of the Giant, for instance, was a difficult role for her young boys to confront, but not for her girls. In other cases, the tales themselves "show girls as passive, boys as strong, and old women as witches." (Howgarth, 1989, 63) But because both boys and girls have the opportunity to act out both male and female roles during the story re-enactment, they gain first-hand experience in what each role is like.

 Red Riding Hood *(1987), by James Marshall, New York: Dial Books.* This version of *Red Riding Hood* follows the traditional storyline with modern words and interesting cartoon-like full-page illustrations. The little girl takes a custard to her grandmother, meets the wolf in the woods and disregards her mother's warning about talking to strangers because the wolf has such charming manners. The wolf interrupts Granny's reading, eats her up, and soon also has swallowed Red Riding Hood whole. A passing hunter hears the wolf snoring, comes in and kills him, thus releasing Granny and Red Riding Hood. In the last scene she promises never ever to talk to strangers (as a crocodile with hat and cane stands behind her eyeing her hungrily).

+ Tell   Speaking for the characters of mother, Red Riding Hood, the wolf, and Granny, you should make their voices as distinct as possible. The final dialog between Red Riding Hood and the wolf who speaks as Granny is the most dramatic moment, ending with: "And Granny what big teeth you have." "The better to eat you with, my dear." Your biggest challenge here is to change your wolf's voice to that of the wolf trying to sound like Granny. In this version of the tale, the hunter acts but does not speak.

+ Dramatize Through Story Re-enactment   If your children perform this popular tale a number of times, individuals will eventually work their way through the different characters' roles. No props are necessary, although some Red Riding Hoods like to carry a basket. This can become complicated if you have more than one child playing this role at the same time, and all want baskets.

AUTHORS
of INTEREST

JAMES MARSHALL's drawings here are typical of the cartoon-like characters in many of his books. He became interested in children's books after seeing one by Maurice Sendak. His first book featured the two lovable hippos with the rocky relationship, *George and Martha*. Many of his books contain cats, his great interest, and allusions to Texas, his home state. (Hurst , 1990, 87)

Leave it up to the children to derive their own meaning from this tale. As Bettelheim says:

> All good fairy tales have meaning on many levels; only the child can know which meanings are of significance to him at the moment. As he grows up, the child discovers new aspects of these well-known tales, and this gives him the conviction that he has indeed matured in understanding, since the same story now reveals so much more to him. (Bettelheim, 1976, 169)

For an adult to interpret a tale like this for a child deprives him of his own discovery of its meaning, and interferes with the child being able to make the story his own.

Strega Nona (1975), by Tomie de Paola, Engelwood Cliffs, N.J.: Prentice-Hall, Inc. This Italian version by Tomie de Paola of "The Sorcerer's Apprentice" is a welcome addition to children's folklore. Strega Nona (Grandma Witch) is accepted by the townsfolk in her Medieval Calabria town because she can cure headaches, make love potions, and get rid of warts. When she puts up a notice in the town square advertising for someone to take care of her little house and garden, Big Anthony answers the ad and is hired. But he secretly listens to Strega Nona saying magic words over an empty pasta pot, and then sees the pot magically filling up with pasta. Afterwards she says more magic words and the pot stops filling. What he doesn't see is the three kisses that Strega Nona blows to the pot to stop its filling. One day when Strega Nona is out of town, Big Anthony says the magic words over the pot and it works. While the pot is filling he rounds up the villagers for free pasta for all. Then when everyone has had his fill, Big Anthony repeats the magic words to stop the pot, but it keeps on bubbling. Eventually the pasta fills the house and starts down the hill to engulf the town. Only Strega Nona's timely appearance halts a catastrophe. For a punishment that fits the crime, Big Anthony must eat up all the pasta.

+ Tell   It is a joy to tell this delightful story about the good witch and her bumbling assistant. Keep the witch's voice low to show authority, and Big Anthony's high to show his immaturity. The story can be made as long or short as you want by the number of townspeople you describe coming to see Strega Nona for her cures. If you tell the story enough times everyone will have learned the magic words before the acting begins. And the children love to blow the magic kisses.

+ Dramatize Through Story Re-enactment   Here is a fairy tale where everyone wants to play the witch the first time through. Let them have fun with the role. You may have to be Big Anthony at first, but eventually others will try it. You will want at least one townsperson coming for each of Strega Nona's three cures. This time you may also want a prop: the magic pot. Use a waste basket or plastic pan or cooking pot from home.

Zomo the Rabbit: A Trickster Tale from West Africa (1992), by Gerald McDermott, San Diego: Harcourt Brace Jovanovich. Gerald McDermott, an artist/author who creates children's picture books about myths and legends has given the world of children's literature a wonderful new hero: Zomo, an African trickster. American children may know him as "Brer Rabbit," but in this tale he is Zomo, who is not big, not strong, but he is very clever. However, Zomo wants more than cleverness. He wants *wisdom*. So he goes to the Sky God and asks for it. As is traditional in folktales of this sort, he must earn wisdom by completing three tasks: bringing to the Sky God the scales of Big Fish in the Sea, the milk of Wild Cow, and the tooth of Leopard. When Zomo eventually completes these tasks he is given wisdom. Your children may be surprised about what wisdom turns out to be. Are you, also?

+ Dramatize Through Story Re-enactment   In this story the characters have definite actions. As you write down the names of the children who want to play the parts of Big Fish, Wild Cow, and Leopard, talk about the actions they will need to do: dance to the drum beat for the fish; charge and get her horns stuck for the cow; and slip and fall down for the leopard. Let the children actors practice before the drama begins. Children can look at the book to see how the character they are going to portray handles the role. The illustrations are geometric in a stylized, folk-art manner, but brilliant in color against a golden African background.

Because this chapter does not describe different activities for each book, but rather the same activity, "Dramatizing Through Story Re-enactment," no outline of "Activities in Chapter 7 to Promote Children's Development" is included here. Story re-enactment promotes development in all areas of child development.

The examples of books described in this chapter should help you to select other folk- and fairy tale books to be used with your children. Read them over carefully to make sure they are appropriate for the age level of the children you teach. Many beautifully done folktale picture books are really suitable for older children because of the sophisticated concepts involved. "Simplicity" should be your rule-of-thumb. Make sure the story is a simple one. Not only will the children understand it more readily, but you will be able to dramatize it through story re-enactment more effectively.

How many times should you "let the play go on"? That is entirely up to you and your children. Youngsters at the *mastery* level of involvement want and need

AUTHORS *of INTEREST*   **GERALD McDERMOTT** began his career when his parents enrolled him in art school at the age of four! His book writing/illustrating grew from his work as an animated film artist, in which he retold legends such as *Anansi the Spider* (African) and *The Stonecutter* (Japanese) on film. These he later transformed into picture books. His book *Arrow to the Sun* (Pueblo) was awarded the Caldecott Medal. He was greatly influenced by mythologist Joseph Campbell and especially by his now classic book *The Hero with a Thousand Faces* (1949, Princeton University Press).

to repeat activities many times. Use your own judgment. When the acting begins to disintegrate, just as it does in dramatic play, then it may be time to go on to something else.

If children want their parents to come and see them perform, use your judgment on this, as well. These story re-enactments are for the children first of all. It is the process that counts and not the finished product. If a few parents want to drop in when a re-enactment is in progress, and if they can accept the rather chaotic goings-on as several children play one part, then let them come. They need to know, however, that this is not a traditional play with parts memorized and children in costume. Rather it is a role-play where children try out powerfully psychological roles that come to have a deep meaning for them.

REFERENCES CITED

Beaty, J.J. (1992), *Preschool Appropriate Practices*. Ft. Worth, Tex.: Harcourt Brace Jovanovich.

Bettelheim, B. (1976), *The Uses of Enchantment: The Meaning and Importance of Fairy Tales*. New York: Alfred A. Knopf.

Bosma, B. (1987), *Fairy Tales, Fables, Legends, and Myths: Using Folk Literature in Your Classroom*. New York: Teachers College.

Campbell, J. (1972), *Myths To Live By*. New York: Viking Penguin.

Cherry, C. (1976), *Creative Play for the Developing Child*. Belmont, Calif.: Fearon Publishers, Inc.

Crowley, D.J. (1966), *I Could Talk Old-Story Good: Creativity in Bahamian Folklore,* Berkeley: University of California Press.

Hedrick, B.C. and Letson, C.A. (1975), *Once Was a Time, A Wery Good Time: An Inquiry into the Folklore of the Bahamas*. University of Northern Colorado, Museum of Anthropology.

Howarth, M. (1989), "Rediscovering the Power of Fairy Tales: They Help Children Understand Their Lives," *Young Children* 45(1) 58–65.

Hurst, C.O. (1990), *Once Upon a Time... An Encyclopedia for Successfully Using Literature with Young Children*. Allen, Tex.: DLM.

Ishee, N. and Goldhaber, J. (1990), "Story Re-Enactment: Let the Play Begin!" *Young Children* 45(3), 70–75.

Mermin, J. (1991), "Hearing The Guten Sweeten Song: Children Choose Folktales," *Day Care and Early Education* 18(4) 8–12.

OTHER PICTURE BOOKS ABOUT *FOLKTALES TO TELL OUT LOUD*

Aardema, V.; Brown, M. (ill.) (1984), *Oh, Kojo! How Could You!* New York: Dial Books.

Aardema, V., Dillon, L., and Dillon, D. (ill.) (1975), *Why Mosquitoes Buzz in People's Ears*. New York: Dial Books.

Brown, M.; (1961), *Once a Mouse...* . New York: Charles Scribner's.

Duff, M. and Aruego, J. and Dewey, A. (ill.) (1978), *Rum Pum Pum*. New York: Macmillan Publishing Co.

French, F. (1991), *Anancy and Mr. Dry-Bone*. Boston: Little Brown.

Galdone, P. (1968), *Henny Penny*. New York: Scholastic.

Galdone, P. (1974), *Jack and the Beanstalk*. New York: Clarion Books.

Goble, P. (1991), *The Great Race of the Birds and Animals*. New York: Alladin Books.

Haley, G.E. (1986), *Jack and the Bean Tree*. New York: Crown.

Haley, G.E. (1970), *A Story A Story*. New York: Atheneum.

Lee, J.M. (1985), *Toad Is the Uncle of Heaven*. New York: Holt.

McDermott, G. (1972), *Anansi the Spider*. New York: Holt.

Perrault, C., Ehrlich, A.; Jeffers, S. (ill.) (1985), *Cinderella*. New York: Dial Books.

Siberell, A. (1982), *Whale in the Sky*. New York: E.P. Dutton.

Xiong, B., and Spagnoli, C.; Hom, N. (ill.) (1989), *Nine-In-One Grr! Grr!* San Francisco: Children's Book Press.

TASTY TALES

LET'S EAT!   *Action Chant*

Munch, munch,
What's for lunch?
Yum, yum,
Try some,   *(hold out hand)*
Time to bake,
Carrot cake;   *(stir with hand)*
Time to mash
Succotash;   *(pound with hand)*
Time to stop
Licking chops;   *(cover mouth with hand)*
LET'S EAT!   *(uncover mouth and shout)*

❦ Cooking in the Classroom

Why would someone want to teach three-, four-, and five-year-old children how to cook? Aren't they too young? Wouldn't it be better to wait until their motor skills are better developed so that they won't spill things or cut themselves? What's the point, anyway?

That is the point: to help young children develop small motor skills and coordination. What better way to help preschool and kindergarten children than one in which they must practice the important eye-hand skills of scrubbing, washing, cutting, coring, dicing, tearing, slicing, peeling, chopping, grating, shredding, measuring, sifting, mixing, stirring, beating, spreading, kneading, rolling, shaking, sprinkling, grinding, pouring, ladling, squeezing, mashing, balling, breaking eggs, and turning a food mill or egg beater?

In other words, cooking in an early childhood classroom has little to do with "teaching children to cook." The point of the activity is to provide an opportunity for the youngsters to develop small motor skills. Of all the small motor experiences you could provide for the children, cooking is the best. It is the best because it is real, not pretend. It is something adults do and therefore children take great satisfaction in being able to accomplish themselves. Furthermore, it is best because it offers unparalleled opportunities to practice small motor skills in so many different ways.

Cooking in the classroom is even more important in helping youngsters develop nutritious food habits, contend other early childhood specialists. Says Professor Maryellen S. Cosgrove:

> Early experiences with food preparation may lay the foundation for a lifelong habit of eating nutritious foods...I can't think of a more appropriate way to involve children in accepting responsibility for their own eating habits than involving them in the preparation of food. (Cosgrove, 1991, 43)

The list of justifications for children's cooking goes on from there. It is an excellent teacher of scientific concepts in concrete ways, such as, that heat and cold change things, and that liquids dissolve things. It helps teach math concepts such as sequencing (following recipes), measuring, and counting. It engages all five of the youngster's senses (smelling, tasting, seeing, hearing, and touching), the principal way young children learn. It gives children practice in following directions, and it promotes the social skills of cooperation, sharing, taking turns, and waiting your turn. Furthermore, it is an excellent pre-reading activity that engages children in "reading" illustrated recipe charts. All-in-all, cooking is an experience young children can hardly afford to miss.

• *Setting Up a Cooking Center*

The location in the classroom of your cooking activities depends upon several factors. It is essential to be near an electrical outlet if you are using electrical appliances. Being close to a sink is also important. Some classrooms that have low counters against the wall with a built-in sink and electrical outlets make ideal Cooking Centers. Others keep their appliances on high shelves for safety's sake, and have children's food preparation on low tables nearby. It is good to have nearby storage shelves where bowls and pans can be selected and returned by the children. A pegboard with hooks for utensils and outline drawings of the utensils mounted behind them is an especially effective method for placing cooking tools at the children's disposal. Some of the equipment you may need can include:

Microwave oven	Food mill	Mixing bowls
Toaster oven	Colander	Measuring cups & spoons
Electric cook pot	Potato masher	Spoons (wooden, slotted)
Electric fry pan	Egg beater	Knives (paring, plastic)
Blender	Flour sifter	Vegetable peeler
Cutting board	Sieve	Scrub brush

Specific recipes may call for other implements. The electric appliances can be borrowed or brought from home if the center does not provide them.

Who will do the cooking in your classroom? It is so easy for the adult in charge of the activity to take over when children fumble, work slowly, or make a mess. Keep in mind that the purpose for the activity is to help *children* develop small motor skills as well as self-esteem as they participate in this grown-up experience. Thus, it is important for the children to do everything they can in each food preparation activity. With proper precautions they can even cut with a sharp knife. The *process* of food preparation is the important thing here and not the *product,* just as it is in art activities.

Be sure to have a simple, illustrated recipe chart located close to the food preparation area for the children to see as they work, and for you to refer to. Hang it on an experience chart holder, a painting easel, or mount it on the wall or cupboard. Following an illustrated recipe chart is an excellent real life pre-reading activity for children whose teachers subscribe to the whole language philosophy of learning.

• *Using Parent Volunteers*

If parents or relatives of the children have special knowledge of the food being prepared (for example, if they are from or have visited the Caribbean islands when pumpkin soup is on the menu), they may want to participate in this cooking experience. Talk with them beforehand about your learning goals for the children, and what you expect from adult volunteers. Don't assume that they will know what they should do when they come into the classroom. Otherwise, they may take over the cooking, and your children will miss the experience. If they want to help prepare the food, decide ahead of time what they should do and what the children will be doing. Some visitors may want to share photos of the islands or talk about their experience, rather than cook with the children.

Picture books about food experiences can motivate children to prepare food in the classroom.

• *Food Allergies; Religious Restrictions*

Be sure to talk to the parents of your children before embarking on your food preparation activities. Check to see what, if any, food allergies the children might have. Also ask if there are other restrictions on foods the children can eat. Some religions restrict the eating of pork products, for instance. If even one child cannot participate with certain foods, then you should change the activity to something else.

✿ Picture Books to Motivate Cooking Activities

Stories featuring foods abound in children's literature. Already we have mentioned: *Keep Your Mouth Closed Dear* (birthday cake), *The Doorbell Rang* (cookies), *Rise and Shine, Mariko-Chan* (rice balls), *Cleversticks* (cookies), *Even That Moose Won't Listen to Me* (garden vegetables), *The Extraordinary Ordinary Everything Room* (jello), *Much Bigger Than Martin* (apples), *Daddy Makes the Best Spaghetti* (spaghetti), *Blueberries for Sal* (blueberries), *The Mysterious Tadpole* (cheeseburgers), *The Knight and the Dragon* (barbecue), *Where the Wild Things Are* (supper), *Jack and the Beanstalk,* (beans; supper), *The Gingerbread Man* (gingerbread), *Goldilocks and the Three Bears* (porridge), *Strega Nona* (pasta), *The Turnip* (turnips), and *Red Riding Hood* (custard).

Stories like these can be the motivation for fascinating food activities, from growing vegetables, shopping at food stores, visiting farms and orchards, picking fruits, preparing snacks, and cooking from recipes, to putting on a meal for parents and friends.

This chapter features other books with a focus on food, and describes how children can prepare each food in the classroom, starting with simple foods and following with more complicated preparations. The chapter concludes with several books on eating.

Pumpkin Pumpkin (1986), by Jeanne Titherington (Toasted Pumpkin Seeds)
My Little Island (1985), by Frane Lessac (Pumpkin Soup)
Apple Pigs (1981), by Ruth Orbach (Raw or Cooked Applesauce)
Don't Forget the Bacon (1976), by Pat Hutchins (Stuffed Pear and Bacon Snack)
Bread and Jam for Frances (1964), by Russell Hoban; Lillian Hoban (ill.) (Strawberry Jam)
The Giant Jam Sandwich (1972), by John Vernon Lord; Janet Burroway (ill.) (Flatbread)
The Best Peanut Butter Sandwich in the Whole World (1990), by Bill MacLean; Katherine Helmer (ill.) (Butter; Peanut Butter)
Nothing Else But Yams for Supper! (1988), by Joan Buchanan; Jirina Marton (ill.) (Yams)
Mashed Potato Mountain (1988), by Laurel Dee Gugler; Leonard Aguanno (ill.) (Mashed Potatoes)

Stone Soup (1987), by Tony Ross (Stone Soup)
Curious George and the Pizza (1985), by Margaret Rey and H.A. Rey (Personal Pizza)
Pancakes for Breakfast (1978), by Tomie de Paola (Pancakes)

 ***Pumpkin Pumpkin** (1986), by Jeanne Titherington, New York: Mulberry Books.* Here is a book to read to your youngest children at Halloween time. Two lines of large print text on a white horizontal page face sensitive close-up drawings of Jamie on the opposite page, a little boy who plants a pumpkin seed and watches it page after page as it sprouts, grows a pumpkin plant, a pumpkin flower, and finally a pumpkin that gets larger and larger. Jamie picks his full-grown pumpkin, scoops out the pulp, carves a jack-o-lantern face, and puts it in the window. But he saves out six pumpkin seeds for planting in the spring.

+ Read   Read to a small group of children before you plan to cut out a pumpkin for a jack-o-lantern. After small groups of children have each made their toasted pumpkin seed snack, carve out the face of the pumpkin or draw on face features in colored felt-tip markers.

+ Make Toasted Pumpkin Seeds   You should cut the top from the pumpkin yourself as it is difficult, unwieldy, and unsafe for most young children to handle. Have children help scoop out the seeds. (They can each save out a few seeds for planting, so be sure to bring in plastic cups and potting soil another day.) With the remainder of the seeds, you and the children can make a simple snack using the following:

Utensils	Ingredients
Colander or plastic bowl	Pumpkin seeds
Aluminum foil pie plates	Vegetable oil
Toaster oven	Salt

Make a recipe chart on newsprint or experience chart paper and mount it next to the work table for all to see. Illustrate each step by drawing simple pictures, and refer to each step as the children perform it. Work with one small group of children at a time (the children you have just read the story to). For each of the recipes in this chapter, the first step for the children before handling food should always be: "Wash your hands."

Toasted Pumpkin Seeds

Directions:

1. Scoop seeds from pumpkin (have each child scoop out a few seeds to get the feel and smell of the pulp)
2. Place seeds in colander or bowl and wash off pulp
3. Spread seeds on small aluminum pie plate

After hearing the story "Pumpkin Pumpkin" children may enjoy toasting pumpkin seeds.

4. Sprinkle lightly with vegetable oil
5. Toast seeds in 350° oven or toaster oven for 30 minutes
6. Sprinkle with salt

Toaster ovens are convenient but small for classroom cooking. This means that only a small group of children will prepare food for themselves at one time. It is actually better for young children to cook in small groups like this so that everyone can see what is happening and everyone gets a turn fairly quickly.

My Little Island *(1985), by Frane Lessac, New York: J.B. Lippincott.* This gorgeous book illustrated in "Caribbean island style" shows a white and a black boy visiting a little Caribbean island and experiencing all aspects of island life in vibrant tropical colors on the opposite pages. Frane Lessac, an American artist who has lived on the island of Montserrat, painted the pictures and wrote the fascinating text about barking frogs, steel bands, and the tasty fruit, fish, and food that the children enjoy. The cousins they visit gobble up pigeon peas, goat–water stew, red snapper fish, fried bananas, and pumpkin soup. Your children and you can make pumpkin soup.

+ Read   As you read to individuals or small groups, give the children time to look at the details of the illustrations. Can they find the barking frogs? The iguanas? Can they identify the tropical fruits mentioned at the market and at the square where the children stop to eat?

+ Make Pumpkin Soup   You can use a pumpkin you purchased or buy canned pumpkin. Because making soup takes time, start the process at the beginning of the day so that the soup will be ready for snack or lunch. You may want to integrate this cooking with your Halloween pumpkin activities or save it for a Thanksgiving meal or for the children's experiences with ethnic foods.

Utensils	Ingredients
Electric cooking pot or hot plate and pot	2½ cups pumpkin
	3 cups water or chicken broth
Wooden spoon	1 chopped onion
Slotted spoon	1 cup light cream or milk
Cup and half–cup measures	Salt and pepper to taste
Tablespoon measure	1 tablespoon curry powder
Knives	
Cutting board	
Food mill, sieve, colander, ricer, or blender	

For each of the recipes in this chapter, be sure to make a simple, step-by-step illustrated recipe chart that you mount near the cooking area and save afterwards. Children need to work at a low counter or table to prevent spills and accidents. Discuss the different steps of the process as you go along. Have the children themselves measure, grind, and stir. In this case an adult will need to peel and chop the uncooked pumpkin, but the children can do most of the other steps including chopping the onion with your supervision. If they do not open their mouths and talk during the onion chopping, they may not "cry." Some children, however, may want to experience how raw onions bring tears to the eyes when chopped. Be sure they do not wipe their eyes with "oniony" hands.

Pumpkin Soup

Directions:

1. Add pumpkin and onions to water or chicken broth
2. Bring to boil uncovered for 10 minutes

Mount the recipe chart on an experience chart holder near the cooking area.

3. Lower heat and simmer covered till vegetables are soft, stirring occasionally (45 minutes)

4. Remove pot from heat and scoop out vegetables with slotted spoon

5. Puree vegetables in food mill, collander or blender

6. Return puree to liquid in pot and heat

7. Add cream or milk, salt and pepper, curry powder, stirring constantly for 5–10 minutes.

Although using a food blender is more effective, children's small motor skills are better practiced through grinding the vegetables in a food mill, or pressing them through a collander or sieve with the wooden spoon. The vegetables are very hot, so do it carefully. Have a child help taste the soup after salt and pepper are added, to see if more is needed. Pour the soup into cups and let it cool before eating. Serve it with crackers for a snack or for lunch.

Apple Pigs *(1976), by Ruth Orbach, New York: Philomel Books.* This clever rhyming story tells about an old apple tree that nobody cared for, until a little girl came along and cleaned up the rubbish, and raked and hoed, to show the tree she cared. The tree did more than its part by bearing so many apples that the family was totally overwhelmed. After eating all they could, they began storing apples everywhere including in bathtubs, in rolled up rugs, and even inside the grand piano. Finally they invited "man and bird and wooly beast" to their wonderful apple feast. Elephants, hippos, yaks and giraffes helped them consume the apple hoard, plus all of the apple delacacies the family cooked or carved. Mother made "apple pig" carvings which your children can make also, following the directions in the book. In addition your children may want to make applesauce, either raw or cooked.

+ Read   Children will want to sit close to this book with its zillions of red apples stashed everywhere in the house. Can they identify the animals from behind as they enter the house? Children may want to repeat the rhymes they like the best.

+ Make Applesauce   Take a field trip to an apple orchard or fruit stand and gather or buy tart cooking apples. If you have a blender you can make raw applesauce without cooking. With a microwave oven, cooked applesauce takes only ten minutes.

Utensils	Ingredients
Blender	4–8 apples
Knives	1–2 tablespoons water
Cutting board	2–4 tablespoons brown sugar
Tablespoon measure	
Mixing bowl	

Make an illustrated recipe chart, mount it near the cooking area, and refer to the steps to take as the children and you follow this recipe. Children can cut apples with serrated plastic knives if you object to their use of paring knives. Children enjoy taking turns adding apples to the blender. For safety purposes, an adult should control this machine. When using a microwave oven, be sure you do not use any metal containers or foil wrapping.

Raw Applesauce

Directions:

1. Wash apples
2. Cut unpeeled apples into small pieces
3. Remove apple cores
4. Blend a few apple pieces at a time with water

5. Add more pieces

6. Pour into bowl

7. Add sugar and mix

Cooked Applesauce

Utensils	Ingredients
Microwave oven	6–8 cooking apples
Half cup measure	½ cup water
Casserole dish and cover	½ to 1 cup sugar
Wooden spoon	
Knives	
Cutting board	

Directions:

1. Wash apples

2. Peel apples (adult)

3. Cut apples in quarters

4. Place apples and water in dish

5. Bake in covered dish 8–10 minutes until apples are soft

6. Stir once during baking

7. Remove from oven and stir in sugar

8. Put through collander or food mill (optional)

 Don't Forget the Bacon *(1976), by Pat Hutchins, New York: Greenwillow Books.* Pat Hutchins' pictures tell the tale in this amusing, confusing story of little Sam going on an errand for his mother to buy: "six farm eggs, a cake for tea, a pound of pears, and don't forget the bacon." He repeats the shopping list as he and his dog walk along, but somehow things get mixed up so badly he has quite a different collection of things before his memory sets him straight, except for ... yes, he does forget the bacon!

+ Read   Children need to watch the illustrations closely to see what new item Sam is substituting for the thing his mother wants. Can they remember which item is right and which is not? After the story is finished, you can discover who really sees details in the pictures by asking the children: what was Sam's dog chasing throughout the book? Do *you* remember?

+ Make Stuffed Pear and Bacon Snacks   We do not know why the mother wanted a pound of pears or the bacon, but your children can put them to good use by making this unusual snack. You may want to shop with your children to buy the ingredients of this recipe. Will they forget anything if you don't write it down?

Utensils	Ingredients
Microwave oven	Pear halves enough for
Small bowl	2 each
Teaspoons and knives	10 slices of bacon
Paper towels	A container of cream cheese
Baking dish	

Use canned pears or raw pears washed and cut in two. Have children follow the recipe you have made. They especially love to crumble the bacon. Be sure to wait until it is cool enough.

Stuffed Pear and Bacon Snack

Directions:

1. Place strips of bacon in baking dish between layers of paper towels
2. Cook in microwave oven 8 minutes or until crisp
3. Wash, slice in two and core raw pears
4. Place cream cheese in bowl
5. Crumble bacon into cheese and mix
6. Dip out cheese with teaspoon and drop into center of each pear slice

Bread and Jam for Frances (1964), by Russell Hoban; Lillian Hoban (illustrator), New York, Harper & Row. This classic book about the little badger Frances (see also *Best Friends for Frances*, p. 85) is the ultimate story of children and their eating habits. Because Frances will eat nothing but bread and jam, her mother serves her only that—both at home and for her school lunches. Frances finally relents when she sees everyone but herself eating all kinds of tempting foods. One of Frances' most endearing traits is her habit of singing to herself songs that she makes up about things. Her "egg songs" and "jam songs" are high points of this book, as is the whole page description of an extraordinary school lunch on the last page.

+ Read   Kindergarten children find this story fascinating, but three-year-olds prefer stories with shorter texts for each page. The topic of food, though, is one all children are attracted to, so you may uncover attention spans you never knew you had—especially if their owners realize that the book is a lead-in to a cooking experience.

+ Make Strawberry Jam   If you have access to a U–Pick–M strawberry patch, make arrangements for your class to visit it and pick their own strawberries. Otherwise, purchase fresh berries in the supermarket. Then make your illustrated recipe chart:

Utensils	Ingredients
Heavy electric pot or hot plate and pot Serrated plastic knives Long knife Paper towels Wooden spoon Cup measure Kitchen timer	1 quart strawberries 4 cups sugar

Strawberry Jam

Directions:

1. Wash berries, dry well on paper towels
2. Cut off berry stems
3. Put berries in pot and cover with 4 cups of sugar
4. Cut into berries to let out juice
5. Cook over low heat, stirring gently
6. When juice has formed, turn heat up to moderate and stop stirring
7. When berries are bubbling, set timer for exactly 15 minutes
8. Take pot off heat and allow to cool uncovered (adapted from Rambauer, 1975, 835)

The jam will thicken as it cools, but this takes awhile. Plan to make strawberry jam a day before you use it. Bring in bread to make a Frances-style bread-and-jam sandwich, or wait and use it on a flatbread sandwich from the next recipe.

 The Giant Jam Sandwich *(1972), by John Vernon Lord; Janet Burroway, illustrator, Boston: Houghton Mifflin Co.* This riotous story in verse starts out: "One hot summer in Itching Down, four million wasps flew into town." No one knows how to get rid of the pesky nuisances until Bap and Baker have a brainstorm at a town meeting and convince the citizens that they should create a giant strawberry jam sandwich to trap the wasps in. So they do. After baking a gigantic loaf of bread, they slice it with a cross-cut saw and haul it out to Farmer Seed's field. Children enjoy the picture details showing the townsfolk spreading butter and jam on the giant bread slice with trowels, spades, and a tractor with a blade. In the sky above hover five helicopters and a tractor with the second bread slice, ready to drop it onto the sandwich, once the wasps have flown in. That's exactly what they do, trapping all the wasps but three, and making a giant jam and wasp sandwich which the birds carry off.

+ Read   This is your children's kind of story, with nonsensical ideas carried to exaggerated extremes. After you have read the story, ask them how else the town could rid itself of wasps. Or ants, or flies, or mosquitoes? What do ants like best? Does anyone suggest making a giant picnic cake with gooey frosting? You will know, then, that they have got the point of this book.

+ Make Flatbread   Making bread is more complicated than the previous recipes in this chapter. Flatbread, however, also called "pocket" or "pita bread," is somewhat simpler, yet just as satisfying for children. Start it early in the day, so children have time to finish it. This is the bread of the Middle East, also called Greek, Armenian, Arab, or Syrian bread; so you may want to make it when you are featuring ethnic foods in the classroom. Don't forget to make the illustrated recipe chart. This is a long recipe and may take two sheets of paper.

Utensils	Ingredients
Toaster oven	1 package active dry yeast
2 large bowls	1 cup warm water
Wooden spoon	3 cups sifted all-purpose flour
Measuring cups	1 teaspoon salt
Measuring spoons	1 tablespoon sugar
Small foil pans	1 tablespoon soft shortening
Flour sifter	

Flatbread

Directions:

1. Mix in bowl: yeast and 1 cup warm water (let stand 3–5 minutes)
2. Add 1½ cups sifted flour and the salt and sugar
3. Beat until smooth
4. Add remaining 1½ cups sifted flour
5. Mix or knead in flour by hand until smooth
6. Place in greased bowl, cover and let rise until double in size (about 45 minutes)
7. Punch down and divide into 2 balls
8. Flatten dough into foil pans
9. Brush with milk
10. Let rise again until almost double in size
11. Bake in preheated 425° oven for about 20 minutes (adapted from Rombauer, 1975, p.610)

Flatbread tastes best when warm. Children can tear off a piece and eat it, or pull it apart and spread it with strawberry jam (made earlier) for their own giant jam sandwich.

The Best Peanut Butter Sandwich in the Whole World (1990), By Bill MacLean; Katherine Hunter (illustrator), Ontario, Canada: Black Moss Press. Children seem to love sandwiches, and Billy is certainly no exception. His favorite is peanut butter sandwiches, and he never gets tired of eating them. Finally his mother suggests that since he likes peanut butter sandwiches so much, he should learn to make them himself. So he does. All by himself he buys the ingredients one at a time: fresh whole wheat bread from the bakery, fresh churned butter from the dairy, and fresh ground peanut butter from the health food store. When he puts them altogether he finds that he really does have the best peanut butter sandwich in the whole world. So good is it that the baker, the clerk from the dairy, and the clerk from the health food store invite themselves to lunch!

+ Read   Children enjoy the full-page pictures showing how Billy bought the ingredients and concocted his super sandwich. They will soon want to do the same.

+ Make Butter   Billy bought his butter fresh from a dairy, but your children can have the fun and experience of making their own. Have each small group of six children make their own butter from an illustrated recipe chart after you have finished reading them the story. Even this short recipe should be written down, so that children have yet another meaningful prereading experience, as well as a visual sequence of actions they must follow in order.

Utensils	**Ingredients**
6 baby food jars and covers	1 pint heavy whipping cream
Plastic knives	
Plastic cups	

Butter

Directions:

1. Refrigerate cream for at least 2 days (needs to be very cold)
2. Divide cream into 6 baby food jars
3. Screw on covers very tightly
4. Shake jars until cream turns to butter (5–10 minutes)

Children can stop briefly to notice when the cream turns to buttermilk. They may want to chant or sing in rhythm as they shake the jars. To the tune of *The Farmer in the Dell,* they can sing:

We're making butter now,
We're making butter now,
Shake, shake, shake, shake,
We're making butter now.

After the butter is finished, pour out the buttermilk into plastic cups for the children to drink. Then they can butter their bread as the first step in making "the best peanut butter sandwich in the whole world."

+ Make Peanut Butter   The next step in making this scrumptious sandwich is to make the peanut butter. Although Billy bought freshly ground peanut butter from a health food store, your children will enjoy making their own peanut butter. Shelling peanuts is an activity of great interest for them, and although it may not be easy, it surely provides good small muscle practice. Purchase a bag of peanuts roasted in the shell, and have the children shell peanuts enough to make one cup. Using a grinder makes coarser peanut butter than a blender, but gives children more exercise of muscles. Don't forget the illustrated chart: another short but important one.

Utensils	**Ingredients**
Grinder or blender	1 cup shelled peanuts
Cup measure	1½ tablespoons vegetable oil
Tablespoon measure	
Bowl	
Wooden spoon	
Table knife	

Peanut Butter

Directions:

1. Add 1 cup of peanuts gradually and blend or grind
2. Blend until spreadable
3. Add 1½ tablespoons vegetable oil and blend

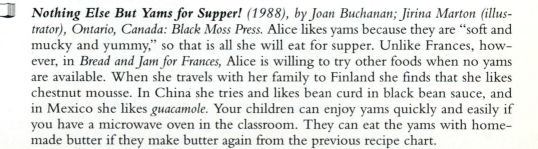

Nothing Else But Yams for Supper! *(1988), by Joan Buchanan; Jirina Marton (illustrator), Ontario, Canada: Black Moss Press.* Alice likes yams because they are "soft and mucky and yummy," so that is all she will eat for supper. Unlike Frances, however, in *Bread and Jam for Frances,* Alice is willing to try other foods when no yams are available. When she travels with her family to Finland she finds that she likes chestnut mousse. In China she tries and likes bean curd in black bean sauce, and in Mexico she likes *guacamole.* Your children can enjoy yams quickly and easily if you have a microwave oven in the classroom. They can eat the yams with home-made butter if they make butter again from the previous recipe chart.

Utensils	Ingredients
Microwave oven	Medium-sized yams
Knife	
Paper towels	

Yams

Directions:

1. Wash yams
2. Puncture each with knife
3. Place on paper towels and bake in microwave oven for the following times:
   1 yam.....4 minutes
   2 yams....6 minutes
   4 yams....8 minutes
   6 yams...10 minutes

In addition the children may want to make their own *guacamole* from ripe avocados (most supermarkets carry them). Mash the pulp with a fork and mix it with enough Italian salad dressing to make it creamy. This can be used as a dip for tortilla chips or as a spread for crackers.

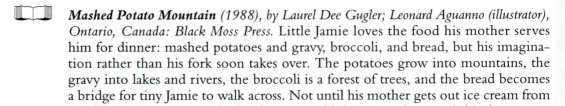 ***Mashed Potato Mountain*** *(1988), by Laurel Dee Gugler; Leonard Aguanno (illustrator), Ontario, Canada: Black Moss Press.* Little Jamie loves the food his mother serves him for dinner: mashed potatoes and gravy, broccoli, and bread, but his imagination rather than his fork soon takes over. The potatoes grow into mountains, the gravy into lakes and rivers, the broccoli is a forest of trees, and the bread becomes a bridge for tiny Jamie to walk across. Not until his mother gets out ice cream from the freezer does Jamie make his fantasy world disappear along with his dinner.

+ Read   Children will want to sit close to this simple story to see the mashed potato mountains grow and Jamie shrink smaller than his knife and fork. He later becomes a monster that eats up the mountains, river, and bridges in order to enjoy the ice cream.

+ Make Mashed Potatoes   Once again children appreciate making the food they eat. It gives them tremendous personal satisfaction to be able to achieve this grown-up task—and they can eat the results! Peeling potatoes is not all that easy for little hands, so select the largest, smoothest potatoes you can find. Don't forget to make an illustrated recipe chart.

Utensils	Ingredients
Electric pot or hot	6 potatoes
plate and pot	½ cup milk
Scrub brushes	3 tablespoons butter or

Vegetable peelers   Margarine
Serrated plastic knives   Salt
Measuring cups
Tablespoon measure
Potato masher
Wooden spoon

Mashed Potatoes

Directions:

1. Wash and scrub potatoes

2. Peel potatoes

3. Cut potatoes into quarters

4. Bring to boil 4 cups salted water

5. Boil potatoes covered (approximately 30 minutes)

6. Drain off water

7. Mash potatoes with masher

8. Add ½ cup milk, 3 tablespoons butter

9. Mash together and mix well

Potatoes can, of course, be whipped with an electric mixer, but children gain more experience and have more control using a potato masher. Children can eat the mashed potatoes with their own homemade butter if they want to make it one more time.

 Stone Soup (1987), by Tony Ross, New York: Dial Books. This classic tale of an unwanted visitor stopping by for something to eat takes a new twist in Tony Ross' book. Instead of three French soldiers or a peddler (as in earlier versions of this story), here we have the Big Bad Wolf dressed like a dandy in coat, vest, and tie, stopping at the Little Red Hen's house to eat her up and steal all her goodies. She invites him in for a big bowl of soup first, and he agrees. So she proceeds to make her grandmother's favorite stone soup, a very special treat. As the wolf waits for each new ingredient of the soup to cook, the Little Red Hen keeps him busy washing the dishes, vacuuming the house, bringing in the wash, cutting up a tree, fixing a TV antenna on the roof, and sweeping the chimney. When at last he gets to eat the soup, he finds himself too full to eat the Little Red Hen as well, so he snatches her secret soup stone and runs away.

+ Read and Discuss   Tony Ross's extravagant illustrations make this a book for children to laugh at as the story is being read. Exaggerated details, such as the hundreds of dirty dishes in dozens of piles, add to the fun as the over-sized wolf tries to do chores in the under-sized house. Ask your children why they think the hen uses a stone to make soup. Children tend to take these things literally. Should people really eat a stone? Help your children to see the joke.

+ Make Stone Soup   Children will, of course, want to make stone soup. The ingredients are mentioned, one by one, as they are gathered up by the Little Red Hen and popped into the soup kettle. Your children can act out the story, making real stone soup, once they have prepared the vegetables. The variety of vegetables as mentioned in the story will give your children a wonderful range of experiences in peeling, cutting, slicing, and dicing. The amount of vegetables and water depends upon the number of servings you want. For eight half-cup servings, the following ingredients should be sufficient:

Utensils	**Ingredients**
Electric pot or hot plate and pot	1 quart water
	1 large clean stone
Measuring spoons	1 teaspoon salt
Measuring cups	2 scraped and sliced carrots
Vegetable peelers	2 peeled and diced potatoes
Serrated plastic knives	1 scraped and sliced turnip
Cutting board	½ cup barley
Wooden spoon	½ cup sliced mushrooms
	1 cup "snapped" beans
	¼ head shredded cabbage
	½ cup lentils
	½ cup peeled & sliced zucchini
	4 bouillon cubes

Stone Soup

Directions:

1. Bring water with salt to boil

2. Add stone

3. Add vegetables

4. Add barley, lentils, and bouillon cubes

5. Simmer soup until vegetables are tender (about 1 hour total)

 Curious George and the Pizza (1985), by Margret and H.A.Rey, Boston: Houghton Mifflin Co. Many children are familiar with the mischievous monkey, Curious George, and his owner, the man with the yellow hat, through the series of Curious George books written in the 1960s. Here is one of a more recent series written for younger children with only a line or two of text at the bottom of each three-quarter page illustration. When George and his master go out for pizza, George is intrigued by Tony the Baker who makes pizza by flattening a ball of dough and throwing it in the air. When George tries tossing the dough himself, the pieces land everywhere and the monkey only escapes Tony's wrath by running out and hiding in the pizza delivery truck. As usual, George later saves the day when Tony is unable to make an important pizza delivery because of a locked gate. Tony rewards George with his own special pizza.

+ Make Personal Pizza   Each child can make his or her own Personal Pizza by following this recipe chart that you prepare. Children can select any or all of the toppings. Because the toaster oven is small, read the story to a small group of children at a time, after which they can make their own pizzas for snack time.

Utensils	Ingredients
Toaster oven	English muffins
Table knives	Cans tomato sauce
Tablespoons	Can oregano
Small foil pans	Salami slices
Serrated plastic knives	Mozzarella cheese slices
Cutting board	Mushroom slices
	Pepperoni slices
	Bell pepper chopped

Personal Pizza

Directions:

1. Preheat oven to 425°
2. Prepare toppings by slicing mushrooms, peppers
3. Slice English muffins in two
4. Spread ½ English muffin with 1 tablespoon tomato sauce
5. Sprinkle with pinch of oregano
6. Put 1 slice salami on sauce
7. Top with 1 slice cheese
8. Add other toppings
9. Bake in foil pan at 425° for 10 minutes (adapted from Wannamaker, 1979, p.18)

 Pancakes for Breakfast (1978), by Tomie DePaola, New York: Harcourt Brace Jovanovich. Another unique DePaola book has a little old woman with a cat and a dog deciding, in wordless book manner, to make pancakes for breakfast. Only her pancake recipe appears in words so that she and the children "readers" will know how to make "pancakes for breakfast." However, as she goes about gathering the ingredients, she finds that she is missing a few things: no eggs, so she must go out to the henhouse to gather them; no milk, so she must go out to the barn and milk the cow; no butter, so she must make it herself in her butter churn; no maple syrup, so off she goes to her neighbor who taps his maple trees and makes syrup. Meanwhile, back home, her cat and her dog have a wild romp scattering all her carefully gathered ingredients. Her plans are ruined until she smells a delightful aroma coming from her next door neighbors' house. So she invites herself to their "pancakes for breakfast," and eats a huge stack.

+ Tell Wordless Story   Have only one or two children at a time "read" this wordless book with you, so that they have a close look at the pictures and can tell you what is happening. Young children tend to describe the pictures rather than read a story (see p. 107) in a wordless book. But in this horizontal book with double-page illustrations all the way across, they may be able to follow the little old woman's actions more easily. Have your "reader" look at the whole double-page (sometimes separated into four pictures with "comic strip" borders), and think to him- or herself what the main character of the story is doing, before trying to tell you the story in words.

+ Make Pancakes   By now children have had experience cooking in the classroom. Have them look at the little old woman's recipe and make an illustrated recipe chart of their own.

Utensils	**Ingredients**
Electric fry pan	2 cups flour
Large bowl	2 teaspoons baking powder
Flour sifter	3 tablespoons melted butter
Egg beater	3 tablespoons sugar
Small bowl	1 teaspoon salt
Measuring cups	3 eggs
Measuring spoons	2 cups milk
Wooden spoon	
Spatula	

Pancakes

Directions:

1. Sift all dry ingredients into bowl
2. Beat eggs lightly
3. Pour eggs and milk into flour mix
4. Mix with large spoon only long enough to blend; batter should be lumpy
5. Stir in melted butter
6. Cook on hot griddle

This is the first recipe that talks about "dry ingredients." Have the children decide what are the dry ingredients in this recipe that should be sifted into the bowl. Butter can be melted in a metal measuring cup on the heated fry pan. The fry pan is hot enough to make pancakes when sprinkled drops of water "dance" on the hot surface. Alert children to the danger of touching the hot implement. When the batter is ready to be poured onto the hot griddle, have each child pour his own from a small pitcher and make any shape pancake he or she wants. Be sure the fry pan is on a table or counter low enough that the child can flip over a pancake with ease. This may be the most difficult action in the entire procedure. Encourage your "flap jack flipper" to keep trying until he or she succeeds!

Picture Books Featuring Eating

One of the best parts about cooking for young children is that they can eat the results. Not many classroom activities have such satisfying consequences. Eating is an activity that is meaningful for children in many different ways. Most obvious are its nutritional aspects. We talk to children about eating healthy, foods; about not eating "junk foods"; about cleaning your plate if you want any dessert; about not eating between meals. Most of this talk has little affect on young children. It is just another set of rules in one of the games adults seem to play. The reasons behind the eating rules are just as mysterious to many children as the rules themselves.

Then there are the social aspects of eating. When should you start to eat? How do you divide up portions? How do you use eating utensils? What about second helpings? What about foods you don't like? When can you leave the table?

Real experiences with food and eating are the best teachers. When children have the opportunity to prepare nutritious foods, they learn to like them. When healthy foods are served in the classroom, children make them part of their diets. Then when young children have the opportunity to eat with others and see how they handle food, to set the table, to pass the food, to take their own portions, to pour their own drinks, to try new foods, to wait until everyone is served or until everyone is finished, they also incorporate these habits into their own behavior.

But picture books can still help. It is good for young children to see in books the concepts they are experiencing in the classroom. Stories about eating are a good follow-up for the food experiences children are practicing. The following books can be especially helpful:

Gregory, the Terrible Eater, Mitchell Sharmat; Jose Aruego and Ariane Dewey (ill.), 1980
The Very Hungry Caterpillar, Eric Carle, 1981
How My Parents Learned to Eat, Ina R. Friedman; Allen Say (ill.), 1984

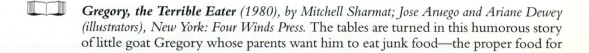

Gregory, the Terrible Eater *(1980), by Mitchell Sharmat; Jose Aruego and Ariane Dewey (illustrators), New York: Four Winds Press.* The tables are turned in this humorous story of little goat Gregory whose parents want him to eat junk food—the proper food for a goat, but all he will eat is human food. They finally lure him into eating goat junk food by giving him one new food every day, but then he turns the tables again by eating too much of everything. When this gives him a stomachache, he finally achieves a balanced breakfast at the end of the book: scrambled eggs, two pieces of waxed paper and a glass of orange juice.

+ Read   Once again illustrators Aruego and Dewey have created a wonderful critter's world of colorful junk and tasty ideas. Children will applaud Gregory's attempts to do the right thing even if it is wrong—for a goat. Read the book to a few children at a time who can sit close enough to pick out details.

+ Pretend to Be an Animal   Children who like this story can pretend to be an animal of their own choosing who wants to eat human food while you (or another child) try to tempt it to try animal food. You'll need to know what the particular animal likes to eat.

The Very Hungry Caterpillar (1981), by Eric Carle, New York: Putnam Publishing Group. Carle's *The Very Hungry Caterpillar* has long been a favorite of early childhood teachers who read it to their children when they are hatching out a butterfly from a caterpillar and cocoon. This time consider the story from the point of view of eating. The hungry caterpillar eats his way through an apple, two pears, three plums, four strawberries, and five oranges on each of the week days, and then splurges on Saturday with a double-page spread of ten different human foods, before changing himself into a cocoon and later a butterfly. To better identify various fruits, it is helpful to have on hand Lois Ehlert's *Eating the Alphabet* (1989) with its brilliantly colored collection of fruits and vegetables from Apricots to Zucchini.

+ Read   Children are fascinated with the actual holes left behind in the food as the caterpillar advances through a progressively larger number of fruits day by day.

+ Make a Fruit Salad   This story easily leads into making a salad from apples, pears, plums, strawberries, and oranges. Be sure to talk about the huge meal the caterpillar devours on Saturday, why he got sick, and what made him well.

AUTHORS
of INTEREST

ERIC CARLE, born in Syracuse, New York of German parents, spent many years in Germany. A high school teacher there recognized his talent and encouraged him to draw. Today he lives in Massachusetts. In his studio he first sketches his ideas, mainly about animal characters, then cuts painted-over tissue paper to the shapes he wants and pastes them down. Finally he draws around the pasted paper to complete the illustrations. (Hurst, 1990, 26)

Fruit Salad

Directions:

1. Wash fruit in collander or bowl
2. Slice fruit into salad bowl
3. Mix pear juice and mayonnaise in small bowl or use whipped cream product to make salad dressing
4. Pour dressing over fruit in bowl and mix

 How My Parents Learned to Eat *(1984), by Ina R. Friedman; Allen Say (illustrator), Boston: Houghton Mifflin Co.* A little girl opens this first person story by telling us that "some days we eat with chopsticks and some days we eat with knives and forks." Then she proceeds to relate the story about how her father, an American sailor, and her mother, a Japanese schoolgirl, first met when her father's ship was stationed in Japan, and how they almost missed getting married. The father wanted desperately to take her mother out to dinner but didn't know how to eat with chopsticks. Her future mother did not know how to handle a Western knife, fork, and spoon. The two of them learn how, and just in time before the sailor's ship leaves.

+ Read   Have your children sit close in order to see the carefully drawn pictures of Japan and its eating customs. The text may be too long for the youngest children. If so, "read" the pictures to them, or ask them what they think is happening.

+ Eat with Chopsticks   Cook boil-in-a-bag rice for a snack, and have the children learn to eat with chopsticks just as the father did in the story. It is difficult to eat rice with chopsticks unless the rice is sticky or unless you hold the plate or bowl close to your mouth and "shovel" in the rice. Japanese porcelain soup spoons are also available in import stores. Your children may enjoy trying them with the pumpkin soup that they make.

Do these books make your mouth water? Cooking with young children is one of the most satisfying activities you can do with them because it is such a grown-up experience, it is real, and they can eat the results. Many children's picture books feature food. See what other ones you can discover, and prepare simple recipe charts for your children's food activities.

REFERENCES CITED

Amster, B. (N.D.), *Stone Soup to Bagels: A Children's Literature Cookbook.* Farmingdale, N.Y.: SUNY Farmingdale.

Coody, B.(1992), *Using Literature With Young Children.* Dubuque, Iowa: Wm. C. Brown, Co.

Cosgrove, M.S. (1991), "Cooking in the Classroom: The Doorway to Nutrition," *Young Children* 46(3) 43–46.

Dedeaux, D.(1991), *The Sugar Reef Caribbean Cookbook*. New York: Dell.

Ehlert, L. (1989), *Eating the Alphabet,* San Diego: Harcourt Brace Jovanovich.

Endres, J.B. and Rockwell, R.E. (1986), *Food, Nutrition, and the Young Child*. Columbus, Ohio: Merrill.

Good Times With Good Foods (1976), Greensboro, N.C.: Learning Institute of North Carolina (LINC).

Hurst, C.O. (1990), *Once Upon a Time…An Encyclopedia for Successfully Using Literature with Young Children*. Allen, Tex.: DLM.

Marotz, L., Rush, J., and Cross, M.(1985), *Health, Safety, and Nutrition for the Young Child*. Albany, N.Y.: Delmar Publishers.

McClenahan, P. and Jaqua, I. (1976), *Cool Cooking for Kids*. Belmont, Calif.: Fearon Publishers, Inc.

Modern Maid Microwave Cooking (1971), Chattanooga, Tenn.: Modern Maid.

Paul, A. (1975), *Kids Cooking Without a Stove: A Cookbook for Young Children*. Garden City, N.Y.: Doubleday & Co.,Inc.

Rombauer, I.S. and Becker, M.R. (1975), *Joy of Cooking,* New York: The Bobbs-Merrill Co., Inc.

Wanamaker, N., Hearn, K., Richard, S., and Idaho-Washington AEYC (1979), *More Than Graham Crackers: Nutrition Education & Food Preparation With Young Children*. Washington, D.C.: National Association for the Education of Young Children.

OTHER PICTURE BOOKS ABOUT TASTY TALES

Barrett, J.; Barrett, R., illustrator, (1978), *Cloudy with a Chance of Meatballs,* New York: Atheneum.

Brown, M. (1947), *Stone Soup*. New York: Charles Scribner's Sons.

Carle, C. (1990 reprint) *Pancakes, Pancakes*. Natick, Mass.: Picture Book Studio.

De Paola, T. (1975), *Strega Nona*. Englewood Cliffs, N.J.: Prentice-Hall, Inc.

De Paola, T. (1974), *Watch Out for the Chicken Feet in Your Soup*. Englewood Cliffs, N.J.: Prentice-Hall, Inc.

Degen, B. (1985), *Jamberry*. New York: Harper & Row.

Dooley, N.; Thorton, P.J. (Ill.) (1991), *Everybody Cooks Rice*. Minneapolis, Minn.: Carolrhoda Books, Inc.

Hutchins, P. (1986), *The Doorbell Rang*. New York: Mulberry Books.

Kaza, K. (1987), *The Wolf's Chicken Stew*. New York: Putnam.

Khalsa, D. K. (1989), *How Pizza Came to Queens*. New York: Crown.

Krahn, F. (1987), *A Flying Saucer Full of Spaghetti*. New York: E.P. Dutton. (wordless)

Kroll, S.; Bassett, J. (ill.) (1984), *The Biggest Pumpkin Ever*. New York: Scholastic, Inc.

Lester, H.; Munsinger, L. illustrator (1985) *It Wasn't My Fault*. Boston: Houghton Mifflin Co.

McGovern, A.; Pels, W. P. (ill.) (1968), *Stone Soup*. New York: Scholastic, Inc.

Numeroff, L.J.; Bond, F. (ill.) (1985), *If You Give a Mouse a Cookie*. New York: Harper Collins.

Polacco, P. (1992), *Chicken Sunday*. New York: Philomel Books.

Sawyer, R.; McCloskey, R. (ill.) (1953), *Journey Cake, Ho!* New York: Viking Penguin.

Sendak, M. (1970), *In the Night Kitchen.* New York: Harper & Row.

Seuss, Dr. (1960), *Green Eggs and Ham.* New York: Random House.

Stobbs, W.; Jacobs, J. (1972), *Johnny-Cake.* New York: Viking Penguin, Inc.

Van Rynbach, I. (1988), *The Soup Bone.* New York: Greenwillow.

Wells, R. (1985), *Max's Breakfast.* New York: Dial Books.

SPACE STORIES AND THE GOOD EARTH

WON'T YOU RIDE A ROCKET SHIP?

Action Chant

Won't you ride a rocket ship, Up to the moon?	(circle with hand)
Ring around the planets, In a balloon?	(turn around in place)
Won't you snare a satellite Or comet by the tail?	(grab air above head)
Only if you find them In the pages of a tale!	(open hands and clap)

What Is "Space" to Young Children?

Ask children what they think about "space." The answers you get will be as different as the children you ask. But they may sound like this: "It's something up there." "It's where you go when you go to the moon." "It's where the astronauts are." "You can't see space but it's there." "It's where God lives." "You have to wear a space suit." "I'm going there when I get big."

Children know about space. They may not know a lot, but then, how many of us do? Children are interested in space. They want to know more about it. They want to be a part of what's going on there. Whereas many adults approach the unknown with caution, even anxiety, most children look at unknown vistas with excitement—as something to explore and find out about.

After all, young children's entire world is "the unknown" to them. Yet most of them can't wait to rush around the corner and see what's there; or to run down the beach and plunge into the water before they know what it's about. They learn by doing. And they want to find out. It's as simple as that. We talk about space with some hesitation as "a new frontier to explore." Children talk about space with great gusto and say "Let's go!"

Picture Books About Space for Young Children

The writers who have produced the books discussed in this chapter are those especially noted for their creative imaginations. What else might you expect in books about a world so unknown and mysterious? Just as children would do, these authors have used their imaginations to tell us about it.

Regards to the Man in the Moon, by Ezra Jack Keats, 1981
Brendan, Morgan and the Best Ever Cloud Machine, by Gerrem Evans; Scot Ritchie (ill.), 1985
Moon Jump, by Mustapha Matura; Jane Gifford (ill.), 1988
UFO Diary, by Saroshi Kitamura, 1989
Professor Noah's Spaceship, by Brian Wildsmith, 1985

Regards to the Man in the Moon *(1981), by Ezra Jack Keats, New York: Collier Books.* One of the best books to start with is this exciting story of Keats' inner city kids using their imaginations to "get out of this world." It all begins with Louie and his new father, Barney, whom the kids tease as "the junk man." But Barney gives Louie some very wise advice: "They should know better than to call this junk. All a person needs is some imagination! And a little of that stuff can take you right out of this world." (Keats, 1981, 2) Louie and his parents convert an old washing machine tub, a clockface, and a few pieces of pipe into the red-white-and-blue *Imagination I.* While the kids continue teasing in the background, Louie in his inverted collander space helmet and Susie in her propeller beanie, get in the space craft and blast off. When they open their eyes they find themselves really in space, staring down at Planet Earth. They're scared when they realize they're all alone, floating past a gorgeous Saturn with its colorful rings and moons. Suddenly they're jerked to a halt by a rope from an old bathtub "space ship" operated by Ziggie and Ruthie who have followed them. These two are stuck in space because they've used up their imagination. Louie guides them all through a meteor rock storm, past the moon, and back to the streets of Manhattan, where all the kids—and even the cats and dogs—are now ready to take off.

+ Read and Discuss   Children follow this story with great delight. It is something they themselves would do if they had Barney's wonderful "junk" or Louie's super imagination. Did it really happen? Children often mix reality with fantasy just as Keats does in this book. How about your children? Can they think up new adventures for Louie and his spaceship?

+ Space Stories   This is the time for children to explore their imaginations about space. What would they do if they were Louie and stranded in space? They may want to write their stories about this challenge in the Writing Center or tell their stories aloud to a cassette recorder in the Sound Center.

+ Dramatic Play   Bring in your own "space junk" and put it in the Dramatic Play Center for children to use on their own imaginative space flights. Bring boxes, cartons, collanders, pans, paper towel rollers, empty oatmeal boxes, plastic aquarium hoses, a windup clock, cleaned-out plastic bleach bottles, pieces of styrofoam packing material, dials from old appliances, pipe cleaners, aluminum foil, belts, gym bags, sun glasses, flashlights, football helmets, safety goggles, and whatever else you can think of to stimulate "space travel." What other items can the children find in Keats' illustrations that can be used imaginatively? Do you already have an old claw-foot bathtub for a private reading area in your Story Center? Now is the time to get one and convert it into a space ship as Louie's friends did.

Brendan, Morgan and the Best Ever Cloud Machine *(1985), by Gerrem Evens; Scot Ritchie (illustrator), Toronto, Canada: Annick Press, Ltd.* Here is another story of imaginative children building a flying machine. This time they go up only as far as the clouds, but that is their purpose. Bigger brother Brendan wants to be like a cloud floating high above the mountains and rivers, so he figures out how to build a cloud machine, and enlists his little brother Morgan to come along. After two attempts, they finally get their machine to work right, even after a near-collision with a cloud-dispersing dirigible.

+ Read   Children need to see the illustrations to follow this story. Would they build their own cloud machine like Brendan does?

+ Take a Cloud-viewing Field Trip   Choose a day with a sky full of puffy cumulus clouds and go outside with a group of children to see what shapes they can see in the clouds. Take pictures of the clouds with an instant-print camera and talk about them afterwards.

+ Do Cloud Drawings with Chalk   After viewing clouds, give children blue construction paper and white chalk to try making their own clouds. Many young children are still in the scribble stage of drawing, but scribbles are fine for clouds. Let them explore using chalk, both the end and the side. Also read the book *It Looked Like Spilt Milk* (Shaw, 1947), a picture book classic with a white shape on each blue page that is really a cloud, but looks like something else.

+ Make Model Cloud Machines with Wood   Do you have a Woodworking Center? Now is the time to start one. Bring in hammers (small adult hammers are best), nails of different sizes, pieces of wood, ceiling tiles, a box of "pounding junk" (pull tabs, Tinker Toy wheels, metal nuts, washers, and so forth). If you do not have a work bench, bring in several tree stumps for pounding on. Then encourage children to build their own cloud machines. Have the pounders wear safety goggles.

Moon Jump (1988), by Mustapha Matura; Jane Gifford (illustrator), New York: Alfred A. Knopf. This child's imagination carries him to the moon without a space ship. Cayal jumps and jumps and jumps so high he finally reaches the moon. There a moon man takes him jumping across the moon to his house. Finally Cayal with his teddy bear jumps home again, landing where he started in his mommy and daddy's bed.

+ Read and Search   Large colorful illustrations almost fill every page, with a line or two of text underneath. If children like this story, give them the challenge of finding items in the illustrations that relate to space and the moon. How many can your sharp-eyed youngsters find? Do these items help to explain why Cayal jumped to the moon?

+ Have a Moon Jump   Bring in a small child-sized trampoline and let children pretend to make their own moon jump. If no trampoline is available, use a sturdy inflated plastic mat. For safety purposes put down gym mats and have an adult nearby.

UFO Diary (1989), by Satoshi Kitamura, New York: Farrar Straus. The silky blue of space sets off the golden little UFO as it glides across Kitamura's glossy full-page illustrations to Earth. As the blue turns to green, the UFO lands when it sees a creature, a little boy. This diary kept by the occupant of the UFO records what happens on his brief stop on Earth: how the boy shows him around the fields and ponds; how he points out to the boy his planet in the sky at night, how he gives the boy a ride around Earth before he leaves, and how the boy gives him a yellow gift, a dandelion that he promises to plant.

+ Read and Discuss   This calm and matter-of-fact approach to UFOs is much more level-headed than most science fiction that looks at aliens as enemies who must be destroyed. In this case the aliens are us. The UFO occupant is the diary writer who tells this story from his first-person point of view. We never see the UFOer who decides that the boy creature is friendly because he smiles. They do indeed become friends. What would your children do if they met a space person? "Are UFOs real?" the children may ask. How will you answer? That some people believe they are real because they have seen them? That others believe they are imaginary? Isn't it best to keep an open mind about things we cannot explain?

+ Keep a Space Diary   Bring in a blank diary book and show it to the children. Would they like to keep a diary about an imaginary trip into space? They can pretend to blast off and go into space; pretend to visit a planet or the moon. Afterward ask the children what you should write in the diary for them about their first day's trip. Tell them they can continue the trip tomorrow, and you will record for them their next day's adventures. Be sure to read from the previous days' recordings. Keep the diary going as long as your children show interest. Put a second blank diary in the Writing Center for the children to record their own adventures.

Children can make their own cloud machines from wood after hearing "Brendan, Morgan, and the Best Ever Cloud Machine".

Professor Noah's Spaceship (1980), by Brian Wildsmith, Oxford, England: Oxford University Press. All the animals in the jungle come to life through Brian Wildsmith's talented pen in this clever variation of the Noah's Ark story. Wildsmith's gift for creating colorful animals with eyes that see through you is given full sway here as the animals gather in their polluted forest to determine what to do. Owl has seen a huge and wondrous object being built on the other side of the forest. So the animals troop over there to find an extraordinary space-ship being built by Professor Noah. He is going to another planet where the forests are still beautiful and he invites them to come along. They help him complete the ship just in time, as their forest has been set on fire. The exciting trip for forty days and forty nights is saved by Elephant who makes a dangerous space walk to fix a damaged "time guidance fin." But elephant has twisted the fin the wrong way, they find out when they land. Instead of going into the future they have flown backwards in time to the beginning of the Earth before the forests were polluted. They joyfully disembark, promising to keep the world wonderful from then on.

+ Read and Search   How good are your children's powers of observation? As you read this book, have them try to distinguish the different animals (easy to do), but also to pick out the robots that Professor Noah uses to build his spaceship. Can the children distinguish one of these colorful mechanical critters from another? How do the animals play with the robots?

+ Read the Noah's Ark Story and Compare   Peter Spier's wonderful wordless *Noah's Ark* (1977) is the perfect book to compare with *Professor Noah's Spaceship*. Although the first page of the book contains a sixty-line poem describing the ark and its occupants, the rest of the book is completely wordless. Spier, who is noted for his detailed drawings, has outdone himself in this book, filling every corner, roost, perch, deck, shelf, cage, nest, stairway, loft, rafter, stable, jar, hutch, fence, trough, manger, basket, ladder, clothesline, and even the bilge water in the hold of the ark with animals, birds, snakes, and insects. Have two or three children at a time look closely to see what is happening on each page. Do they notice any changes among the animals as the great flood continues to cover the Earth? Why do there seem to be so many more animals?

Then have the children make a comparison between the two books. Are any of the animals the same? Are any of the incidents the same? What happens in the original story to make Noah build an ark? How is this like the Wildsmith book? What role does the elephant play in both books? What about the dove? Which are the last animals out the door? Why? What happens to the animals in each book when the danger is past and they disembark?

Preschool and kindergarten children are not too young to make these compar-isons. Their visual skills are at their peak before age seven. They can pick out details that adults often overlook. If you want someone with sharp eyes to help you find something, ask one of your children!

These two books are, of course, an excellent lead-in to the remainder of the chapter on "The Good Earth."

AUTHORS
of **INTEREST**

BRIAN WILDSMITH grew up in a mining village in Yorkshire, England. He loved sports and music, but did not become interested in illustrating children's books until he began reading them to his own children in London. He wanted something better in art for children, and so began his career in illustration. His art is striking and distinctive with its shimmering watercolors and whimsical animals, sometimes shown from behind. (Hurst,1990)

❧ The Earth That Touches Us

Whether your children live in city apartments, Indian pueblos, townhouses, farmhouses, or cottages by the sea, they are somehow touched by the good Earth every day. Quenching rain falls on them; grass grows under their feet; trees make oxygen for them to breathe. Soil produces fruit and grain and vegetables to eat. Flowers and trees bloom with beauty for them to enjoy. It all seems to happen without much effort. It all seems so commonplace that no one gives it a second thought. Surely it will go on forever just as it always has.

But will it? These days we are picking up signs that our good Mother Earth may be hurting. Forests are dying from car exhausts and factory smoke. Lakes are dying from pollution and acid rainfall. Tropical reefs are dying from a change in water conditions. Rain forests are being cut and burned and cleared away. Beaches are being polluted and wildlife is dying from oil spills. Wetlands are being bulldozed into the sea. An opening in the ozone layer above the earth is letting in harmful rays from the sun. Rainfall is decreasing and crops are drying up and dying. Where will it all end?

As teachers of young children you are in an extremely sensitive position of influence in the lives of your charges. You may well be their first teacher outside the home. They look to you for support, for assistance, for advice, and for knowledge about this brand new world around them. How should they behave in it? They look to see how you behave. What should they know about it? They ask you to share your knowledge. What should they believe about it? They want to know your opinions.

What are your beliefs and opinions concerning the good Earth? It is important that you sort them out for yourself. "I'm not an environmentalist," you may declare, "I just don't want to get involved." That is not what your children are asking of you. They want to know what you know about birds and animals, trees and flowers, rain and snow, mountains and seashores. They are asking you to introduce them to these commonplace marvels. Then they will make up their own minds.

❧ Criteria for Choosing Books to Awaken Children's Interest in the Earth

1. Should help children become aware of the natural world
2. Should appeal to one or more of children's senses

3. Should present the message of caring for the resources of the Earth

4. Should lead children out into the natural world for hands-on experience

The picture books you select should be books that help children to *become aware of the natural world around them.* This is the time to do it—when children's development concentrates on sensory skills. Their eyes and ears need to focus on the fascination of the natural world. Otherwise, when they become adults they may look but not see. They may listen but not hear. If their eyes have never been trained to notice the flight of a bird, the flutter of a butterfly, the yellow of a dandelion in a sidewalk crack, the song of a house finch, they may pass them by unnoticed.

The books you select should also appeal to children's sensory nature: their sense of seeing, hearing, smelling, tasting, touching. Children explore their environment first through their senses. Babies use taste at first, putting everything into their mouths. Your children have expanded their tools of exploration to include all of the senses. Choose books with stories about the natural world, therefore, that appeal to and engage children's senses.

Also choose picture books about *caring* for the world around them. Young children need to learn how the Earth and its resources care for us, and how we in turn must care for the Earth. These stories should feature children or talking animals that demonstrate caring for something in the natural world. We humans tend to concentrate on *taking:* food, shelter, clothing, land, trees, animals. At this point in time, we need to shift our pattern of thinking, and concentrate in like measure on *giving:* on giving back something of ourselves to the world around us—our time, our effort, our interest, our money, *our caring.* The time to bring about a balance in giving and receiving between the Earth and its people is now. We caregivers of young children must make it our responsibility to teach our youngsters this message of caring for the Earth and its creatures.

The books you choose should have at least one more quality: they should lead children out into the real world for hands-on experiences with nature. Books are wonderful motivators, but it is the follow-up experiences that make things real. Every time you read one of the following books to your children, be thinking of ways you can put the youngsters in actual touch with the topics mentioned.

• Help Children Become Aware of the Natural World.

Brother Eagle, Sister Sky, a message from Chief Seattle, by Susan Jeffers (ill.), 1991
Where Butterflies Grow, by Joanne Ryder; Lynne Cherry (ill.), 1989
Sunflowers for Tina, by Anne Norris Baldwin, 1970

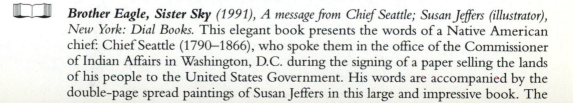

Brother Eagle, Sister Sky *(1991), A message from Chief Seattle; Susan Jeffers (illustrator), New York: Dial Books.* This elegant book presents the words of a Native American chief: Chief Seattle (1790–1866), who spoke them in the office of the Commissioner of Indian Affairs in Washington, D.C. during the signing of a paper selling the lands of his people to the United States Government. His words are accompanied by the double-page spread paintings of Susan Jeffers in this large and impressive book. The book begins: "How can you buy the sky?...How can you own the rain and wind?" and goes on to describe natural wonders experienced by Native American people. Jeffers' sumptuous drawings look up at Native Americans on horseback through the golden poppies and white daisies that flood their meadows; look down from the eyes of an eagle swooping out of the trees, with a scream of surprise; look with joy from the backs of galloping pinto ponies as Native American children race the wind.

The last pages show Native Americans looking out from their forests over a barren landscape of clear-cut trees, with the chief declaring: "The voice of my grandmother said to me, Teach your children what you have been taught. The earth is our mother. What befalls the earth befalls all the sons and daughters of the earth." (Seattle, 1991) The story ends, however, on a positive note with a modern father, mother, and two children planting new trees among the stumps, as viewed through an intricate spiderweb among pink daisies and white Queen Anne's lace:

> "We did not weave the web of life. We are merely a strand in it. Whatever we do to the web, we do to ourselves." (Seattle, 1991)

+ Read and Search   Children should sit close enough to savor the pictures in detail from the front endpapers with the chief's spirit advancing through the forest, to the back endpapers with a forest full of animals all eyeing the reader as if to say: "Did you get the message?" Can your children find the faces hidden in the birch woods, the rocks, and the pond? Whose faces are they? "Reading" Jeffers' illustrations is always a joyful experience for children. How many animals can they find in the book? Do they know their names?

+ Go for a Woods Walk   This book should inspire you and your class to go for a walk in the woods; or if you don't have woods, then a park or a meadow or a desert or a beach. Just enjoy the out-of-doors. Walk or sit or picnic and breathe in the fresh air. Close your eyes and listen for sounds: the wind in the trees, the lapping of water, the calls of birds, the buzz of insects. Enjoy.

Where Butterflies Grow *(1989), by Joanne Ryder; Lynne Cherry (illustrator), New York: Lodestar Books.* This book is another visual feast that should help children become aware not only of the beauty on the ground around them, but also of the tiny bits of very active life: the insects. It begins with a boy and girl down among the daisies in a meadow, lifting up a leaf and discovering a tiny black caterpillar bursting out of an egg. From then on it engages the readers' imaginations, asking them to imagine being a "creeper" like the caterpillar, crawling through meadow grasses and flowers, past animals and other insects as it eats and eats. There is even excitement and danger in such a life when a female cardinal tries to eat it, causing orange horns to pop out of its head in defense. Excellent scientifically accurate artwork shows the caterpillar turning into a chrysalis, developing within its case, and finally crawling out "wet, crumpled, and new" as a gorgeous black swallowtail butterfly.

+ Read and Search   Turn your children's attention to the double-page spreads of meadow grasses and flowers to see what other insect life they can spy. They'll need to look sharply for the praying mantis.

+ Go on an Insect Walk   If you live near weeds, wild grasses or a meadow, take your children on a walk to see what they can see at their feet. Can they pretend to be a bug? Have them choose one and watch what happens to it. Take a tape recorder along and have them record what their insect is doing. If you should find a butter-fly chrysalis bring it into the classroom along with some nearby vegetation, and watch it hatch. Then release it. Are any of the flowers they see like the ones in the book? Be sure to take the book along with you.

Sunflowers for Tina (1970), by Anne Norris Baldwin, New York: Scholastic, Inc. What if you don't have a meadow or forest to visit? Tina is an inner city African-American girl who longs for flowers of any kind. She lives in a tenement apartment with her mother, her brother Eddie, and an aged grandmother who never smiles. She tries planting the fresh vegetables her mother brings home from the store, but they only wilt. Then Eddie discovers a wonderful sunflower that has somehow sprung up on a nearby vacant lot. As a surprise he takes Tina to see it, and afterwards she puts on a yellow skirt and swirls around the apartment like a sunflower herself. Her grandmother smiles.

+ Read and Search   Children living in any location can enjoy this story and empathize with the girl who longs for flowers and beauty in her life. Afterwards, ask your listeners what things of beauty they see in the book. Do any of them mention Tina? The hidden message to your listeners is that the girl herself is beautiful. So are they!

+ Go for a Living Things Sidewalk Walk   This time take your children for a sidewalk field trip. What living things can they see on the sidewalk or nearby? Do they mention dandelions growing from the cracks between the sidewalks? Any insects? Worms? Seeds or nuts? Grasses and weeds along the sides? Blue bachelor buttons or white Queen Anne's lace? Do they think any of the things they see are beautiful? As we know, beauty is in the eye of the beholder. Do they want to collect the things they discover, or should they leave them there for others to enjoy? Take along an instant print camera to record their discoveries. Then they can take the beauty back with them as well as leaving it where it is.

• *Appeal to One or More of Children's Senses.*

Planting a Rainbow, by Lois Ehlert, 1988
The Hunter and the Animals, by Tomie de Paola, 1981
White Snow, Bright Feather, by Julie Downing, 1989

Planting a Rainbow (1988), by Lois Ehlert, San Diego: Harcourt Brace Jovanovich. Here is another wonderfully colorful book about living things by Lois Ehlert. This time the topic is planting flowers from bulbs, seeds, and seedlings. In large bold type the first-person narrator declares, "Every year Mom and I plant a rainbow." In large shapes and bold colors the artist illustrates the process of bulbs developing underground and sprouting in the spring; of sowing seeds and setting out plants; and finally of watching the rainbow grow. The center of the book consists of color-coded page sections starting small and getting progressively larger, showing in rainbow order, the flowers they have grown by color: red, orange, yellow, green, blue, purple.

+ Read This book is a visual feast of colors from the front cover flowers in orange and red to the back cover flowers in purple and blue. For children who are just learning their colors it is an eyeful indeed. Children can take turns "reading" the book to each other once you have gone through it with them.

+ Go on a Rainbow-Flower Field Trip Cut up colored construction paper into playing-card sizes with enough of the six rainbow colors for all of the children to have a card. Have each child select one color card. Take the children on a flower-seeking field trip where children will try to find flowers the same color as their card—not to pick but to look at. These can be wild flowers in a meadow or woods, commercial flowers in a greenhouse or florist shop, supermarket plants or bouquets, flowers growing in a formal garden, or potted flowers in a building (hotel lobby, museum, etc.) Invite someone who knows flowers to come along and tell the children the names of the flowers they are seeing. Purchase a potted flowering plant and bring it back to the classroom. (Make sure the plant parts are not poisonous.) Does anyone find flowers that are different in color from any of the cards? Mention the names of some of these in-between colors (for instance, magenta, pink, rose, violet). Why do they think that some colors are named for flowers?

The Hunter and the Animals *(1981), by Tomie DePaola, New York: Holiday House.* "Read" this wordless story to yourself before continuing. (This is a test of your own visual acuity!) Now continue. In this book DePaola cleverly uses Hungarian folk art to depict the plight of a hunter who goes into the woods, hunts all day without seeing any animals because they are hiding, and finally falls asleep under an oak tree. At this point the animals come out and play a trick on the hunter. One by one they remove the stylized oak branches from the trees and substitute pine branches. They also hide his gun and bag. When he wakes up in the light of a full moon and looks around him, he panics, hysterically running this way and that. When he begins to cry, the concerned animals come out of hiding, approaching him with gifts of fruit, returning his gun and bag, and finally leading him home—all wordlessly. In return, he breaks his gun over his knee and makes them a promise.

+ Read and Search This story also engages the sense of seeing. As you "read" the wordless story—or have one of the children read it, encourage one or two others to sit close and look at the pictures. What do they see happening? DePaola has found that many children discover the trick that the animals played on the hunter, while many adults do not. (DePaola, 1982) Did you? Did you realize this was happening in the story before reading about it here? Don't be discouraged if you did not. Children see details that adults overlook. Because they don't know what to look for or what to expect, children tend to look at things more carefully. It behooves us to do the same. We see mainly what we look for. Thus we often overlook important things: like the leaves of trees turning brown when they should be green; like the absence of birds in the bushes where they always have been; like the water of the lake turning green with algae. Ask your listeners what they think the promise was that the hunter made to the animals. What promise would your children have made if they were there?

+ **Go for a Seeing Walk**   Go outside with your children for a walk around the building. When you come to a familiar tree or bush, have them all turn their backs to it (you,too), and without looking, describe what the tree or bush looks like. (Don't tell them ahead of time that this will happen.) Then have everyone turn around to see if they were right. What details did they miss? What about you? Continue your walk until you come to another natural object of interest. Then, everybody turn around again, and describe it. If you have an instant print camera you can photograph these objects, and start a scrapbook, recording your descriptions. Several weeks later, take another walk and repeat the experience. Have the objects changed? In what ways?

 White Snow, Blue Feather *(1989), by Julie Downing, New York: Bradbury.* A little girl narrates this simple but lovely winter story about her trek outside through the snow from her house to the woods to feed the birds. Each double-page spread is a single large picture of the snowy woods and the girl's footprints. A simple text tucked here and there in phrases or a sentence or two makes up the story. The little girl hurries back to show her mother what she found: a blue jay's feather—a piece of the sky—and it's for her mother. The jay shown is a Steller's Jay from west of the Rocky Mountains.

+ **Read and Search**   Show this book to your youngest children as you read the brief text. Let them use their senses to find other objects partly buried in the snow, not mentioned in the text.

+ **Go for a Snow Walk**   What can your children find on a walk through the snow? They can carry paper sacks for leaves, twigs, nuts, pebbles, and maybe a feather. If there is no snow where you live, go for a walk outside anyway. Children use their senses to see and find things overlooked by many adults.

+ **Make a Collage and Story**   Put out the items collected by the children on their walk and make a collage of them by gluing them to sheets of colorful backing paper. Children can make individual collages or put all of the items together for a group collage. Have them dictate a story about the experience for you to write on an experience chart.

• *Present the Message of Caring for the Resources of the Earth.*

The Legend of the Bluebonnet, by Tomie de Paola, 1983
The Great Kapok Tree, by Lynne Cherry, 1990
Tacky the Penguin, by Helen Lester; Lynn Munsinger (ill.), 1988
The Butterfly Hunt, by Yoshi, 1990

The Legend of the Bluebonnet *(1983), by Tomie DePaola, New York: G.P. Putnam's Sons.* Native Americans have always lived close to the Earth and revered it. They have long understood the message: you get back from the Earth what you give to it. This message has been passed along from one generation to the next through stories, especially legends that tell how things came to be. Tomie DePaola retells in this book one of these legends of the Comanche people.

This is the story of the girl She-Who-Is-Alone, the only survivor in her family of the terrible drought that is devastating the land and People. All the girl has left from her family is the warrior doll that her mother made for her and her father decorated with bluejay feathers. The shaman, who has been listening for the words of the Great Spirits, finally returns and tells the People what they must do. He says that the People have been selfish; that they have taken from the Earth without giving back; that now they must sacrifice in a burnt offering the most valued possession among them; that when the ashes of the offering are scattered to the four points of the Earth, the drought and famine will end.

The People talk about what the Great Spirits want, surely not their special bow or prized blanket. But the girl knows that it is her doll, her most valued possession, that is wanted. When everyone is asleep she goes to the top of the hill, builds a fire, and puts her beloved warrior doll in it. When there is nothing left but ashes, she scatters them to the four points of the Earth, and lays down to sleep. In the morning she awakens to find the ground all around covered with blue flowers as far as she can see. Then it begins to rain. For her great sacrifice the People change the girl's name to One-Who-Dearly-Loved-Her-People. Every year thereafter the bluebonnet flowers have appeared on the land now called Texas as a sign of forgiveness from the Great Spirits.

+ Tell   This is a story for telling. Just as the original storytellers of the Native Americans did, you also can tell this legend to your children. Make it dramatic. Use a booming voice when the shaman speaks. Use whispers when the girl is thinking what she must do, and then doing it. Use gestures when the girl describes her beloved doll. It is more effective to let the listeners imagine the doll, rather than using a real doll. If the children respond well to this story, they will want to be the tellers next time.

+ Make Puppets   Children can make puppets of the characters out of small paper bags. The brown of the bag is the color of the buckskin clothing worn by the Comanches. Put out felt-tip markers for children to draw their character's face on the folded end of the bag. Bring in black yarn and let children cut pieces for hair which they can glue to their puppet's head. They can decorate their bags with colored lines and dots as shown on the clothing in the book. They can make a fringe at the bottom of the bags by making parallel cuts all around with scissors. Bring in very small candy bags and blue feathers from a craft shop for making the warrior doll in the same way.

+ Dramatize Through Story Re-enactment   When the dolls are finished the children can re-enact this story with puppets, just as they did with the folk tales in Chapter 7 with you as narrator.

The Great Kapok Tree *(1990), by Lynne Cherry, San Diego: Harcourt Brace Jovanovich.* The lushness of the Amazon rain forest is brought to life by author/artist Lynne Cherry who traveled to a real rain forest in Brazil in order to illustrate this book. Every page is engulfed in green leaves, stems, vines, and branches right out to the ends of the pages. Text is tucked in a bordered square on every other page, although vine flowers, frog toes, and butterfly wings droop over its borders. The story is about a man who is brought into the forest and directed to chop down a giant kapok tree. He takes a few swings at its buttressed roots and then sits down to rest. As the heat and hum of the forest lull him to sleep, the animals, snakes, and birds come out one by one to whisper in his ear why he should not chop down the tree. He awakens with a start when a rain forest child implores him to look upon them all with new eyes. The man does just that. He picks up his ax, looks around at all the living creatures, then drops his ax and walks out of the forest.

+ Read   Have a few children at a time sit close to this large, beautifully done book to gaze at the incredible life of the rain forest. As you read the words of each forest creature, make your voice sound different: Squawk for the toucan, squeak for the tree frog, growl for the jaguar, speak deep and lazily for the three-toed sloth.

+ Photocopy the Animals and Put Them in a Tree   Make photocopies of all of the animals shown. Let children choose an animal, cut it out, and color it with crayons. Bring in a potted tree of some kind and have the children place their animals in its branches. You cut out and complete the photocopy of the sleeping man and his ax and place them under the tree.

+ Dramatize Through Story Re-enactment   You be the narrator and have the children re-enact the story, bringing each of their animals out of the classroom tree to speak to the man about why he should not cut down their tree. Can they change their voices to imitate the animals just as you did in your reading?

Tacky the Penguin *(1988), by Helen Lester; Lynn Munsinger (illustrator), Boston: Houghton Mifflin Co.* Tacky the Penguin is not like any other penguin that ever lived. In this rambunctious talking-animal tale, Tacky shakes up everybody with his hearty backslaps, unpenguin-like marching, splashy cannonball dives, and screechy singing. He is definitely an odd bird. But when the rough and tough hunters come with their "maps and traps and rocks and locks," Tacky is definitely the bird to have around.

+ Read   Lester's stories should be read aloud, at least the first time through, so children can see the absurd animal characters and hear their hilarious rhymes. Ask the children: Who was the caring character in this story? Would they like to have Tacky around? Is it good to be different from everyone else?

+ Tell   Then tell this story aloud to your whole group of children. By now they should know the rhythmical description of the ferocious-looking hunters, as well as their repetitious saying about what they are going to do to the penguins. Have them repeat these refrains with you as you tell the story. Just as in folktales, it is easy to remember the four repeated incidents in this story: greeting, marching, diving, and singing.

+ Do a Penguin Ticket March   Make "Penguin Tickets" by photocopying several pages of this story that show the penguins and Tacky marching. Cut out the individual penguins and have the children color them black and white. (These young artists don't need to stay within the lines!) Be sure to have them make several wild-colored penguins to represent Tacky. Then have your children march around the room in a line to the beat of a drum, tambourine, or marching record. As they march have them reach in a box and take a Penguin Ticket. If they get a regular Penguin Ticket they should keep on marching as they are doing. If they get a Tacky Ticket they should begin doing outlandish marching steps like Tacky does. After a few minutes have them march past the box again, return the tickets, and start the whole process over again.

 The Butterfly Hunt *(1990), by Yoshi, Saxonville, Mass.: The Picture Book Studio.* At first glance this book with its rows of real-looking butterflies on the cover and endpapers may look like a nonfiction butterfly book. Keep turning the pages. When you see that it starts with the words "Once there was a boy..." and shows him walking down a country lane, you know there is a story to follow. This boy is surprised by a huge yellow butterfly, and determines to catch it and take it home for a pet. He gets a net and collecting jar and begins his quest. He catches all kinds of butterflies and fills up many jars, but the elusive yellow butterfly is still out there fluttering. His net gets ripped in a tree; the boy falls in the mud. Then SWISH, the yellow butterfly is his at last! He looks at it in his net, and then at all the other butterflies in jars and bags and boxes. And he sets them free. "And forever and ever the butterfly was his very own," as the story ends.

+ Read and Discuss   This also is a book for your children to sit close to and savor the pictures. The butterflies in the air are beautiful to see. What about the butterflies that the boy has caught? Can a butterfly be your very own if you let it go? How is this possible?

+ Color Butterflies   Draw an outline of a butterfly and duplicate it for all of the children to color their own butterflies. Have them paint with water colors. Cut out the butterflies so that the children can also paint the reverse side. When they are dry attach them to a string for a mobile of butterflies fluttering in your classroom.

• *Lead Children Out into the Natural World for Hands-on Experience*

Wild Wild Sunflower Child Anna, by Nancy White Carlstrom; Jerry Pinkney (ill.), 1987
Where Does the Trail Lead?, by Burton Albert; Brian Pinkney (ill.), 1991.
The Whale's Song, by Dyan Sheldon; Gary Blythe (ill.),1990

Wild Wild Sunflower Child Anna *(1987), by Nancy White Carlstrom; Jerry Pinkney (illustrator), New York: Macmillan Publishing Co.* Anna is as Tina *(Sunflowers for Tina)* might have been if she had had a meadow to romp in. This is a story about a little African-American girl in a yellow dress "jumping silly and loud" among the flowers in the field and meadow. She talks to the flowers, whispers to the seeds, sifts soil through her fingers, picks berries, hops through the frog pond, climbs a tree, rolls down a hill, looks under a stone, and picks a yellow daisy.

+ Read   A feast of colors, an envelopment of daisies, an engulfment of berries, a splashing of frog's legs, and an enchantment of Queen Anne's lace greet the eyes of the readers of this book. Be sure your listeners can see these wonders closeup. Can they identify with this Anna? Maybe. Maybe not. Would they like to?

+ Take Field Trips   If yours are country children, take them on a field trip into a meadow. Let them experience the same things that Anna does. It's all right. You don't have to know anything about a meadow. You don't have to teach them anything. They don't have to do anything—except enjoy. If they are city children, take them to a park, an arboretum, or a greenhouse. Is there a botanical garden they can visit? Somehow, somewhere, your children need to experience wild, growing things. Get out the yellow pages and start calling. Where can my children see a wildflower firsthand? This is truly the birthright of every child. If you can't find any place within the city, charter a bus. This is extremely important. If children grow up without firsthand experiences of living, growing things, they will not treat the Earth with the respect and reverence it is due. It is up to you!

Where Does the Trail Lead? *(1991), by Burton Albert; Brian Pinkney (illutrator), New York: Simon & Schuster.* If the previous book has not carried your children into the field, maybe this one will. Here an African-American boy explores Summertime Island (Nantucket) in wonderful scratchboard illustrations that fill the pages with a trail through the dunes, a lighthouse, tide-pools of periwinkles, gulls, a ghost town of shanties, an old boat in the cattails, and the "roar of surfers' waves." This unusually effective art form should help your children to see the good Earth from an entirely new perspective, as the boy finally comes back to the crackle of the campfire on Summertime Island.

+ Read and Discuss   Children should see these illustrations. Have them sit close. Scratchboard is different from any other book illustration described here. Children should experience it, as well as see it. This book is for all children, not just African Americans. What do your listeners think about the topic of this book? Have any of them ever spent a summer vacation at the beach? Did any of them ever explore in the way of this boy? You may have children who say they did, but that you know have never been out of town. That is not unusual, and you must accept it. These are children who would like to have such an experience, so they project themselves into it.

+ Go to the Beach in Your Dramatic Play Center   How good is the imagination of your children? Can they pretend to go to the beach? Even children who have never been to the beach have often seen enough television to pretend about it. Bring

Children can take an imaginary trip to the beach in the Dramatic Play Center if you provide beach props after reading this story.

in props like beach bags, towels, sunglasses or straw hats, sandals, and a big beach umbrella, and let your children take it from there.

+ Do a Scratchboard Etching   For older children, they may want to try doing a scratchboard etching themselves. Have them take a small square of posterboard and color it completely with crayons of different colors. Put newspapers underneath and have them bear down hard, coloring to the edge of the posterboard, until every bit is covered. Then they should paint over the entire board with a dark wash of watercolor or tempera paint. (India ink is not safe.) When you mix the wash add a few drops of liquid detergent. Let this dry. Then unbend a paper clip and use it to scratch the posterboard. The colors will show through the scratchings. The children can make scribbles or waves or any kind of design. (Warner, 1989, 19–20)

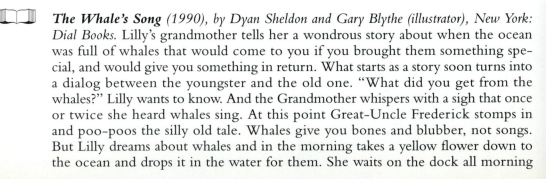

The Whale's Song *(1990), by Dyan Sheldon and Gary Blythe (illustrator), New York: Dial Books.* Lilly's grandmother tells her a wondrous story about when the ocean was full of whales that would come to you if you brought them something special, and would give you something in return. What starts as a story soon turns into a dialog between the youngster and the old one. "What did you get from the whales?" Lilly wants to know. And the Grandmother whispers with a sigh that once or twice she heard whales sing. At this point Great-Uncle Frederick stomps in and poo-poos the silly old tale. Whales give you bones and blubber, not songs. But Lilly dreams about whales and in the morning takes a yellow flower down to the ocean and drops it in the water for them. She waits on the dock all morning and all afternoon but nothing happens. Then at night a sound wakes her. She races down to the shore and there are the whales, leaping and singing. Then all is silent. Was it a dream? Far out to sea she hears them again, calling her name.

+ Read   The art in this book could be hung in a gallery. Each stunning picture covers one and two-thirds horizontal pages, with the text accompanying each picture in a white vertical box off to one side. Closeups of whales and girl and grandmother show only parts of the whole scene. Dark or muted colors dominate, giving the book a dreamlike, mystical air. Children should sit close to savor these unusual illustrations as the book is read aloud.

+ Talk about Gifts   What would your children give to the whales if they were Lilly? Ask each one. Can they tell why? Does it matter how much such a gift costs? What makes a gift valuable? What is more important than the cost of such a gift?

+ Listen to Whale Music   Today it is possible to listen to whales singing on tape. One such tape is *Whales Alive* by Paul Winter and Paul Halley with narration by Leonard Nemoy and the voices of humpback whales (Living Music Records, Inc., Litchfield, Conn.). Some science museums also feature exhibits where whales' singing is heard, such as the Smithsonian Institution in Washington, D.C.

It is not only the books about space and the good Earth that can make a real difference in your children's lives. It is also the follow-up activities into the natural world around them that are so critical. If children are the ones to make a difference in how natural resources are managed in the future, then these future citizens need to broaden the base of their experiences now, so that their choices will not be limited—so that their decisions will be wise ones.

ACTIVITIES IN CHAPTER 9 TO PROMOTE CHILD DEVELOPMENT

Physical Development

Make model cloud machines with wood *(Brendan, Morgan and the Best Ever Cloud Machine)*
Have a moon jump *(Moon Jump)*
Do a penguin ticket march *(Tacky the Penguin)*

Cognitive Development

Read the Noah's Ark story and compare *(Professor Noah's Spaceship)*
Go for a woods walk *(Brother Eagle, Sister Sky)*
Go on an insect walk *(Where Butterflies Grow)*
Go for a living things sidewalk walk *(Sunflowers for Tina)*
Go on a rainbow-flower field trip *(Planting a Rainbow)*

Go for a seeing walk *(The Hunter and the Animals)*
Go for a snow walk *(White Snow, Bright Feather)*
Take field trips *(Wild Wild Sunflower Child Anna)*
Talk about gifts *(The Whales' Song)*

Language Development

Keep a space diary *(UFO Diary)*
Dramatize through story re-enactment *(The Legend of the Bluebonnet)*
Dramatize through story re-enactment *(The Great Kapok Tree)*
Tell *(Tacky the Penguin)*

Creative Development

Dramatic play *(Regards to the Man in the Moon)*
Take a cloud-viewing field trip *(Brendan, Morgan and the Best Ever Cloud Machine)*
Do cloud drawings with chalk *(Brendan, Morgan and the Best Ever Cloud Machine)*
Make a collage and a story *(White Snow, Bright Feather)*
Make puppets *(The Legend of the Bluebonnets)*
Photocopy the animals and put them in a tree *(The Great Kapok Tree)*
Color butterflies *(The Butterfly Hunt)*
Go to the beach in your Dramatic Play Center *(Where Does the Trail Lead?)*
Do a scratchboard etching *(Where Does the Trail Lead?)*
Listen to whale music *(The Whales' Song)*

REFERENCES CITED

Beaty, J.J. (1992), *Preschool Appropriate Practices.* Ft. Worth, Tex.: Harcourt Brace Jovanovich.

Hurst, C.O. (1990), *Once Upon a Time…An Encyclopedia for Successfully Using Literature with Young Children.* Allen, Tex.: DLM.

Shaw, C.G. (1947), *It Looked Like Spilt Milk.* New York: Harper.

Spier, P. (1977), *Noah's Ark.* Garden City, N.Y.: Doubleday & Co.

Warner, S. (1989), *Encouraging the Artist in Your Child (Even If You Can't Draw).* New York: St. Martin's Press.

OTHER PICTURE BOOKS ABOUT *SPACE STORIES AND THE GOOD EARTH*

Aardema, V. and Vidal, B. (ill.) (1981), *Bringing the Rain to Kapiti Plain.* New York: Dial Books.

Baylor, B. and Parnall, P. (ill.) (1974), *Everybody Needs a Rock.* New York: Charles Scribner's Sons.

Breadman, T. (1992), *It Came from Outer Space.* New York: Dial Books.

Burningham, J. (1989), *Hey! Get Off Our Train*. New York: Crown Publishers, Inc.

De Paola, T. (1988), *The Legend of the Indian Paintbrush*. New York: G. P. Putnam's Sons.

Ets, M. H. (1963), *Gilberto and the Wind*. New York: Viking

Greenfield, K. and Ewart, C. (ill.) (1992), *Sister Yessa's Story*. New York: Harper Collins.

Haley, G.E. (1979), *The Green Man*. New York: Charles Scribner's Sons.

Haley, G.E. (1984), *Birdsong*. New York: Crown Publishers, Inc.

Kellogg, S. (1988), *Johnny Appleseed*. New York: Morrow Junior Books.

Mazer, A. and Pedersen, J. (1990), *The Yellow Button*. New York: Alfred A. Knopf.

Pinkwater, D. (1989), *Guys from Space*. New York: Macmillan.

Ryder, J. and Cherry, L.(ill.) (1982), *The Snail's Spell*. New York: Viking Penguin.

Teague, M. (1990), *Moog-Moog Space Barber*. New York: Scholastic.

Waterton, B. and Blades, A. (ill.) (1980), *A Salmon for Simon*. Toronto, Canada: Douglas & McIntyre, Ltd.

RHYTHMS AND RHYMES

Action Chant

Plunk on the banjo,   *(imitate instruments and movements)*
Stomp your feet;
Strum on the guitar,
Feel the beat;
Blow on the mouth harp,
Hear that sound!
Saw on the fiddle,
Sashay around!

Children's Involvement with Rhythms and Rhymes

Children love a beat. They will get up and move to it, if the beat is strong enough. They will memorize long verses of chants and songs, if the beat can be heard. Adolescents love a beat. Think about rock music. Think about rap. It is the beat that captivates, mesmerizes. Adults love a beat. They may criticize the loudness of rock music, but secretly tap their feet to the rhythm. We all, in fact, respond to a beat. It is not only universal, but also elemental. Our heartbeats set the pattern. Our breathing follows suit. You could even say the human species lives within a rhythmical pattern of beats.

If the beat also includes a pattern of rhyming words, it is "unbeatable"—irresistible to young and old alike. That is the reason you must be sure to include rhythm and rhyme in your classroom. Whenever you stumble upon an idea or thing or activity that your children find "irresistible," then you must use it for all it's worth! If children need help improving their self concepts, use rhythm and rhyme; if they need to improve their large or small motor coordination, rhythm is the thing; if, later on, they have difficulty learning to read, have them learn to the lyrics of songs! Strong interest on the part of the youngsters is an unfailing key for activities that will improve their growth and development. Tap into it, and you will succeed against all odds!

Children's Picture Books Using Rhythms and Rhymes

You may agree with the concept, but wonder about the application. What does this have to do with picture book storytelling for young children? Preliterate children learn songs and singing games without books. That is the way it should be. Nevertheless, it is fortunate that today's authors and publishers of picture books have also come to realize the value of rhythm and rhyme. The market responds to current interests, and this is definitely one of them. More and more picture books illustrating children's songs and singing games have appeared than ever before. But is it necessary, you may wonder? Do my children need a book about the songs and singing games they already know and enjoy? Yes, they do indeed. It is, first of all, a validation for your efforts to involve children in their rhythmic birthright. Important ideas are printed in books. Children's songs and singing games have finally made it into picture books! That is an affirmation of their importance. Children will be just as happy as you are, to see books that illustrate these favorite activities.

Secondly, such books are a bridge between the spoken (sung) and written word. When children see that the songs and singing games they have been enjoying are right there for them to see in written form, their excitement knows no bounds. So this is what our singing looks like when it is put into words and pictures! Whole language teachers call such books *predictable books*. Research has found that the best beginning books for helping children learn to read are predictable books that "contain selections with repetitive structures which enable children to anticipate the next word, line, or episode." (Bridge, 1986, 82) Although it may not be your purpose to "teach" reading, predictable books like these help children learn how print and speech are related, a necessary element in children's literary emergence.

Unlike adults, children do not look upon such books as a way to learn a song or a game. Instead, they see these books as a wonderful follow-up activity. Since they already know the words, seeing the words written down along with illustrations helps them to bridge this gap they eventually must overcome in learning to read: the gap between spoken words and written words. As reading specialists Barclay and Walwer point out:

> Like predictable books, song lyrics contain features that help children to more easily make the link from oral to printed language...These song picture books are becoming increasingly popular and *available* as more teachers discover the powerful appeal that these books hold for learners—young and old. (Barclay and Walwer, 1992, 76)

❧ Singing Games and Song Picture Books for Young Children

Old MacDonald Had a Farm, by Glen Rounds (ill.), 1989
Fiddle-I-Fee, by Melissa Sweet, 1992
This Old Man, by Carol Jones (ill.), 1990
The Wheels on the Bus, by Maryann Kovalski, 1987
We're Going on a Bear Hunt, by Michael Rosen; Helen Oxenbury (ill.), 1989
The Lady with the Alligator Purse, by Nadine Barnard Westcott, 1988
Mama Don't Allow, by Thacher Hurd, 1984
Abiyoyo, by Pete Seeger; Michael Hays (ill.), 1986

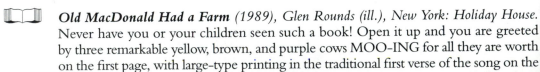

Old MacDonald Had a Farm *(1989), Glen Rounds (ill.), New York: Holiday House.* Never have you or your children seen such a book! Open it up and you are greeted by three remarkable yellow, brown, and purple cows MOO-ING for all they are worth on the first page, with large-type printing in the traditional first verse of the song on the opposite page. EE-AY, EE-AY, OH! stands half an inch tall, shouting its refrain as loud as possible, and COWS is even larger. Then comes: "With a MOO-MOO here," and so forth, telling children in print what they already know in words. Your prereaders have to see it only once to identify most of the words. Ask them to find the word that says COWS, and most will point to it with no hesitation. Turn to the next page and there is a big brown pig oinking with a similarly presented verse opposite. And so it goes. Raggedy roosters, face-forward sheep, floppy-eared hound dogs, fat and scrawny cats, guinea hens that squawk POT-RACK, and finally one huge skunk that old MacDonald runs from saying PEE-YOO, adorn the remainder of the book.

+ Read and Sing   First of all, before you read any of these song picture books, be sure your children already know the songs, have sung them many times, and have played the singing games that accompany them. To gain the most benefit from the books, children should be familiar with the words of the songs. The back pages of this book contain the music to the traditional Old MacDonald song.

Once again, read the book to a small group of children so that they can look closely at the pictures and the words. Read, don't sing, the words the first time through. Once the children catch on—that the printed words they are looking at are actually the words of the song they know—they may want to read them to you. Fine. Then go through the book again, singing the words as you turn the pages. Have fun with the children by skipping around the pages and trying to mix them up as you sing!

+ Make a Feltboard   These large and heavily outlined animals make excellent feltboard characters when cut from an extra paperback copy of the book. You, rather than the children, need to do this privately. Mount them on cardboard with sandpaper backing as described on pp. 74–75. Have children lead the group in singing the verses by putting the next animal character on the feltboard to indicate what verse to sing next. Store the characters in a labeled manila envelope in the Story Center along with the book for the children to play with independently.

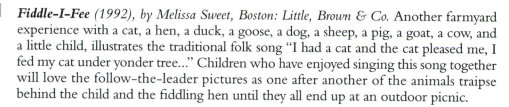

Fiddle-I-Fee *(1992), by Melissa Sweet, Boston: Little, Brown & Co.* Another farmyard experience with a cat, a hen, a duck, a goose, a dog, a sheep, a pig, a goat, a cow, and a little child, illustrates the traditional folk song "I had a cat and the cat pleased me, I fed my cat under yonder tree..." Children who have enjoyed singing this song together will love the follow-the-leader pictures as one after another of the animals traipse behind the child and the fiddling hen until they all end up at an outdoor picnic.

+ Read   Say the words of this cumulative rhyme as you read the book to individuals or small groups of children. Do they notice that the animal names are colored and in big print? Can they figure out what each name says by using the picture cue?

+ Play the Singing Game   First sing the song together verse by verse, then have children represent each animal and join your follow-the-leader line has you march around the room. Have more than one child represent each animal so everyone can be involved.

+ Invite a Fiddle Player   Does someone in the children's families play the fiddle? Can they visit the class and play square dance music for the children to move around the room? If not, perhaps someone from a square dance club could play music or bring a tape to play.

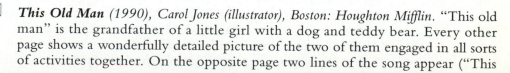

This Old Man *(1990), Carol Jones (illustrator), Boston: Houghton Mifflin.* "This old man" is the grandfather of a little girl with a dog and teddy bear. Every other page shows a wonderfully detailed picture of the two of them engaged in all sorts of activities together. On the opposite page two lines of the song appear ("This

old man he played...ONE He played nick nack on my....") with a peep hole cleverly cut through the center of the page, showing through to the next picture, and
giving the reader a clue to the missing word. Turn the page and the missing word
appears along with the refrain. This time the hole lets the reader look back to the
previous picture and see the little girl again. Grandfather uses toy drumsticks to
do his "playing on." The dog, of course, collects his many bones on every other
page. At the end of the book the music and verses for the song appear.

+ Read   Again, be sure the children already know the words and melody to this
singing game. It is a favorite one. Then they will appreciate the illustrations as you
read the book to one or two children at a time, so that they can peek through the
hole in the page to answer aloud the missing word. The pictures will also help
them to understand meanings of the words to the song: e.g., did they know what
"hive" meant before they saw the illustration?

+ Play the Game with Drumsticks   As the whole groups sings the song, instead
of doing it as a fingerplay, choose someone to be "this old man"; give that child a
pair of drumsticks; and have him or her drum lightly on an object for each verse of
the song. Can your "old man" find objects to rhyme with the numbers as in, one—
thumb? Repeat the game so that several children get a chance to be the old man.

The Wheels on the Bus (1987), by Maryann Kovalski, Boston: Little, Brown and Co.
This book incorporates a favorite nursery school fingerplay song into a wonderful
story about Grandma taking Jenny and Johanna downtown shopping for new winter coats. As they get tired of waiting in their new coats for the bus that never seems
to come, Grandma suggests they sing the song her Granny taught her: *The Wheels
on the Bus.* The music appears on the next double-page spread along with a visu-
alized scene of a red double-deck bus on Picadilly Circus in London. From then on
every other page shows this bus and its passengers hilariously illustrating the words
of the song on the opposite page. Wipers, people, horns, money, babies (go waaa,
waaa, waaa), parents (go ssh, ssh, ssh), and so forth, get progressively wilder.
Grandma and the girls get so carried away with their singing that when their own
bus finally arrives—they miss it! So—they take a taxi.

+ Read and Sing   Children should sit close to the reader to see these marvelously
detailed illustrations of Londoners hopping on and off the bus, giving clinking coins to
the concertina player's monkey, and what happens when the monkey gets loose. Does
anyone spot the man-with-the-monocle's hairpiece on the floor? Once you have
read the story, have the children sing it again. Make up different fingerplay motions
each time. Then take hold of hands and sing it one more time. The children will
have to make the motions for each verse differently when their hands are not free.

+ Dramatize Taking a Bus Ride   Set up a pretend bus in your Dramatic Play
Center. The only prop you might need is a peaked hat for the driver. If you have a
"riding bench" with a steering wheel, place that first with a line-up of chairs, one
behind the other, for bus seats. Otherwise, the driver can steer with a pretend wheel.
Will you need play coins and tickets for this bus? That is up to your children. Many

of them have undoubtedly experienced riding on a bus, perhaps a school bus. If not, you may want to arrange a bus ride field trip first. Where will your pretend bus go? That is up to the driver.

We're Going on a Bear Hunt (1989), By Michael Rosen; Helen Oxenbury (illustrator), New York: Margaret K. McElderry Books. While this is not a song, it is a traditional action chant or fingerplay done in unison much like a singing game. In this case the children move hands, feet, and body with you as leader. The book shows a father with three children, a baby, and a dog "going on a bear hunt." As they come to each obstacle: they can't go over it; they can't go under it. Oh, no, they've got to go through it. So they do, with wonderful sound words such as "swishy swashy!" for the grass, "splash splosh!" for the river, "squelch squerch!" for the mud, and so on. When they finally confront the bear in his cave, they have to retrace all of their steps—and quickly. The illustrations in this large book showing father, children, and dog becoming progressively more soggy, are done in double-page spreads of color in every other scene.

+ Read and Dramatize   If your children have not "gone on a bear hunt" with you, be sure to take them before reading this book. In case the words you know are somewhat different, try changing them to these words, so that the book will fit what the children are used to. Then when you read the story, the children can chime in as you come to the repetitions. Afterwards, take them all on the bear hunt one more time.

+ Have a Shadow Play   The bear hunt game makes an excellent shadow play. Do it on a day when it is overcast or dark outside. Then draw your window blinds and turn off the lights to make it dark in the room. Hang a sheet from a clothesline stretched across the room near one end. Have a goose-neck lamp or similar light source on a stand somewhat behind the sheet to project light onto the sheet. The shadows are made by you and one or two children who enact the bear hunt game with voices and motion between the light and the sheet. All of the other children should be sitting as the audience on the other side of the sheet. Try it out ahead of time to see how close to place the light to the sheet in order to cast shadows. You may want only your head and hands projected as shadows on the sheet. In that case, be seated behind a table and do all your motions like fingerplays with your head and hands. Repeat the shadow play as many times as you have children who want to participate. The audience can join in on the words.

The Lady with the Alligator Purse (1988), by Nadine Bernard Westcott, Boston: Little, Brown & Co. Here is another rhyming story rather than a song. Many older children will recognize it as a jump rope rhyme:

> Call for the doctor,
> Call for the nurse,
> Call for the lady
> With the alligator purse.

It has a captivating rhythm and rhyme that make people want to tap their feet, clap their hands, or jump to the slap of a jumprope on the sidewalk. This hilarious

After hearing this story, children can re-enact the rhyme with a real purse and a cracker feast.

variant of the original rhyme has Lucy's baby Tiny Tim drinking up all the water in the bathtub, eating up all the soap (with a cloud of pink bubbles), and trying to eat the bathtub but it wouldn't go down his throat. When the doctor arrives and says "penicillin" and the nurse says "castor oil," the lady with the alligator purse saves the day by saying "pizza," as she pulls out several pizzas from her huge green 'gator handbag. It ends up as a pizza feast for all on top of the bed, including a cat, a dog, and a baby alligator(!) or is it a frog? Out went the doctor (with a button popping from eating too much); out went the nurse (with flies buzzing to get at the pizza pieces sticking out of her bag); but when the lady with the alligator purse goes out, she goes in Mary Poppins style by sliding down the bannister!

+ Read   Your children will crowd close to this book to see the silly pictures of Lucy's bathroom with goggles on a coat rack, swim fins on the floor, and waves in the toilet bowl. What are they to think? Can a baby pick up a bathtub? Can pretend ideas be illustrated? After you have read it once or twice, see if the children can say the verses aloud (even the new ones).

+ Play a Pocketbook Game   Bring in a large purse or bag and put a silly item in it. Then give it to a child who wants to take the part of "the lady with the alligator purse." Now all of you together can say the rhyming verses. When it comes time for the lady with the alligator purse to call out "pizza," have your pretender, instead, draw the item out of the purse, hold it up, and say its name. Put in a different item for each different "lady." If you want, you can fill the purse with crackers, for instance, and have a "cracker feast" with all your listeners.

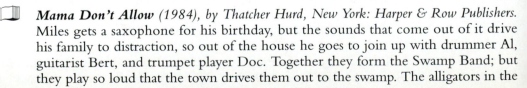

Mama Don't Allow *(1984), by Thatcher Hurd, New York: Harper & Row Publishers.* Miles gets a saxophone for his birthday, but the sounds that come out of it drive his family to distraction, so out of the house he goes to join up with drummer Al, guitarist Bert, and trumpet player Doc. Together they form the Swamp Band; but they play so loud that the town drives them out to the swamp. The alligators in the swamp simply *love* the Swamp Band, and invite them to play for the Alligator Ball on the Swamp Queen riverboat. After the ball is over the band is hungry, but so are the alligators. They seem to be smacking their lips as they look at the Swamp Band! Before the band members are put into a boiling pot, they persuade the alligators to hear one more song before dinner. It is a lullaby of Swampland that puts all the alligators to sleep, and allows the band to escape.

+ Read   Here is another song your children should know before you read this book. The music and lyrics are on the last page. The illustrations in bright cartoon colors against the blues and greens of the river and the swamp will entice any listener. As you read about the song that the Swamp Band plays for the alligators, have your children sing "Mama Don't Allow..."

+ Have Children Form a Swamp Band   This story calls for the children to form their own Swamp Band with instruments they can make themselves with your help. Make a shoe box banjo by removing the cover, cutting four small slots equidistant in the top at either end, and stringing four rubber bands around the box so that they are held in place by the slots. Get a collection of shoeboxes first so that everyone who wants to make one has the opportunity. To make a tambourines, bring in foil pie tins, punch holes in the sides and tie pull tabs to the holes so they dangle from strings. To make drums or tom-toms, bring in oatmeal boxes, coffee cans, or salt boxes. Children can beat on the box tops or make their own tops with wrapping paper secured tightly across an open top with string, tape, or rubber bands. To make blowing instruments like a kazoo, fold waxed paper over a comb and hum on it. To make a "tooter," fasten waxed paper over the end of a paper towel or tissue tube for children to blow sounds through. (Beaty, 1992, 207–211) Have the children sing "Mama Don't Allow" and play their instruments. Also play a record or tape of New Orleans Dixieland music for the children to accompany with their Swamp Band.

Abiyoyo (1986), by Pete Seeger; Michael Hays (illustrator), New York: Macmillan Publishing Co. This storysong based on a South African lullaby and folk tale, tells of a little African boy who plays the ukelele and his father, a magician who can make things disappear. The little boy goes around town playing on his ukelele until the grown-ups tell him to take that thing out of here. His father goes around town making glasses and saws and chairs disappear, until the people drive him and his boy out beyond the village walls. Then one day the giant monster Abiyoyo who eats people appears on the scene. The people are horrified to see him grab a whole sheep and a whole cow and eat them in one gulp. Everyone grabs their most precious possessions and runs. The boy and his father, however, run out to meet the monster. The boy begins playing his ukelele faster and faster which makes the monster dance faster and faster until he falls down. At this moment the father steps up and Zoop! The monster disappears. Everyone, of course, now welcomes the two back joyfully.

+ Read and Discuss   Your children should look closely at the outstanding drawings of people of all races gathered in this rural village. The dancing sequence of the angular silvery monster is a wonder to behold. Words and music of the simple song appear on several pages.

+ Have a Monster Dance   Children can make box heads from cardboard cartons by painting them with poster paints and cutting out eye holes. They may want to paint on monster-looking noses and mouths with teeth, or tape on matchbox or paper tube noses. Put on appropriate "monster music" for them to dance to, or have the children sing the Abiyoyo song.

Traditional Children's Poems and Nursery Rhymes in Picture Books

Not only have singing games and songs made it into picture books, but so have nursery rhymes and poems. There have always been collections of illustrated nursery rhymes. However, the picture books considered here contain only one entire poem with accompanying illustrations. The point is for children to have a book they can almost "read." If children know the poem, then the words in the book are "predictable." In other words, if children already know the oral words, when they see the same words in written form, they can predict what they say.

You are not formally teaching children to read at the preschool level, it is true; but preschoolers should have access to these books, nevertheless. The poems were written for children of this age group; and such familiar (and thus predictable) nursery rhymes can help young children make this important connection between oral speaking and written talk. Reading specialist Connie A. Bridge points out:

> Throughout the ages, children have been enchanted with rhymes and chants to the extent they have been passed on from generation to generation as nursery rhymes, jump rope rhymes, and songs. These predictable snatches of language become part of the child's language repertoire. Once they have been so deposited in the minds and hearts of children, it is an easy and logical next step for them to read these memorable phrases in printed form. Because the children can predict what is printed on the page, they can "read" the lines even though they might not be able to recognize the individual words in isolation or in other contexts. (Bridge, 1986, 83)

The nursery rhyme and poem picture books discussed here include the following:

Old Mother Hubbard and Her Wonderful Dog, by James Marshall (ill.), 1991
The Owl and the Pussycat, by Edward Lear; Jan Brett (ill.), 1991
Wynken, Blynken, and Nod, by Eugene Field; Susan Jeffers (ill.), 1982
The House That Jack Built, by Jenny Stow (ill.), 1992

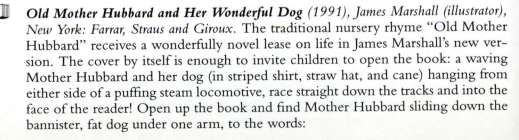

Old Mother Hubbard and Her Wonderful Dog *(1991), James Marshall (illustrator), New York: Farrar, Straus and Giroux.* The traditional nursery rhyme "Old Mother Hubbard" receives a wonderfully novel lease on life in James Marshall's new version. The cover by itself is enough to invite children to open the book: a waving Mother Hubbard and her dog (in striped shirt, straw hat, and cane) hanging from either side of a puffing steam locomotive, race straight down the tracks and into the face of the reader! Open up the book and find Mother Hubbard sliding down the bannister, fat dog under one arm, to the words:

Old Mother Hubbard
Went to the cupboard,
To fetch her poor dog a bone;

When she gets there on the next page, the cupboard, of course, is bare, but on one of its shelves two mice are seated at a miniature table having tea served. From page to page and verse to verse the poem continues with the old woman and dog getting wilder and weirder and more wonderful in their outlandish outfits and bizarre activities.

+ Read and Repeat Lines   Large type, two lines to a page, keeps the reader turning the pages and the looker laughing at what comes next. After the first time through, have the listeners join in with the words that they know. Before long, everyone will know all of the verses.

+ Play Toss-Doggie-the-Bone Game   Draw a simple picture of the face of Mother Hubbard's dog on the side of a cardboard carton. Draw a large round circle for his mouth and cut it out. Purchase several plastic doggie bones from a pet store or drug store, and have children try tossing them into the dog's "mouth" in a bone-toss game.

The Owl and the Pussycat *(1991), by Edward Lear; Jan Brett (illustrator),* New York: G.P. Putnam's Sons. Never has Edward Lear's classic nursery poem enjoyed such a lush Caribbean setting as Jan Brett's drawing pen has created for it. Above blue-green and pink cottages, red and yellow hibiscus, wild poinsettias, red ginger, white orchids, anthuriums, and bird-of-paradise blooms decorate the page corners, while palm and palmetto thatch or bamboo and pandanus outline the top borders of the pages. Borders are a Jan Brett trademark (see p. 141), thus the bottom borders in this tropical sea extravaganza are of course brain coral, conch shells, sand dollars and sea fans. In between the borders, the Owl and the Pussycat float away in their "beautiful pea-green boat" on a romantic idyll in this talking-animal tale to "the land where the bong-tree grows."

+ Read and Search   Read the poem through to a small group of listeners. They may or may not have heard it. But its intriguing and nonsensical Edward Lear lyrics should capture their fancies, while Jan Brett's art does the rest. Where does Miss Pussycat come from? Where does the Owl find the ring he needs to marry Miss Pussy? What do the listeners think about the Piggy-wig beachcomber? The magistrate Turkey? And what about the "runcible spoon"?

Next time through have them look for fishes. The cross-section ocean drawings disclose more than a dozen species of rainbow reef fish carrying on a drama of their own under the pea-green boat. Do the children notice Miss Pussycat's fish-bowl fish, a yellow butterfly fish who seems to be looking for someone? Can they discover who? Are the youngsters happy with the way the poem ends?

+ Make a Shoebox Underwater Peep Show   Shoeboxes are valuable items in preschool programs, as you have discovered. In this case you and the children can make a lovely underwater peep show following directions similar to those on p. 87. Cut away one end of the box and cover it with cellophane paper (can be colored

After seeing Jan Brett's illustrations in "The Owl and the Pussycat," children can help create an underwater peep-show inside a shoe box.

cellophane). Cover the inside of the remaining three walls, as well as the bottom and the inside of the cover with blue construction paper. You can trace the sizes needed, and most of the children can cut them out. Then have them paste these papers inside the box to create an undersea effect. Next draw fish outlines on white construction paper and have the children, who can, cut them out. Let them color their fish on both sides. You can now help them tape (with cellophane tape) a piece of thread to their fish at one end and to the cover of the box at the other. Make the threads of different lengths, so that when you put on the cover of the box, it appears that the different fish are swimming in the ocean. Make a small hole in the cardboard end of the box for the children to peep through. If they aim their box toward the light, it should give an underwater effect of fish swimming in the ocean. Children can make separate shoebox peep shows or group peep shows for the whole class. Some children may want to elaborate by cutting out a "diver" to hang from the cover, or pasting cutout "starfish" and "seashells" on the bottom of the box.

Wynken, Blynken, and Nod *(1982), by Eugene Field; Susan Jeffers (illustrator), New York: E.P. Dutton.* Here is another classic nursery poem loved by an earlier generation of children, but made available here by Susan Jeffers' contemporary illustrations. The pages are blue to represent night. The three children who represent Wynken, Blynken, and Nod are two modern-day boys (one little and one bigger) and a girl, who climb the stairs to the attic of their old Victorian house and play "pretend" in the moonlight. The first verses take place in the attic. Then the fantasy enlarges as the children sail out the attic window in their wooden shoe boat and onto a sea of clouds.

+ Read and Search   Read the poem all the way through, letting your small group follow along with the pictures. Then take them through the verses again and ask them what is real? What is imagination? How can they tell? What about the father and mother who finally find their children asleep in the attic? How do they feel? How can you tell? Do your children like the song that the Daddy sings? Do it again, teacher. You can ask the children the same questions every time you read this book. They expect it. Some children do not respond at first. It takes them several readings to understand what you are asking.

+ Make a Fishnet Wall Hanging   The children in this poem fish for stars in their net. Bring in a fishnet or transparent curtain that can be hung on the wall as a hanging. Have your children cut out stars (or whatever) from colored construction paper to be hung on the net you provide. Make large cardboard stars for the children to trace around on the construction paper. Some will be able to, others not. Whatever they trace can be cut out by them. Some will be able to follow the lines as they cut. Others will not. That's okay. Whatever they produce can be taped or stapled to your "net."

 The House That Jack Built *(1992), Jenny Stow, (illustrator), New York: Dial.* This house that Jack built is an orange-trimmed Caribbean cottage in a lush tropical setting of coconut palms, banana trees, and hibiscus blooms. Each double-page spread is a brilliant tropical scene showing the rat, cat, dog, cow (with the crumpled horn), maiden (all forlorn) and all the other timeless characters acting out their roles in this classic rhyming cumulative tale.

+ Read, Clap, and Tap   Read to one or two children at a time, holding them close to see the splendid illustrations and hear the rhythmical lines. They'll want to hear it over and over, and may soon join in with the rhyming. This is a toe-tapping, hand-clapping story. Have them clap or tap to the beat. Some children may want to get up and move around while the others say the lines in a chorus.

+ Build a House   Have children cut out pictures of houses from magazines and mount them at child's eye-level in the Block Center. Be sure to have doll house furniture and figures of people in the center as accessories. Then have a house-building week. Beginners may make only a rectangular room with one layer of blocks. Skilled builders may create an entire apartment building. All attempts should be accepted and photographed with the builders, if they agree.

Picture Books in Rhyme

A growing number of children's picture books contain rhymes and rhythms without being singing games or traditional poems. They are the books that are written in rhyme in the first place. All of the popular Dr. Seuss books are written in rhyme, for example. (See p. 17) Many other authors have found that rhyme is the best way to present their stories.

Kindergarten teacher Janice Hayes Andrews agrees. She believes that children should be taught to love reading before they are taught the mechanics of it:

Sadly, the drilling in phonics and structural analysis can turn children off to literature before they ever get turned on to it...Poetry is part of the magic that motivates children to love reading. (Andrews, 1988, 17)

For teachers who would like to turn children on to the magic of books and reading through poetry, here is another group of picture books from simple to elaborate that are written in rhyme:

I Went Walking, by Sue Williams; Julie Vivas (ill.), 1989
Sheep in a Jeep, by Nancy Shaw; Margot Apple(ill.), 1986
Silly Sally, by Audrey Wood, 1992
Barn Dance!, by Bill Martin Jr. and John Archambault; Ted Rand (ill.), 1986
I Like the Music, by Leah Komaiko; Barbara Westman (ill.), 1987

I Went Walking *(1989), by Sue Williams; Julie Vivas (illustrator), San Diego: Harcourt Brace Jovanovich.* From Australia comes this catchy rhyming story for your youngest children. Julie Vivas' distinctive illustrations (see her *Wilfrid Gordon McDonald Partridge*) show an orange-haired child in blue-green jacket and multicolor shorts going walking and seeing animals, one at a time, that look at him, much in the manner of Bill Martin's *Brown Bear, Brown Bear, What Did You See?*

+ Read and Respond   The large print and illustrations against a white background make this book one you can read to more than one or two children at a time. The book is actually a question and response story with a child saying: "I went walking," and someone else asking: "What did you see?" The child then answers with the name of the animal. Once your children get the point, have each of them in turn take the role of the child. They can answer according to the pictures of the animals as you turn the pages at first. Later have them make up their own animals for the response.

+ Play a Rhyming Follow-the-Leader Game   You be the leader at first with children following behind you as you walk around the room, saying "I went walking." The children in line should respond together: "What did you see?" Then you can reply about the animal "looking at me" as you march around the room. Then you should go to the back of the line while the next person in line takes a turn as leader.

Sheep in a Jeep *(1986), by Nancy Shaw; Margot Apple (illustrator), Boston: Houghton Mifflin Co.* From its "Beep! Beep!" first page with a sheep in a cowboy hat driving off in a red jeep, to its last page wreck with "Jeep for sale—cheap," this book is a rhyming, rollicking tale of a jeep ride down a hill, through the mud, and into a tree.

+ Read   Children enjoy the pictures of the silly sheep forgetting to steer their jeep, along with the simple one-line rhymes: "Sheep in a jeep on a hill that's steep." Can they think of other "eep" words that rhyme?

+ Make Shoebox Jeeps   Your collection of shoeboxes should include enough of them to make several cardboard jeeps. The children can discard the covers; paint the boxes red; punch two holes on either side of the boxes at the ends; insert Tinkertoy rods, and fasten Tinkertoy wheels to the outside. A Tinkertoy wheel can also serve as a steering wheel. These homemade jeeps can carry a full load of wooden or plastic farm animals from your Block Center.

***Silly Sally** (1992), by Audrey Wood, San Diego: Harcourt Brace Jovanovich.* Silly Sally in purple dress with pantaloons protruding, wends her way to town upside down through a brilliant buttercup countryside in this rollicking cumulative tale. The simple verse "Silly Sally went to town, walking backwards, upside down," is repeated each time she meets an even sillier animal who shows her how to dance backwards, leap backwards, sing backwards, and sleep backwards. How did she finally get to town? Read it and find out!

+ Read   Children should sit close to the reader in order to see the details in this merry romp. Can they tell who Sally is going to meet next from the upside down picture cues?

+ Act It Out   Read the story aloud while certain children perform the actions. Be sure to put out mats or floor pads. Then children can do somersaults or play leapfrog. Singing a tune and going to sleep backwards can also be fun, but don't encourage head stands.

***Barn Dance!** (1986) by Bill Martin Jr. and John Archambault; Ted Rand (illustrator), New York: Henry Holt and Co.* Rural children should enjoy this rollicking midnight dance of the farm animals who are lured to the barn by the scarecrow's fiddle music. The skinny kid in the farmhouse hears the sounds and sneaks out to join the jamboree. The entire book features toe-tapping, hand-clapping, square-dance-type verse in the dark of the night against a full moon.

+ Read   First read the book aloud to yourself to be sure you've got the rhythm of the square dance calls down pat—otherwise, you're likely to stumble. Children like to hear this different kind of country beat.

+ Have a Square Dance   Bring in a square dance record or tape and play it for the children's creative movement. Most preschoolers have not yet developed the skill to follow a beat for long, but there are always some exceptions. A few children seem to be born with the ability to keep good time to music of all kinds. If children are interested, you can teach them a few square dance steps. Have two partnered children stand across from and facing two other little partners. Have one set of partners hold hands and move forward to the other set of children; then back again to their own place. Have the second set do the same thing. Let all the children who are interested try these steps without the music. Then form a "square" with four sets of partners facing one another. Have one pair at a time move forward and backward to their place while the others clap. Most square dance tunes will be too fast for most of the children to follow. Try them and see. You can also try reading the *Barn Dance* verses like a square dance caller to accompany this simple dance your children do.

***I Like the Music** (1987), by Leah Komaiko; Barbara Westman (illustrator), New York: Harper & Row Publishers.* Here is a city musical feast told in rhythmical first-person verses by a little girl narrator who doesn't like the symphony: "But Grandma says the symphony/The symphony's the place to be." She likes, instead, the music of the street:

I like the beat
Of my feet
When my shoes hit the street

Then Grandma takes her to an outdoor symphony concert in the park. Here she not only likes the music, but gets to help conduct it!

+ Read   Children enjoy hearing this story in rhyme with its strong street beat. In addition, those close to the reader get to see what a concert hall looks like, and what instruments like the bassoon, the harp, the tuba, and the French horn are all about.

+ Have a Street Beat Jam   Have the children look closely at the illustrations to see what the street people use to make music: sticks, pots and pans, a garbage can top, a mop, the backs of chairs, a boombox. Bring in a boombox and some tapes of contemporary music and challenge your children to find their own unique ways to accompany the sounds. What do you have on your art shelves? Margarine cups filled with beans make great shakers; Tinkertoy sticks make great drumsticks; combs with waxed paper folded over them make good kazoos.

It is obvious that children's picture books featuring rhythms and rhymes can inspire children to sing, move, read, count, create, dramatize, dance, and especially have fun with language. That's what counts the most. For children to be successful with speaking, listening, reading, and writing in the future, they need a strong foundation today of happy, successful, and fun experiences with language.

ACTIVITIES IN CHAPTER 10 TO PROMOTE CHILD DEVELOPMENT

Social Development

Dramatize taking a bus ride (The Wheels on the Bus)

Physical Development

Play a game with drumsticks *(This Old Man)*
Have a shadow play *(We're Going on a Bear Hunt)*
Play toss-doggie-the-bone game *(Old Mother Hubbard and Her Wonderful Dog)*
Clap, tap to rhythm *(This Is the House That Jack Built)*
Build a house *(This Is the House That Jack Built)*
Play a rhyming follow-the-leader game *(I Went Walking)*
Act it out *(Silly Sally)*
Have a square dance *(Barn Dance!)*

Language Development

Make a feltboard *(Old MacDonald Had a Farm)*
Play a pocketbook game *(The Lady with the Alligator Purse)*
Play a rhyming follow-the-leader game *(I Went Walking)*

Creative Development

Have children form a swamp band *(Mama Don't Allow)*
Have a monster dance *(Abiyoyo)*
Make a shoebox underwater peep show *(The Owl and the Pussycat)*
Make a fishnet wall hanging *(Wynken, Blynken and Nod)*
Have a shadow play *(We're Going on a Bear Hunt)*
Build a house *(This Is the House That Jack Built)*
Make shoebox jeeps *(Sheep in a Jeep)*
Have a street beat jam *(I Like the Music)*

REFERENCES CITED

Andrews, J.H. (1988), "Poetry: Tool of the Classroom Magician," *Young Children* 43(4) 17–25.

Barclay, K.D. and Walwer, (1992), "Linking Lyrics and Literacy Through Song Picture Books," *Young Children* 47(4) 76–85.

Beaty, J.J. (1992), *Preschool Appropriate Practices.* Ft.Worth,Tex.: Harcourt Brace Jovanovich.

Bridge, C.A. (1986), "Predictable Books for Beginning Readers and Writers," in Sampson, M.R., ed., *The Pursuit of Literacy: Early Reading and Writing.* Dubuque,Iowa: Kendall/Hunt Publishing Co.

Fox, M. and Vivas, J. (ill.) (1985), *Wilfred Gordon McDonald Partridge.* Brooklyn,N.Y.: Kane/Miller.

Martin, B. and Carle, E., (ill.) (1983), *Brown Bear, Brown Bear, What Do You See?* New York: Holt, Rinehart & Winston.

OTHER PICTURE BOOKS ABOUT *RHYTHMS AND RHYMES*

Carlstrom, N.W. (1986), *Jesse Bear, What Will You Wear?* New York: Macmillan Publishing Co.

Hood, T. and Begin-Callanan, M. (ill.) (1990), *Before I Go to Sleep.* New York: G.P. Putnam's Sons.

Keats, E.J. (1968), *The Little Drummer Boy.* New York: Collier Books.

Keats, E.J. (1971), *Over in the Meadow.* New York: Scholastic, Inc.

Lawson, C. (1991), *Teddy Bear Teddy Bear.* New York: Dial.

Mosel, A. and Lent, B. (1968), *Tikki Tikki Tembo.* New York: Scholastic, Inc.

Oppenheim, J.; Schindler S.D., illustrator (1991), *Eency Weency Spider,* N.Y.: Bantam.

Peek, M. (1969), *Mary Wore Her Red Dress and Henry Wore His Green Sneakers.* New York: Clarion Books.

Pomerantz, C. and Alley, R.W. (ill.) (1987), *How Many Trucks Can a Tow Truck Tow?* New York: Random House.

Shannon, G., Aruego, J., and Dewey, A. (ill.) (1981), *Lizard's Song.* New York: Greenwillow Books.

Wescott, N.B. (1989), *Skip to My Lou.* Boston: Little Brown & Co.

Wolkstein, D. and Brown, M. (ill.) (1981), *The Banza.* New York: Dial Books

SUNLIGHT AND SHADOWS

LIGHTS   *Action Chant*

Blazing,
Blinding,
Brilliant,
Bright;
That is how
The sun gives
Light.

Gleaming,
Glimmering,
Glistening,
Glow;
That is how
The moonbeams
Show.

❧ Children's Involvement with Beauty and Aesthetics

The brilliance of sunlight, the shadows of night, the colors of the natural world around us: too often we take them for granted. Young children are different. Because they do not know what to expect of their world, they look for all the possibilities. They try out. They explore. They discover. Then they try to make sense of what they have experienced. Our roles as teachers and parents in the lives of young children is to encourage their explorations, to suggest directions they should take, and to help them understand what it is they are experiencing.

We do a good job for the most part, giving them knowledge and helping them to understand the whats, whys, and hows of objects and animals, people and places, facts and figures in the world around them. But there is one area we sometimes miss: *beauty.* We teach them to know their colors, it is true. But what do we say about the beauty of the colors? They learn facts about the sun and the moon, but do we help them to appreciate the glow of a sunset, or the marvel of moonlight? Do we ever point out the beauty of rainbow colors reflected in a puddle...even one that is muddy? The pleasing patterns of bricks in an old wall...even one that is crumbling?

It is important for their sake and ours that we take time to help children recognize and develop the aesthetic side of their nature. Now is the time to do it—while they are still open and accepting. A great deal of what they see around them may not seem all that beautiful. Yet if children learn to look for beauty, they will find it. Then when they mature, they too will insist on preserving the beauty around them for everyone to appreciate. Or as Stephanie Feeney and Eva Moravcik of the University of Hawaii state:

> For if children are not exposed to beauty in childhood, we fear, they may not learn to create or to appreciate beauty as they might if attention were paid to this aspect of development. (Feeney and Moravcik, 1987, 8)

And what is this beauty? It is different for every person. It may be dew on a spider's web, the peels of paint on a rickety fence, the comforting creak of a rocking chair. Or it may be a scarlet oak tree in autumn, the smell of burning leaves, or moonlight flickering through pine branches. The old cliche is true: that beauty is in the eye of the beholder. Yet if beauty is so many different things, how can we possibly teach young children what it is all about?

Quite simply. We have to alert our youngsters to listen for the creaks, to look for the gleams, and to recognize the tingles of wonder that beauty of all kinds arouses in us. You be the model. Look for beautiful things in your own life. Mention them to children when you recognize your own glimmers of beauty. Ask the children to acknowledge their delights,too: when they burst into a wonderful room like yours for the first time; when they feel the first snow of winter; when they see the sidewalk glisten on a rainy day; when they hear the rattle of palm fronds in a freshening breeze; when they smell the first raindrops spattering in desert dust; when they look at the pictures and listen to the words in the books you will be reading to them. Young children are sensory beings. Talk to them in terms of the five senses: how does it look, feel, sound, smell, or taste in a way that is unique...in a way that is beautiful? Again, as Feeney and Moravcik declare:

> Children are fascinated by beauty. They love nature, and enjoy creating, looking at and talking about art. They express their feelings and ideas through succinct and picturesque language; song, sometimes boisterous and sometimes lyrical; and expressive movements—the essence of poetry, music, and dance. Young children have strong preferences for books, objects, and food. They are creative and inquisitive, and have delightful insights into the arts. (Feeney and Moravcik, 1987, 8)

Beauty in Children's Picture Books

More and more picture books currently on the market are marvels of beauty. Already mentioned as particularly outstanding are: *Stopping By Woods on a Snowy Evening, Storm in the Night, Where Does the Trail Lead, Wild Wild Sunflower Child Anna, Where Butterflies Grow,* and *Brother Eagle, Sister Sky.* This chapter presents additional samplings of beautiful picture books or of books to arouse children's interest in beauty under the topics of:

Sunlight
"Children Appreciating the Sunlight"
"Animals Looking for the Sun"

Moonlight
"Children Appreciating the Night"
"Animals in the Moonlight"

Daylight
"Beauty Is Where You Find It"

✧ Sunlight: Children Appreciating the Sunlight

The Way to Start a Day, by Byrd Baylor; Peter Parnall (ill.), 1978
One Light, One Sun, by Raffi; Eugenie Fernandes (Ill.), 1988
Sun up, Sun down, by Gail Gibbons, 1983
A Rainbow of My Own, by Don Freeman 1966
The Day of the Rainbow, by Ruth Craft; Niki Daly (ill.), 1988
Shadows Are About, by Ann Whitford Paul; Mark Graham (ill.), 1992

The Way to Start a Day *(1978), by Byrd Baylor; Peter Parnall (illustrator), New York: Macmillan Publishing Co.* This Southwestern Native American story is a hymn to the sun for children all over the Earth. With the color of sunrise splashed across a horizon of buttes and mesas, the narrator tells the reader to go outside and and greet the sun with some kind of blessing or song you made up yourself. The reader should not try to think of the words to use until he is standing there, feeling the sun on his face just as the cavemen did eons ago, and the Aztecs, Chinese and Egyptians. Some people still know how to start the day, says the author and the artist, with flowing sunrise colors to match the words in blank verse. This book invites your children to go outdoors and say "hello" to the sun.

+ Read   Children should sit close for this story, looking at the way words are arranged in verses on these pages, and how colors flow out to the horizon. If they look closely enough they will experience how other people around the world greet the day, and thus find hints about how they should do it. Ask your listeners what they see or hear that is beautiful in this book.

+ Make Up a Sun Song   Open up the curtains and look out. The sun will already be up when your program is in session, but the children can still make up a song to the sun. What should the words say? Write down the children's suggestions on chart paper. What about the tune? It can be a chant to the notes of the scale with one line sung all on the same note, something like:

"Good morning sun we're glad to see you;
Come in our room and see what we do;
Come be our guest and shine all around...etc."

Children can accompany their song on a toy xylophone, playing one note over and over until the next higher note is reached.

Sun up, Sun down *(1983), by Gail Gibbons, San Diego: Harcourt Brace Jovanovich.* This first-person story by a little girl is flooded with rays of sunshine across the full-color pages inside, outside, throughout the seasons, and throughout the day until rain clouds cover the sun. Afterward a rainbow appears. Although told like a story by the girl and her parents, the book includes factual information about the sun's distance from the earth, the formation of clouds, rainbows, and shadows.

+ Read This very colorful book done in cartoon-like illustrations on glossy pages presents a stylized sun in all its glory shining on the little girl and her cat. Children will see that the text is sectioned off in white space at the bottom or within the pages as the teacher reads the story.

+ Make Sun Collages Prepare this activity ahead of time by making a table full of geometric design cutouts from colored construction paper: circles of red, yellow, orange, and green; long triangles of yellow, red, purple, orange, and white that can serve as sunrays if children want them to; rectangles of brown, red, gray; arches of rainbow colors. Put them all out on the table, along with paste and backing paper of different colors. Children can create their own collages. If they want to make a representational picture, that is fine, but give them the freedom to experiment with the colored cutouts. Can children paste more than one "sun" on their papers? Of course! Do they need to tell you a story about their collage afterwards? Only if they volunteer one.

One Light, One Sun *(1988), by Raffi; Eugenie Fernandes (ill.), New York: Crown Publishers, Inc.* Raffi is one of Canada's most successful children's recording artists. He has converted a number of his popular songs into children's picture books. This book is one of them called "Raffi Songs to Read." As with similar books in the previous chapter, this book illustrates one line of the song on every double-page spread. Illustrations of three houses and their occupants start from a distance on a round globe-like scene, and come closer on every page until they show the inside of the homes themselves and then the inside of a single room. The sun beams brightly on birds, animals, fish, and people of various ages and races (including a boy in a wheel chair), engaged in interactions with one another. It is a one-world story, with one sun shining over all.

+ Read Before you read the book be sure the children know this simple song. If you do not have a recording of it, the words and music are on the last page of the book. Have one or two children sit close to read the words with you and find interesting little details in the illustrations. Do they notice the boy feeding the ducks? Where did he get the food? What happens to each of the people when the sun comes up the second day?

+ Bring in a Globe Do the children know why the illustrations in the book show the houses and people on top of a round ball? Bring in a globe of the world and talk about it to a small group of children at a time in your Science Center. Show them where their country is on the globe, their state, their city or town. Bring in a flashlight to represent the sun and let a child shine it on the globe as you turn the globe around and around. When it is night in their state, what part of the world has daylight? When it is day in their state, what part of the world has night?

A Rainbow of My Own *(1966), by Don Freeman, New York: Viking Penguin.* Children are intrigued by rainbows: their beauty, their elusive nature, their mysterious appearances and disappearances. In this first-person story, a little boy sees a rainbow out the window and wants to catch it for his very own. He puts on his rain gear, runs outside, and begins his chase. What starts as a realistic story suddenly turns to fantasy as the rainbow begins chasing the boy. In the end when the rain is gone and the sun comes out, the boy really finds a rainbow of his own on the wall of his room where the sun is shining through the prism of his fish bowl.

+ Read and Discuss   Children will want to follow the boy's rainbow games through the book. Afterwards can they tell what is *real* in this story and what is *pretend?* How do they know?

+ Have Children Make a Rainbow of Their Own   This is the time to put out several jars of different paint colors at your easels. Children soon catch on that they can make rainbows without your showing them how. Even more exciting for them is to make their own rainbow from the sun shining through a prism or crystal. Buy prisms from science or day care supply catalogs or sometimes from camera shops. Buy crystals from New Age stores or variety stores that sell items like wind chimes. Crystals tied to a thread can be hung in a window where the sun shines through. Rainbows will then be projected on the opposite wall. Have children try holding a prism so that the sun's rays shine through it and are refracted into the colors of the rainbow. Oil on water gives the same effect when the sun shines on it.

The Day of the Rainbow (1988), by Ruth Craft; Niki Daly (ill.), New York: Viking Penguin, Inc. This South African city story brings together a collection of ethnic characters each of whom lose something by accident and then find it again at the end of a rainbow. The East Indian girl Nerinder drops her library book on the pavement when the baby makes her mother spill the groceries. The black African boy Leroy, who is roller skating down the sidewalk with earplugs attached to his "walkman," drops a tiny package with earrings for his girlfriend Lou. The Greek woman Eleni Poppodopolous loses the recipe for her husband's rare raisin cake specialty when she gets on the bus. Then it rains, and when the sun comes out again a rainbow curves over the city and onto the sidewalk. People can find lost and precious things at the end of a rainbow, so these three losers come out to look. Niki Daly's wonderfully funny and expressive portraits of the three city dwellers losing and then finding each other's treasures make this book a joy to behold.

+ Read and Discuss   City children will enjoy comparing their city streets with this South African city. Are they the same? Different? How? What beauty do they see in this "hot and cross" city-scape? Does their own city have similar kinds of beauty? Do they like the way the words of the story rhyme? Could this story be true?

+ Make Chalk Drawings Like the Pavement Chalker   Have the children talk about why a man like the pavement chalker was making chalk pictures in the first place. Take several boxes of chalk outside and let the children make chalk drawings on your sidewalks. If you do not have sidewalks outside or chalkboards inside, use cardboard cartons for children to draw and scribble on with chalk.

Shadows Are About *(1992), by Ann Whitford Paul; Mark Graham (ill.), New York: Scholastic, Inc.* A simple story for your youngest children shows a little boy and girl going about their daily activities from sunup to sundown accompanied by shadows. Each double-page spread is a wondrous picture of children and animals in filmy light and shadows, accompanied by a rhyming line of text in large print. The artist's son is the little boy.

+ Read   As with the Keats' book *Dreams,* children need to sit close to see the illustrations of the children and the shadows that follow them everywhere. Your children should be intrigued to see that shadows can do anything children do, even turn flips.

+ Make Wall Shadows   Use a flashlight for the sun to make shadows against your wall. Can children make animals with their hands? Work with a small group at a time and have each one try it.

+ Find Shadows Inside and Out   Have a small group of children at a time look for shadows in the room and then outside. You can keep a list of shadows that children see. Mount your list in the classroom and add to it as children find more shadows every day. They may be even more perceptive than you!

Sunlight: Animals Looking for the Sun

How the Sun Was Brought Back to the Sky, by Mirra Ginsburg; Jose Aruego and
   Ariane Dewey (ill.), 1975
When the snake bites the sun, by David Mowaljarlai and Pamela Lofts, 1984
Rainbow Crow, by Nancy Van Laan; Beatriz Vidal (ill.), 1989

How the Sun Was Brought Back to the Sky *(1975), by Mirra Ginsburg; Jose Aruego and Ariane Dewey (illustrators), New York: Macmillan Publishing.* Many, if not most, cultures have explanatory folk tales about the sun: why it shines, why it doesn't shine, or how to make it shine. Often it involves animals like the rooster having to wake up the sun, so it will shine. In this Slovenian tale the sun does not come out for three whole days. The baby chicks get worried and set out to find out where the sun lives and to bring it back into the sky. They ask the snail who tells them to ask the magpie who takes them to ask the rabbit who takes them to ask the duck who takes them to ask the hedgehog who knows where the moon lives and takes them there. The moon then continues this cumulative tale by taking them all on to the sun's house. The sun, however, has been shut out of the sky by the gray clouds and doesn't even know how to shine any more. So all of the animals use their particular skills to brighten up the sun, and he bursts forth in golden rays to light up and warm everything everywhere. And if you don't believe this tale just look out and see, say the Slovenian storytellers.

+ Tell   As you did with the tales from Chapter 7, this is also a story to tell out loud before you read it to the children. Its cumulative nature makes it easy to remember the order of the episodes. Your practice with the Chapter 7 tales should make it simple for you to change your voice for the animal characters.

+ Read   It isn't just the sun that brightens things, but in this case, Areugo and Dewey's sparkling drawings. Their cheerful, colorful animals are a joy to see. Children will enjoy the chick's quest to find the sun and wake him up with all the other animals tagging along.

+ Dramatize Through Story Re-enactment   Have children choose the animal characters they would like to portray, as well as the moon and the sun, and you be the remainder of the characters. After children know this story well from your telling it and reading it to them, they should be able to re-enact it with great confidence.

When the snake bites the sun (1984), by David Mowaljarlai and Pamela Lofts, San Diego: Mad Hatter Books, Slawson Communications, Inc. This traditional tale from the aborigines of Australia has been retold and illustrated by Pamela Lofts from paintings by the aboriginal children living in the Kimberleys, Western Australia. The entire story is a splash of wonderful color covering entire double-page spreads in bright brush strokes with the hot primary colors of the sun beating down on Australia. There are two suns in this story: a big fat mother sun and little daughter sun who live in hollow logs. When both of them come out they burn up the earth so badly that the fat mother sends her daughter out of the log alone, where she encounters a good man and then a bad man who eventually drives her into space where she is bitten by a snake. She descends to the edge of the earth and becomes snagged in the fork of a tree. Her mother looks after her until she is strong again to make the same journey from east to west to bring sunlight, but then retires to let the earth cool so that it will never burn up again.

+ Read and Discuss   Children need to view these striking illustrations. Read the story to them first and then let them tell you the story from the illustrations alone. How does this story present day and night? Why do your children think a snake is involved? Do they think that this book is beautiful?

+ Paint Easel Pictures of the Sun, the Snake, and the Earth   Put out jars of colors at your easels: red, yellow, blue, black, and green. Encourage children to paint their own feelings about this story. Preschoolers should not be expected to do representational paintings. Let them paint their own story about the sun, the earth, and the snake in any colors, however they want to do it. In this case, you can ask them afterwards for their story, if they want to tell it—just as the Aboriginal boy who told this story was asked to tell it.

Rainbow Crow (1989), by Nancy Van Laan; Beatriz Vidal (illustrator), New York: Alfred A. Knopf. This Native American explanatory tale comes from the Lenape people, and tells about a time before men walked the Earth when it begins to snow without ceasing. One by one the animals are covered and buried as the snow on the ground grows deeper. Talking among themselves, the animals decide that one of them must visit the Great Sky Spirit to ask him to stop the snow. Rainbow

The folktale "When the snake bites the sun" may motivate children to do easel paintings of the snake, the earth, and the sun.

Crow, the most beautiful bird on Earth with the most beautiful voice, volunteers to go. But the Great Sky Spirit says he cannot stop the snow or the cold. Instead, he gives Rainbow Crow the gift of fire, a blazing stick to take back to Earth to melt the snow and keep the animals warm. Rainbow Crow flies back as fast as he can but the fiery stick finally scorches off all his brilliant colors and makes his beautiful voice hoarse. Later when the Great Sky Spirit visits the Earth and finds the blackened crow weeping, he tells him about men coming who will become masters of all the animals. But to the crow the Sky Spirit gives freedom because he will never be hunted for his meat which tastes like smoke, nor captured for his singing voice which is hoarse, nor for his rainbow colors which are now black. Instead, the crow's feathers will shine and reflect all the colors of the Earth, even as they do today.

+ Read   Children are attracted to this book by its beautiful pictures. The cover shows a gorgeous Rainbow Crow flashing green, blue, red, and purple feathers. Even Black Crow is beautiful in the last illustration with tiny rainbows glistening in his feathers. The Great Sky Spirit is represented by a sun made of concentric rings of rainbow colors.

+ Do a Crayon Etching   Children can create the colors of Rainbow Crow by completely coloring a small sheet of white paper or posterboard with wax crayons of many different colors. Then color over the crayon colors with a with a black crayon until the entire sheet is black like the crow. Finally, children can scratch through the black with a scratcher such as a paper clip until the colors underneath show through. All kinds of lines or scribbles can be etched on the paper by scraping off the black. Give the children large primary crayons so they can press down hard without breaking them. Put a sheet of newspaper under the white paper to allow children to color without marking other surfaces.

❧ Moonlight: Children Appreciating the Night

Owl Moon, by Jane Yolen; John Schoenherr (ill.), 1987
Half a Moon and One Whole Star, by Crescent Dragonwagon; Jerry Pinkney
(ill.), 1986
Ayu and the Perfect Moon, by David Cox, 1984
Shadow, by Marcia Brown, 1982

Owl Moon *(1987), by Jane Yolen; John Schoenherr (illustrator), New York: Philomel Books.* This book with its crispy words and wintery pictures takes a little girl narrator across the snowy fields and into the woods at night following the crunchy tracks of her father. Although she gets progressively colder, she holds her words inside her because: "If you go owling you have to be quiet and make your own heat." At the last minute Pa calls up a great horned owl who swoops out of a shadow and lands in the flare of his flashlight. After the owl lifts off the branch, it is time to go home, and it is finally all right to talk out loud, but: "you don't need words or warm or anything but hope. That's what Pa says."

+ Read and Discuss   Whether or not you live in a winter community, your children can feel this little girl's cold and fear and wonder as she and her father tramp off across the fields and into the woods on a moonlit winter night. The listeners soon learn the rules of the game from the little girl's experience: 1)you have to be quiet; 2)sometimes there's an owl and sometimes there isn't; 3)you have to make your own heat; 4)you have to be brave; 5)you can almost smile if the owl calls; 6)when the owl flies away, you can talk and even laugh out loud. Your listeners may not feel like laughing after this perilous adventure, but they may have many questions: Is this a true story? (Yes, more or less) Can you really call up an owl? (Yes) Why didn't they shoot it? (Oh, yes, be prepared for this one!)

Discuss this last question thoroughly. This is the reason for your bringing the idea of beauty into the classroom in the first place. Is the night beautiful? Are owls beautiful? This Caldecott Medal winning book surely presents them in all their stark wonder. Why do people want to shoot owls? What would happen if we killed all of the owls? If you yourself do not know the answers, then bring in an expert from the Audubon Society, a science museum, the National Park Service, or the State Fish and Game Commission to talk to your youngsters. You need to know and your children deserve to have the facts on this important issue, if we hope to preserve the natural beauty of the Earth for generations to come.

+ Make Night Beauty Chalk Pictures   Chalk scribbles on black or blue backing paper can be beautiful. After hearing this story give children white chalk, a cup of water to dip their chalk in, and dark backing paper. Let them create their own "Owl Moon" scenery.

+ Do Nighttime Fingerpainting   Have children choose either blue or black fingerpaint and spread it across their white paper. Another time have children do fingerpainting with white paint on blue or black paper.

Half a Moon and One Whole Star (1986), by Crescent Dragonwagon; Jerry Pinkney (illustrator), New York: Macmillan Publishing Co. Once again Jerry Pinkney's skill as a nature artist in *Wild Wild Sunflower Child Anna* illuminates the world of Susan, an African-American child, this time asleep in her bed as the nighttime world around her carries on its own doings. Parrots, possums, raccoons, crickets, and yes, an astounding owl float through the sky-dark pages of Crescent Dragonwagon's poem, *Half a Moon and One Whole Star*. It is an evocative hymn to a summer night.

+ Read   Bring your listeners close and read this poem slowly, even sing-songy. If your children like it, read it for naptime to help restless children go to sleep. It makes a wonderful lullaby.

+ Make a Sleepers and Wakers Card Game   Purchase an extra copy of the paperback version of this book to cut out playing-card-sized pictures of "sleepers" and "wakers." Do this privately away from the children. Laminate these pictures onto the front side of an old deck of playing cards with clear contact paper. To play the game with two or three children at a time, first read the book to them. Then have the children draw a card, tell what it is, and whether it is a "sleeper" or "waker" at night. They may need to check back with the book and listen to the story again. The night sleepers include: Susan, Susan's parents, robins, parrots, chickens, minnows, and morning glories. The night wakers include: owls, bats, possums, frogs, crickets, raccoons, Johnny, the baker, and the sailor. What about Susan's toys? What about the half a moon and one whole star? Your children can decide.

Ayu and the Perfect Moon (1984), By David Cox, London, England: The Bodley Head. Old Ayu tells three little girls how she danced the Legong dance of Bali when she was young on one magical night of a full moon. The colorful customs and costumes of the island of Bali come to life in this book through David Cox's pictures and words as old Ayu recreates the scenes of her childhood practicing, waiting, and finally dancing near the banyan tree in the village square.

+ Read   This lovely quiet story should appeal to your children's sense of beauty from an island where beauty is honored both day and night. The processions of giant puppets, dancers in masks, scenes from everyday life, and the beauty of the costumes are things to celebrate in Bali.

+ Have a Stick Puppet Dance   Cut out body parts and costume parts ahead of time from construction paper of different colors. Look at the book to guide you: heads, arms bent in different directions, sarong skirts, feet, headdresses, fans, feathers, neckpieces, flowers. These do not have to be elaborate. Make them plain, but in many colors and shapes. Bring in a few sheets of peel-off circles and stars. Then prepare sturdy oblong body shapes from oaktag or cardboard glued to a tongue depressor. Make enough for each child to use a body shape to make at least one puppet. Put all of these items out on an art table and invite a small group at a time to make Balinese stick puppets. Balinese are renown for their puppet dances.

  For the puppet dance, make a puppet theater out of a cardboard carton. Cut out the back, cut down the sides diagonally, and cut a rectangular opening out of the front.

Paint or decorate it any way you like. Place this box theater on a table. Have two children at a time sit behind the table and dance their puppets in the theater opening. For music bring in a tape from *The King and I* musical, or use drum beats. If your audience is preschoolers, they will want to come behind the theater to see what is happening. Tell them they will all get their chance when it is their turn to dance their puppets.

***Shadow** (1982), by Marcia Brown, New York: Charles Scribner's Sons.* Here is another book that was awarded a Caldecott Medal for the beauty of its art. Marcia Brown's stunning illustrations in collage and block print against an African sunset and night sky background feature shadow, an ash-color image from folklore that appears where there is firelight and a storyteller to bring it to life. African folklore shows "shadow" as white against the black profile of the dancers and dark against the daytime black of the people. In the poetry of its text this book has shadow curling up at the foot of trees and racing with the animals in the daytime. It is the pupil of the eye in the crackling coals of the fire at night.

+ Read   Again children need to sit close to the reader to see the exquisite art of the African village and its people. The words of the story are poetry that your children will feel but may not understand. That makes no difference. This book with its integration of words and art brings shadow to life as something people cannot describe or explain, but only know as they know an old friend. Children will understand that zebra's shadow has no stripes, and that shadow spreads out at night filling every hole and sticking to your footprints.

+ Make Stamped Imprints of Shadow   Give your children black or blue backing paper and let them make shadow's imprint on this night background with stampings. Let them stamp imprints onto the background paper from a dish of white paint with actual rubber stamps of people and animals, or from pieces of raw vegetables such as potatoes, radishes, or carrots.

Moonlight: Animals in the Moonlight

Where Does the Brown Bear Go?, by Niki Weiss, 1989
Fox's Dream, by Tejima, 1985
Northern Lullaby, by Nancy White Carlstrom; Leo and Diane Dillon (ill.), 1992

***Where Does the Brown Bear Go?** (1989), by Niki Weiss, New York: Viking Penguin.* White verses on black double pages ask the reader where particular animals go, while on the right side, each animal is illustrated going somewhere. On the next spread we read and see: "They are on their way." "They are on their way home." The animals asked about include the white cat, the monkey, the camel, the stray dog, the seagull, and the brown bear. These animals accumulate in a row on the "home" pages, until the end of the story when they are all very cleverly "home" as stuffed animals in bed with a sleeping child.

+ Read   Children enjoy following along each of the verses, as the last two lines are repeated. This is a goodnight game played by a parent to put a child to sleep. Can you also play it with your nappers to make them drowsy? Turn off the lights, pull down the shades and try it. You will be able to see the white print no matter how dark you make it.

+ Make a Feltboard Game   Purchase an extra paperback copy of this book to cut out the various animals and mount them as feltboard characters (see pp. 74–75). When you are reading this story to a group, one of the children can put up an animal on the feltboard in any order he or she chooses for you to read about.

Fox's Dream (1985), by Tejima, New York: Philomel Books. Fox's Dream is a book neither you nor your children will forget. The art alone is so striking that everyone's attention is immediately drawn to the brilliant cover of this vertical book, where a fox with golden eyes confronts you against a background of black and white snow-covered pines. The story of a cold and hungry fox walking alone through the forest in the moonlight slowly unfolds on page after page. He races after a snow hare, but finds himself in a strange place of frozen trees where animals of ice nest in their branches. Wordless pages show deer and then geese in black and white trees, and finally a family of ice foxes. The fox closes his eyes and remembers the green and yellow spring and his own family. When he opens them he sees in the distance another fox, a vixen, and runs to nuzzle her. Soon it will be spring.

+ Read and Discuss   Let your children gaze at the pages as long as they want at the black-outlined drawings against white snow and black sky. Which is Fox's dream: the white ice animals or the foxes in spring? Or both? Does this book show the winter that the children know? Is it supposed to? Do they think that the story is beautiful?

+ Do Chalk and Water Art   White chalk dipped in water can be drawn on black construction paper to give a contrasting effect. Let children scribble anything they want on the black night. If they want to add snow, give them pieces of cotton to paste on their creations.

+ Make Spatter Paint Drawings   Another way to show snow against a black or dark background is through spatter paint. Have children dip an old toothbrush or brush into thick white poster paint and spatter it across the paper.

Northern Lullaby (1992), by Nancy White Carlstrom; Leo Dillon, and Diane Dillon, (illustrators), New York: Philomel Books. This story as wide as all outdoors is a goodnight song to the creatures of an Alaskan night: Grandpa Mountain, Grandma River, Great Moose Uncle, Wolf Uncle, Snowshoe Hare, Aunties Willow and Birch, Cousins Beaver, Deer Mouse, and Red Fox, Sister Owl, Brother Bear, and finally the Native American infant in its leather cradle.

+ Read   Children should be up close to see the stunning art of this Alaskan night. Spread across one and two-thirds horizontal pages, each illustration shows the creatures of the night personified as Native Americans spread across the entire black sky in the blues, greens, and pinks of northern lights. Even the snowy ground reflects purple, pink, and blue from the sky. In one corner is a tiny log cabin with a smoking chimney that is finally seen from the inside on the last page.

+ **Make Northern Lights**   The night phenomenon of the aurora borealis is something most of your children will never experience unless they live in the northern regions. They can try making their own northern lights by covering several flashlights each with blue, yellow, and red cellophane. Pull down the shades, turn off the lights and shine the flashlights toward the ceiling, moving them around and around to get the effect. Read the story as the children listen quietly on their cots at naptime, shining their flashlights back and forth. If you do not have enough flashlights for everyone, take turns on several days.

+ **Make Chalk Drawings**   If children enjoyed this story, put out black construction paper and colored chalk for them to color with using the side of the chalk across the paper.

Daylight: Beauty Is Where You Find It

Clementina's Cactus, by Ezra Jack Keats, 1982
Maebelle's Suitcase, by Tricia Tusa, 1987
The Park Bench, by Fumiko Takeshita; Mamoru Suzuki (ill.), 1988
Miss Rumphius, by Barbara Cooney, 1982

***Clementina's Cactus** (1982), by Ezra Jack Keats, London, England: Methuen Children's Books.* In this small-format book, his twenty-fifth children's book, Ezra Jack Keats departs from his inner city settings and collage illustrations. In simple lines and water colors little Clementina and her father are depicted against the vastness of the desert where they live in an old cabin. (Is this "the miner,' forty-niner, and his daughter Clementine" from the old folk song?) The book is a completely wordless story showing daughter and father exploring the desert together until they come upon a stumpy old barrel cactus with prickly buds on top that takes Clementina's eye. She will not leave it, and sits down to wait for it to do something. Her father finally carries her home just in time to avoid a crackling thunder storm, with a rainbow at the end making its promise. Next morning at the crack of dawn Clementina hurries back to her cactus, and sure enough, it has burst into bloom overnight with huge yellow flowers: three on top and one on the side!

+ **Read**   By now your children should be able to read a wordless book. Look through it with them, helping them to concentrate on the main character, the little girl Clementina. Ask them to tell you what she is doing, thinking, or saying, and what is happening in the story. Then go back to the beginning and ask them to read you the story if they will. Or perhaps they can read it to a friend.

+ **Play Desert Music**   Get a record or tape of Ferde Groffe's *Grand Canyon Suite.* Have children close their eyes and imagine the miner and his daughter tramping along behind a pack mule to the "On the Trail" movement. Later play the thunder storm movement. Do the children hear the thunder? What about the lightning? Can the children tell when the storm is over and the sun comes out?

+ Make Your Own Desert Music   Have children try out ways to make thunder (such as, slowly empting a sack of potatoes or something similar into a tin pan). Can they use their toy xylophones for the lightning? For the clip-clop sounds of the donkeys or mules on the trail, have children try clacking blocks together in a rhythm. Tape record the results of the experiments. Then choose the best sound effects and tape record their humming of the "On the Trail" theme with the children's sound effects in the background. Play it back and see how they like their version of the *Grand Canyon Suite.*

+ Visit an Arboretum or Botanical Garden   Many cities have an arboretum or botanical garden in a temperature-controlled greenhouse with a wing or room set aside for cactus and desert plants. Take your group on a field trip to visit such a location. Arrange for an attendant to give you a guided tour. For children living in desert parts of the country, arrange for a field trip to the desert. Perhaps a member of the Audubon Society or garden club can accompany your group.

+ Purchase or Make a Cactus Dish Garden   Take children with you when you make your purchase of cactus. Ask the clerk about watering the cactus and whether it will bloom. Be careful of the cactus spines.

Maebelle's Suitcase (1987), by Tricia Tusa, New York: Macmillan Publishing Co. Maebelle is a remarkable African-American woman who is 108 years old and lives in a treehouse because of her fascination with birds. She makes hats for a living and sells them to a shop in town. This story features a particular hat that she is making for her own entry in the annual hat contest. As she waves goodbye to her bird neighbors who are flying south for the winter, one of them, Binkle, drops in and asks to borrow her suitcase for his long trip south. She watches him fill it with branches, leaves, and even his nest. But when he tries to fly away he finds it too heavy to lift. She invites him inside to watch her make a hat for the contest, and somehow the items she needs to make the hat beautiful are just like those in Binkle's suitcase. She doesn't win the contest for the most beautiful hat, but together the two of them create such an extraordinary hat that it wins a prize as the most original hat and is placed in the town museum.

+ Read   What is beauty to one person means nothing to another. After you have read this book, ask your children which of Maebelle's hats they like the best, and what they think of the one she creates with Binkle's treasures.

+ Tell a Story Using Hat Props   This is a wonderful story for telling aloud using a suitcase or bag with props in it. As you tell the story pull out a plain hat and put it on your head. Then, one by one, pull out other strange items and place them on it. Be sure to practice ahead of time so that you are able to handle the hat items without having them all fall off.

This is a wonderful story for a child to tell aloud as she creates a hat like Maebelle did.

+ Dramatize Through Story Re-enactment   Children who like this story will want to get in on the act themselves. Do a story re-enactment as described on p. 136. Bring in several hats, several bags, and a tableful of items to be placed on the hats as the story progresses, because you are sure to have several Maebelles as characters each time you re-enact the story. Boys as well as girls can take the part of Maebelle.

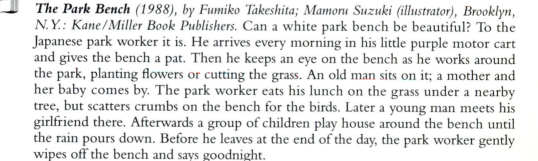

The Park Bench *(1988), by Fumiko Takeshita; Mamoru Suzuki (illustrator), Brooklyn, N.Y.: Kane/Miller Book Publishers.* Can a white park bench be beautiful? To the Japanese park worker it is. He arrives every morning in his little purple motor cart and gives the bench a pat. Then he keeps an eye on the bench as he works around the park, planting flowers or cutting the grass. An old man sits on it; a mother and her baby comes by. The park worker eats his lunch on the grass under a nearby tree, but scatters crumbs on the bench for the birds. Later a young man meets his girlfriend there. Afterwards a group of children play house around the bench until the rain pours down. Before he leaves at the end of the day, the park worker gently wipes off the bench and says goodnight.

+ Read   This park bench is Japanese and so are all of the characters in the book. Don't tell this to your children at first as you read the story. See if they notice anything different. Do any of them see the Japanese writing under the English words? How is this bench and park and people the same or different from any others they have known?

+ Bring in a Japanese Speaker to Read the Story   If possible, find a Japanese reader who will read the story to the children in Japanese. Would the children like to learn a few words in Japanese themselves?

+ Go on a Field Trip to a Park Bench   Now that your children's eyes have been opened to such an unlikely source of beauty and interest as a park bench, maybe they would like to take a closer look at one themselves. Take a picnic with you and spend some time in the park. Take instant photos of the children sitting, eating, and playing around a bench.

+ Make a Book About their Park Bench   Make your own book about the park bench you have visited. Have children contribute to the story in small groups. You can write down their words and later print or type them onto the pages of your book. Children may want to include words about the photos you have taken to illustrate their book. What will they name their book? Be sure to read the finished book to the small groups. Some of the children may also want to read it aloud themselves. Keep their book in the Story Center along with *The Park Bench*.

Miss Rumphius (1982), by Barbara Cooney, New York: Viking Penguin. The tale of Miss Rumphius, the "Lupine Lady," tells the true story of the life of the author's great-aunt, from girlhood to old age. She was once a little girl, Alice, who lived near the sea and helped her grandfather who was an artist. He carved figureheads for the prows of sailing ships and painted pictures of the sea. Alice helped him paint in the skies. Alice told him what she wanted to do when she grew up: to travel to faraway places and to live by the sea. He told her she must do one more thing: "You must do something to make the world more beautiful." When Alice grew up she did travel to far away places and she did live by the sea, but she always wondered what she could do to make the world more beautiful. Then one day she noticed that her blue lupine flowers had somehow escaped from her garden and been seeded by the wind over to the other side of the hill. That was it! She sent for five bushels of lupine seed and began scattering the seed everywhere when she went out walking. Some people called her That Crazy Old Lady. But next spring there were beautiful blue lupines everywhere. She had done the third thing, "the most difficult thing of all."

+ Tell   Because this is a rather long story for reading to preschoolers, try telling the story to your total group. It lends itself well to telling aloud with hand gestures as did the *Cats in Hat Boxes* story on pp. 99–101. Make the story your own in the same way by reading it over, and then silently telling it to yourself several times. Try telling the story as a first-person tale as if you are Alice. Think about how you can use the hand gestures most effectively:

1. *Once upon a time when I was a little girl I helped my grandfather in his shop…*
   Gestures: Use hands to show grandfather carving wood and girl painting picture.

AUTHORS *of* **INTEREST**   BARBARA COONEY has illustrated over a hundred books for children, including two for which she was awarded the Caldecott Medal (*Chanticleer and the Fox* and *The Ox-Cart Man*). She lives in Maine and is a world traveler and a gardener. This grandmother plans to live to be one hundred years old and to enjoy it. (Hurst, 1990, 35)

2. *I told my grandfather I wanted to travel to faraway places when I grew up, and then to live by the sea..*
Gestures: hold up one finger on one hand; motion outwards to the right with other hand; hold up two fingers on one hand; motion outwards to left with other hand.

3. *My grandfather told me that I must do a third thing: that I must do something to make the world more beautiful.*
Gestures: hold up three fingers on one hand; motion outwards and around with other hand.

4. *What could I do?*
Gestures: clap hand to head; shake head; hands on hips; look around.

5. *When I grew up I traveled to a tropical island and drank coconut water out of a coconut…*
Gestures: pick up imaginary nut with both hands; hold it up and drink.

6. *I climbed tall mountains where the snow never melted*
Gestures: move arms and legs as if to climb; hug self with arms and shiver.

7. *I even rode on a camel in the Land of the Lotus Eaters*
Gestures: move upper part of body forward and back.

8. *Then I came home and lived in a house by the sea*
Gestures: stretch out arms.

9. *But what could I do to make the world more beautiful?*
Gestures: clap hand to head; shake head; hands on hips; look around.

10. *One day I discovered some beautiful blue lupine flowers that the wind had seeded from the flowers in my garden; then I knew what I had to do…*
Gestures: bend down to look at imaginary flowers; get up and put hands on hips; nod head.

11. *I bought 5 bushels of lupine seeds and every time I go out walking I scatter seeds all around…*
Gestures: walk in place and throw imaginary seeds out of imaginary bag.

12. *At first people called me That Crazy Old Lady, but when the lupines started blooming they called me the Lupine Lady; and I knew that I had finally done the third thing, the most difficult thing of all…something to make the world more beautiful!*
Gestures: nod head; move hand toward ground; raise both hands above head and shake in victory.

+ Discussing This Story   If children really like this story they will want to be the Lupine Lady and tell their story to the group. Encourage anyone who wants to tell this story aloud. It is a very important story for this day and for these young-sters. Ask them how they will try to do "the third thing" in their own lives. What other kinds of things are there that would make the world more beautiful? Does any-one mention being kind to others? Helping someone who needs help? Smiling at people? Is a smile a beautiful thing?

+ Order Wild Flower Seeds and Take the Children on a Seed-scattering Field Trip: They can all be Miss Rumphius if you take them out in the country to scatter seeds. Tell them to keep their eyes open later in the summer to see if any of these seeds grow up and bloom or if any other wildflowers appear.

So where is it that you and your children can find beauty? In sunshine...moon-light...daybreak...rainbows? In birds, flowers, park benches? They and you will also find beauty if you look for it—deep inside!

ACTIVITIES IN CHAPTER 11 TO PROMOTE CHILD DEVELOPMENT

Cognitive Development

Bring in a globe of the world *(One Light, One Sun)*
Have children make a rainbow *(A Rainbow of My Own)*
Find shadows inside and out *(Shadows Are About)*
Make a sleepers and wakers card game *(Half a Moon and One Whole Star)*
Make northern lights *(Northern Lullaby)*
Visit an arboretum or botanical garden *(Clementina's Cactus)*
Make a cactus dish garden *(Clementina's Cactus)*
Go on a field trip to a park bench *(The Park Bench)*

Language Development

Tell a story *(How the Sun Was Brought Back to the Sky)*
Dramatize through story re-enactment *(How the Sun Was Brought Back to the Sky)*
Take children on a seed-scattering field trip *(Miss Rumphius)*
Make a feltboard game *(Where Does the Brown Bear Go?)*
Tell story using hat props *(Maebelle's Suitcase)*
Dramatize through story re-enactment *(Maebelle's Suitcase)*
Bring in a Japanese speaker to read *(The Park Bench)*
Make a book about their park bench *(The Park Bench)*
Tell a story as Miss Rumphius *(Miss Rumphius)*

Creative Development

Make up a sun song *(The Way to Start a Day)*
Make sun collages *(Sun Up Sun Down)*
Make chalk drawings *(The Day of the Rainbow)*
Make chalk drawings *(Northern Lullaby)*
Make wall shadows *(Shadows Are About)*
Paint easel pictures *(When the snake bit the sun)*
Do a crayon etching *(Rainbow Crow)*
Make night beauty chalk pictures *(Owl Moon)*
Do nighttime fingerpainting *(Owl Moon)*
Have a stick puppet dance *(Ayu and the Perfect Moon)*
Make stamped imprints *(Shadow)*
Do chalk and water art *(Fox's Dream)*
Make spatter paint drawings *(Fox's Dream)*
Play desert music *(Clementina's Cactus)*
Make your own desert music *(Clementina's Cactus)*

REFERENCES CITED

Feeney, S. and Moravcik, E. (1987), "A Thing of Beauty: Aesthetic Development in Young Children," *Young Children* 42(6) 7–15.

Haskell, L.L. (1979), *Art in the Early Childhood Years.* Columbus, Ohio: Merrill.

Janssen, D.H. and Beaty, J.B. (1988), *Storytelling Mark Twain Style.* Elmira, N.Y.: McGraw Bookstore, Elmira College.

Jenkins, P.D. (1980), *The Magic of Puppetry: A Guide for Those Working with Young Children.* Englewood Cliffs, N.J.: Prentice-Hall, Inc.

OTHER PICTURE BOOKS ABOUT SUNLIGHT AND SHADOWS

Berger, B. (1984), *Grandfather Twilight.* New York: Philomel.

Brown, M.W. (1947), *Goodnight Moon.* New York: Harper.

Carle, E. (1992), *Draw Me a Star.* New York: Philomel Books.

Carle, E. (1986), *Papa, Please Get the Moon for Me.* Natick, Mass.: Picture Book Studio.

Crews, D. (1981), *Light.* New York: Greenwillow.

Dayrell, E. and Lent, B. (ill.) (1968), *Why the Sun and the Moon Live in the Sky.* Boston: Houghton Mifflin Co.

Edwards, F.E. and Bianchi, J. (ill.) (1991), *Melody Mooner Stayed Up All Night!* Newburgh, Ontario, Canada: Bungalo Books.

Goodall, J. S. (1972), *The Midnight Adventures of Kelly, Dot, and Esmeralda.* New York: Atheneum. (wordless)

Grifalconi, A. (1987), *Darkness and the Butterfly.* Boston: Little Brown & Co.

Hort, L. and Ransome, J.E. (ill.) (1991), *How Many Stars in the Sky?* New York: Tambourine Books.

Howard, J.R. and Cherry, L. (ill.) (1985), *When I'm Sleepy.* New York: E.P.Dutton.

Hutchins, P. (1972), *Good-Night, Owl!* New York: Macmillan Publishing.

James, B. and Watson, R.J. (ill.) (1990), *The Dream Stair.* New York: Harper & Row.

Lesser, C. and Cauley, L.B. (ill.) (1984), *The Goodnight Circle.* San Diego: Harcourt Brace Jovanovich.

Lobel, A. and Lobel, A. (ill.) (1977), *How the Rooster Saved the Day.* New York: Viking Penguin.

McDermott, G. (1974), *Arrow to the Sun.* New York: Viking Penguin.

McDermott, G. (1980), *Papagayo the Mischief Maker.* New York: Simon & Schuster.

Nunes, S. (1988), *Coyote Dreams.* New York: Atheneum.

Rice, E. (1987), *City Night.* New York: Greenwillow.

Ryan, C. D. and Lobel, A. (ill.) (1971) *Hildilid's Night.* New York: Macmillan.

Sendak, M. (1970), *In the Night Kitchen.* New York: Harper.

Waddell, M.; Benson, P. (ill.) (1992) *Owl Babies.* Cambridge, Mass.: Candelwick Press.

Wiesner, D. (1991), *Tuesday.* New York: Clarion Books. (wordless)

Willard, N. and McPhail, D. (ill.) (1983), *The Nightgown of the Sullen Moon.* San Diego: Harcourt Brace Jovanovich.

Wolff, A. (1985), *Only the Cat Saw.* New York: Dodd.

PICTURE BOOK STORYTELLING AND YOU

BOOKS

Action Chant

Books in piles;
Books on shelves;
Books for smiles;
Books for selves.

Books for looking;
Books for sleep;
Books for cooking;
Books to keep.
I LIKE BOOKS!

❧ The Classroom Story Center

Now that you are familiar with a sampling of picture books for young children; now that you have some ideas about using them with the youngsters, where do you go from here? The first place to go is to your classroom—to your Story Center—to make sure that it is the attractive area you want it to be, so that children will flock to it eagerly. Step back and look at the area through the eyes of a newcomer if you can. Here are some of the details that should concern you:

1. Location
2. Distinctiveness
3. Size
4. Coziness; privacy
5. Attractiveness
6. Book accessibility

1. *Where in the classroom is the Story Center located? Why?*

As you step back and look at your Story Center, you need to think about its location first of all. Is it placed in a comfortable corner away from the noise and traffic of the rest of the activities? It is essential that this important book-and-reading area be as quiet and least active as possible, so that children can enjoy an undisturbed time with books. It is not necessary for it to be in a corner if another location is better for noise control. Perhaps you have a bay window in the middle of the room that is perfect for a book nook. Then try to locate noisy, active play away from this area. This is not always possible in a small room, but you can try. What was your reason for locating the Story Center where you now have it? If you did not have a reason, you may want to reconsider its location, if another spot seems more suitable.

2. *How distinctive is the Story Center from the other activity areas?*

As you look at the Story Center you should be able to distinguish it easily from all of the other interesting classroom centers. You should be able to tell instantly that this is a place for books and relaxation, and that it is an inviting area to visit. Is this the case in your classroom? The Story Center needs to stand out from the rest, to be separated from and differentiated from the other centers around it. If it is not, then you need to make some changes. Be sure that book shelves are pulled away from the wall and placed at right angles to the wall as room dividers. Shelves against the wall make for a flat and undistinguished Story Center. The message such an area gives children is that this is not as important a place as, say, the Block Center, because its space is not that well defined. If you do not use shelves, then use room dividers such as screens or panels. You can make your own attractive screens from a large cardboard packing case, and cover them with decorative contact paper, colored burlap, or colored corrugated cardboard from a teacher's supply store or hobby shop.

3. *What is the size of the Story Center?*

As you focus your concern on the size of the center, you will need to consider classroom space in general, the number of activity centers you include, and the number of children involved. Be aware that your book area is important, and therefore needs to be allotted enough space to accommodate a small group of children comfortably. It should be a medium-to-small learning center. If it is too large, then there tend to be other inappropriate activities happening. Children wander around or fool around and disturb the readers. On the other hand, the Story Center should not be too small. It should accommodate a group of four to six children without crowding, because you will be reading or storytelling to that many at one time.

4. *How cozy is the Story Center? How private?*

One of the most important characteristics for this center should be its coziness. Children are attracted to cozy areas where they can curl up with a book, or snuggle up against large pillows. Small size helps to make an area cozy. So do furnishings. Be sure to have cozy seating: on the floor with shag rugs and big colorful pillows; in one or two beanbag chairs; in an overstuffed easy chair; on a couch or bench covered with pillows; in an old claw-foot bathtub full of pillows. This seating arrangement also makes for privacy. Children need a place and a space to be alone in a busy classroom. Your Story Center can be that place when it is not being used for reading aloud or storytelling. Do not plan to use a large cardboard carton with a door cut in one side as a private reading place. Children tend to fight over who gets to go in the box. Furthermore, it is too dark for book-looking, and is rarely used for such.

5. *How attractive is the Story Center?*

The four items previously considered add to the attractiveness of the center: its location, distinctiveness, size, and coziness. In addition, be sure to make the Story Center colorful. The book covers themselves will be colorful, but you can extend this color by hanging book posters on the wall or on the room dividers. Book posters can be purchased from children's book stores, teachers' supply stores, or suppliers such as:

The Children's Book Council, Inc.
350 Scotland Road
Orange, NJ 07050

*Your Story Center
needs to be a cozy
place where children
can curl up with a
book.*

To make your own posters, remove the book jackets from hardback copies of your books and mount them in the Story Center on backing paper or colored oak-tag. Other colorful items you might consider: balloons make a learning center both attractive and an exciting place to be. Standing inflatables from party stores include Mr. Banana, a pink flamingo, and various cartoon characters.

What else might you display in your center to make it attractive? Children's art from the activities mentioned in this book should be displayed here. Photos of authors of the children's books being used can be mounted and displayed here. The important reference book *Once Upon a Time... An Encyclopedia for Successfully Using Literature with Young Children* includes, in an envelope on the back cover, fourteen separate five-by-seven-inch photographs of children's book authors. (Hurst, 1990) Many publishers will also furnish photos of children's book authors if requested. Photos of your own children should be displayed as they complete books of their own which are on the shelves of the center. Other items to make the center attractive can include stuffed animals, dinosaurs, and pictures of pets.

6. *How accessible to the children are the books in the Story Center?*

This seems to be a strange question to ask. Of course, the books are accessible! But are they? Take a look. Accessible means *visible*. Can you tell at a glance what books are available for the children today? Well, maybe not at a glance; but all of the books are right there on shelves that the children can reach. Sorry. This is not enough. To be accessible in an early childhood center, all of the books should have *their front covers visible to the children*.

If you have traditional shelves where only the spines of the books are visible, then you need to change them. Put a backing on the shelves and display the books with their covers showing. If you say that you have too many books to show them all at once, then you have too many books out. You are not a library. If you have more than fifty books crowded onto shelves with only their spines showing, then you need to store some of them for later use.

Accessible means *choices.* Give children a chance to make a choice. First of all they need to see what books are available for their choosing. They should not be overwhelmed with huge numbers of books. It is too difficult for young children to choose when the choice is overwhelming. Have a core of children's favorite books on hand all of the time (at least two dozen). Then add books from time to time as you need them.

Children should be able to reach and look at these books at their leisure. Make your own book display by cutting off the sides of cardboard boxes diagonally and standing them on a table like an easel to hold books face-side out. In fact, the tray and paper clips of a painting easel can also be used to display books. Or bring in a revolving bookstand from a store. Children love to twirl it around, and eventually they will choose one of its books.

Finally, children should be motivated to choose certain books by the original ways in which you have them displayed. Accessible means *irresistible.* Use your creativity. Hang paperback books on a clothesline. Clip special books to colorful ribbons or streamers hung from a shelf or the ceiling. Place stuffed animals on your shelves and tie appropriate books to their paws. Display puppets next to the books where they can be used. Put a set of miniature dinosaurs next to a dinosaur book. Display the cheeseburger beanbag toss game next to *The Mysterious Tadpole.* This is what makes books accessible: making them irresistible!

It is possible, even probable, that you will end up making your Story Center so attractive and irresistible that more children will want to use it than it can accommodate. If this happens, treat it as you do your other learning centers when they become overcrowded. Have children take tags, use tickets, or whatever other self-regulating device you have invented for them to take turns in the various centers. (Beaty, 1992, 11) And be happy! If children want to crowd into the Story Center, then you have arranged it successfully!

❧ Using Audio-Visual Materials

Should audio-visual materials be located in the Story Center? The answer to this question depends upon your goals for children. If a primary goal is bringing together children and books, then many teachers feel that audio-visual book materials and equipment can be used, but not in the Story Center where they may distract the readers. Materials such as book filmstrips, book videotapes, and book audiotapes do spark children's interest in the real thing: the books. They can be a part of an early childhood program, located perhaps in a learning area such as the Sound Center as discussed in Chapter 1. Their use, however, is somewhat different than many adults might suppose. They are not in the preschool classroom or kindergarten for entertainment purposes, but for child development.

It is important that preschool and kindergarten teachers understand that young children learn best through active participation with hands-on activities and human interaction. Many teachers feel that viewing book films and videos is a passive experience for children, one that should be used sparingly in the classroom. They agree, however, that audio-visual materials have a place in the curriculum for promoting listening skills and visual memory. *So long as the use of book films and videos does not substitute for the actual telling of stories or reading of real books, they can be used in their own special way.*

Such films can best be used by individual children and small groups in the Sound Center where child choice and child interaction can take place. This makes a great deal more sense for child development than having the total class sit passively in front of the television while a book video is being shown. Furthermore, young children love to put on a headset—such a grownup thing—and listen to a tape or watch a filmstrip.

Be sure to have the actual book in the Sound Center whenever a book film or tape is being used. Then children can make the connection that the filmstrip, video, or sound cassette is the same as the book. How exciting for them to be able to pick up the book afterward and take it over to the Story Center to look at privately whenever they want! Be sure that the films and videos you obtain are animated versions made directly from the book itself. A selected list of filmstrips, sound cassettes, and videos appears at the end of this chapter. Such audio-visual materials can be borrowed from many libraries, or purchased or rented from the companies that produce them.

✥ Using Big Books

The use of big books began in New Zealand in the late 1960s. These large-sized paperback picture books were originally made by primary teachers and children to be used in reading groups for shared reading. The large size of the books (fourteen-and-a-half by eighteen inches) made it possible for children to see easily the pictures and text of a book as it was read aloud by a teacher or the children in a reading group. Topics of these teacher-made books were either traditional tales with predictable patterns of language such as *The Three Little Pigs,* or class experiences such as *What We Saw At the Fire Station* (Cowley, 1991, 19).

Eventually publishers in New Zealand and abroad began publishing commercial big books in the late 1970s and 1980s. Although some of these were large-sized copies of traditional children's literature that publishers already had in stock, most were stories made up to teach children to read. Today more and more children's literature (such as the books discussed in this text) is being converted into big books because of the whole language emphasis on the use of children's literature to teach reading.

Big books with predictable stories have caught on both in elementary reading programs and most recently in preschool classrooms. While it is easier for children in a group setting to see the pictures if a big book is being read, what young children especially like is to hold a big book all by themselves or to share it with a friend in the Story Center as they look at the pictures together.

Big books need space for display in your Story Center. Some commercial big book holders are made of fabric with pockets for five books that can be mounted on a wall or hung on a chart holder. Teachers also use easels to display big books or to hold them while they read them aloud to a group of children. Some of the picture books mentioned in this text that also come in big book size are listed at the end of the chapter.

More and more big books are being published every year by an increasing number of picture book publishers. Most are used (along with several copies of the same regular-sized book) in the teaching of reading. Preschool teachers need to be aware of this purpose: that although big books are really essential in whole language reading programs, they are not necessary for the same purpose in preschool. Because they are much more expensive than regular-sized books, big books should be considered carefully before being purchased by preschool programs with limited budgets. For preschools it is more important to have a well-stocked library of regular-sized picture books, than a large number of big books.

Kindergartens involved in early reading programs have a more evident need for big books than do preschools. As the kindergarten teacher reads to an early reading group from her big book, the children can follow along in their own regular-sized copies of the big book being read. This is not necessary in a preschool program. Instead, preschool teachers can consider big books as a wonderful extra-special treat. Keep a few of them on hand for reading aloud to a total group (your small books are for small groups), and for a unique experience in your Story Center for children who love to handle books.

Young children especially like holding a big book all by themselves.

ঞ Obtaining the Books Described Here

You are all set to go. Your Story Center is irresistible. Your ideas for using the books described here are well integrated into your scheme of things. There is only one problem. The books that you want to use are not the ones that you presently own. What do you do? First of all, try the public library. Ask to borrow the particular books by title and author. If the library does not have the books you want, it can obtain them through inter-library loan. Get to know the children's librarian who orders the books, and spend some time discussing the books you need and will be using in the future. Librarians respond well to the needs of their patrons, and may well purchase these particular books on your recommendation.

A second method is to purchase the books yourself. You can buy them from a trade bookstore or order them directly from the publishers, and usually at a discount by using an order form or letterhead stationery that identifies you as an educational enterprise. Any bookseller will give you publisher's addresses if you want to send in your own order. On the other hand, bookstores are happy to obtain books for you that they do not have in stock—and in a much shorter time than your private orders. Most trade bookstores have weekly deliveries of books.

A third method is to order the books yourself from a book supply house rather than from separate publishers. If you are ordering a large number of books, you can obtain a catalog and order them from a supply house. Decide ahead of time whether you want paperback or hardback copies of the books. Paperbacks, of course, are the least expensive but do not last as long in the hands of young children. However, if you plan to cut pictures from extra copies, you will want paperbacks. Most of the books discussed here come in both forms. Three book supply houses that have catalogs and sell many of the children's books discussed here are:

1. Gryphon House
   Early Childhood Books
   P.O.Box 275
   Mt. Rainier, MD 20712

2. The Book Lady, Inc.
   8144 Brentwood Industrial Drive
   St. Louis, MO 63144

3. Redleaf Press
   450 N. Syndicate, Suite 5
   St. Paul, MN 55104

ঞ Choosing and Using Books Other Than Those Described Here

If you plan to use books other than those discussed here, this textbook was created to give you a model to follow in using children's picture books of any kind. Chapter 1 assists you in determining whether books can best be used for storytelling or story reading. It gives suggestions on preparing for storytelling or reading and then delivering the story to the children that can be applied to any book.

In order to choose other books, however, you may need guidance in selecting from the more than *four thousand* juvenile books published annually. Help is available from many sources:

1. Join a book-based network.
2. Join a book-sharing project.
3. Become acquainted with a bookseller.
4. Obtain a book-selection guidebook or list.

1. Join a book-based network.

The Association of American Publishers (AAP) keeps a database of more than 1,500 educators and administrators who share an interest in using children's literature in the classroom. You can join this AAP Reading Initiative Database by writing to:

AAP Reading Initiative Database
Association of American Publishers
220 East 23rd St.
New York, NY 10010

You will receive a kit containing information on choosing good books, on ordering sources, on children's book workshops or conferences, and on working with librarians, authors, and illustrators. In addition, you can request names of other members in your area for sharing book information. *(Instructor,* 1992, 55–56)

2. Join a book-sharing project.

The Association of American Publishers and the American Library Association together sponsor a book-sharing project called "Teachers as Readers" in order to encourage teachers and parents to work together in keeping up with the latest children's literature and purchasing the best children's books for use in the school and home. Teachers and parents are encouraged to form their own group in order to get grants or establish partnerships with businesses. Information on starting and funding Teachers as Readers groups can be obtained from the same address as in #1 above. *(Instructor,* 1992, 54–55)

3. Become acquainted with a bookseller.

Your local bookstore is often one of the best sources for keeping you up-to-date on the newest children's books. Get acquainted with such a bookseller and ask for help in obtaining information on new books or help in developing bibliographies of the best books on certain topics or themes. One such bookseller who puts out a newsletter on current children's books is: Frank Hodge, Hodge-Podge Books, 272 Lark St., Albany, NY 12210.

4. Obtain a book-selection guidebook or list.

An especially useful guide to children's literature is The New York Times Parent's Guide to the Best Books for Children by children's book editor Eden Ross Lipson (Random House, 1991) with book categories that include Wordless Books, Picture Books, Story Books and Early Reading Books, and paragraph descriptions of each of more than seventeen hundred books. Especially helpful are its over fifty special subject indexes from Adoption to War and Peace.

Books Kids Will Sit Still For by Judy Freeman (Bowker, 1990) contains reviews of more than two thousand children's picture books, folklore, poetry, and nonfiction.

A reference book that children's librarians will help you use is *A to Zoo: Subject Access to Children's Picture Books* by Carolyn Lima and John Lima (Bowker, 1989). Almost twelve thousand of the best fiction and nonfiction books are listed in seven hundred subject categories.

The International Reading Association and Children's Book Council puts out a free annual list of children's favorite newly published books that can be obtained by sending a self-addressed nine- by twelve-inch envelope, stamped with first-class postage for four ounces to "Childrens Choices," International Reading Association, 800 Barksdale Rd., Newark, DE 19711.

Creating Book Activities for Books Other Than Those Described Here

This textbook was designed with model activities for each of the books described. When you choose to use a book other than those described here, you will need to invent your own activities. You can create them just as the author of this textbook did by following this procedure:

1. Read the book carefully, looking for topics, themes, or activities.
2. Choose an idea from the book based on how well it fits with a certain type of activity.
3. Make up your own activity or check the activities listed at the end of each chapter for ideas.

For example, the book, *If You Give a Mouse a Cookie* by Laura Joffe Numeroff and Felcia Bond (ill.), Harper/Collins, 1985, is a simple humorous story about what a little boy imagines will probably happen if you give a mouse a cookie. One thing leads to thirteen other things in this story. So you might consider activities that involve *consequences* of an action.

1. What are the consequences? Have children bake cookies and then play the game "If You Give a Child a Cookie." (Have each child tell what might happen in his or her house.)
2. What are other consequences? At snack time have children pour glasses of milk for one another and play the game "If You Give a Child a Glass of Milk." (Go around the group having each child tell what might happen next.)
3. Read the book to the children at naptime, and when you come to the part about the mouse taking a nap, help children get comfortable, fluff up their pillows, and then read them another bedtime-type story.
4. After naps are finished have children get out paper and crayons to draw with just as the mouse did.
5. What other "consequences" activities can you think of?

Plan to read or tell stories to individuals or small groups in the Story Center on a daily basis.

✤ Telling or Reading Stories in the Classroom Curriculum

How frequently should you tell or read stories to the children? Once a day, twice a week, or what? Is there some sort of rule-of-thumb? The rule-of-thumb is always this: "the more, the better." First of all, be sure that the Story Center is open to children's free and independent use at all times. Then one of the staff members should be in charge of this center on a daily or weekly basis. She does not have to be physically in the center at all times, but she should plan to read *at least* one story a day to individuals or a small group in the center. In addition, you or another staff member or volunteer should plan special story readings or tellings on a regular basis. They may or may not be done in the Story Center.

For example, you may read *I Like Me* to a small group of new children at a time in the Story Center and then have them do the mirror-talking activity during the first week of school until everyone has experienced it. While this is happening the other children will have already chosen to work in the Block Center, the Dramatic Play Center, the Manipulative/Math Center, the Art Center, the Large Motor Center, or any of the other learning centers you have arranged. Your assistant will be overseeing such activities as you read to a small group. When you are finished you can switch roles and let her/him do the reading to another small group. (See *Preschool Appropriate Practices,* Beaty, 1992.)

If children are making Halloween costumes and may be somewhat fearful of the trick or treat experience, you may want to read *The Trip* and afterwards help children create their own peep show as Louie did. A grandfather may come to your Music Center one day to play a harmonica after you read to the total group *Song and Dance Man*. You or one of your staff members may be telling the story of *The Turnip* to the total group and then holding a story re-enactment.

Plan to have stories read in the Story Center to individuals or small groups on a daily basis. In addition plan to do one or two other activities weekly with books and stories either in the Story Center or somewhere else. Let the children's interests lead you. On the other hand, your planning should integrate books and book activities into the curriculum you are following for the entire year.

Also have special guests come and read: parents, grandparents, a librarian, a teenage brother or sister, a retired teacher, a children's bookstore owner, a book publisher's representative, an author. Who else in your community can you get? Use your ingenuity. The mayor? A pediatrician? The nutritionist from the hospital? A National Park ranger? A community helper? A television personality? Some of these people will not only be happy to help you, but also respond well to the newspaper publicity you can arrange for them. You can provide them with the book they will be reading or telling the story from. Choose it as a part of your curriculum, on the basis of their particular role and for the follow-up book activities you plan to do.

If you are really clever, you can plan your entire year's curriculum around children's *picture book storytelling*. Go ahead: try it!

✹ Overcoming the Fear of Storytelling

Many people are fearful of performing something new. For instance, teachers often do not feel comfortable leading singing in the classroom unless it is something that they are used to. It is the same with storytelling. Unless this activity is one that you are familiar with, you may not feel comfortable doing it. There are simple ways to overcome this fear.

First of all, you should start with a short, simple story that you like. Practice it by yourself until you know it. Tell it to a pet at home. Say it aloud as you drive to work. Tell it to a cassette recorder and play it back to hear how it sounds.

Mark Twain, one of the great storytellers of all time, wrote this advice in his notebook:

> Drill is the valuable thing. Drill—drill—drill—
> that is the precious thing. For, from drill comes
> the automatic, and few things in this world are
> well done until they can do themselves.
> (Janssen and Beaty, 1988, 38)

He practiced his hour-and-a-half humorous platform lectures over and over until they became automatic, and then he had the fun of telling his stories playfully and enjoying his audience's response. He recommended that the storyteller should first practice his stories:

> ...on a plaster cast [of a statue], or an empty
> chair, or any other appreciative object that will
> keep quiet until the speaker has got his material
> and his delivery limbered up. (Fatout, 1976, xxv)

You can do the same. When your story is "limbered up" and ready to go, then you can tell it first to one child in the Story Center. If this goes well, then ask one or two more children to come and listen. Tell the same story—many times. Your children expect this of you, anyway. A *told* story is a precious one. It is something coming from you, that you have prepared especially for them. Children recognize this. Their appreciative feedback should encourage you to do it again and again.

✿ The Magic of Storytelling

Will you ever become confident enough to tell a story in front of the total group? YES! Yes, you definitely will, because all you have to do is try it once. If you have come this far in reading about and preparing for *picture book storytelling,* then all you need do is *tell your story.* Something MAGIC is going to happen—to you and to your children. You are going to find that children are simply *mesmerized* by stories told by their teacher without a book that you look at! You will be looking at the children. There will be total attention. There will be no rustling around. The children will hang on your every word. They will LOVE it—and therefore, so will you. In the words of Chase Collins:

> Children love to listen to stories. When you tell a good one, you have a very sympathetic audience, listening hard... Your children will be touched to have you affirm the imaginative world they live in, and you will show them that, along with all the facts, you also see some magic in the universe. Children believe there is a place for enchantment in our everyday lives, and as you create stories for your children, you honor it and them. In this land of imagination—this world of the possible—your children will understand you are indeed the good king or queen they believe you are. (Collins, 1992, 3)

REFERENCES CITED

Beaty, J.J. (1992), *Preschool Appropriate Practices.* Ft. Worth, Tex.: Harcourt Brace Jovanovich.

Collins, C. (1992), *Tell Me a Story.* Boston: Houghton Mifflin Co.

Cowley, J. (1991), "Joy of Big Books," *Instructor* 101(3) 19.

Fatout, P.,ed.,(1976), *Mark Twain Speaking,* Iowa City: University of Iowa Press.

"Get the Best Books" (1992), Instructor, 102 (1), 54–56.

Hurst,C.O. (1990), *Once Upon a Time...An Encyclopedia for Successfully Using Literature with Young Children.* Allen, Texas: DLM.

Janssen, D.H. and Beaty, J.J. (1988), *Storytelling Mark Twain Style.* Elmira, NY: McGraw Bookstore, Elmira College.

Numeroff, L.J. and Bond, F. (1985), *If You Give a Mouse a Cookie.* New York: Harpercollins Publishers.

Warner, L. (1990), "Big Books: How to Make Them and Use Them," *Day Care and Early Education* 18(1) 16–19.

A SELECTION OF *BIG BOOKS* FROM BOOKS MENTIONED IN THIS TEXT

Ehlert, L. (1988), *Planting a Rainbow.* San Diego: Harcourt Brace Jovanovich.

Fox, M. (1988), *Hattie and the Fox,* New York: Macmillan.

Friedman, I.R. and Say, A. (1984), *How My Parents Learned to Eat.* San Diego: Harcourt Brace Jovanovich.

Guarino, D. and Kellogg, S. (ill.) (1989), *Is Your Mama a Llama?* New York: Scholastic.

Hutchins, P. (1986), *The Doorbell Rang.* New York: Scholastic.

Numeroff, L.J. (1988), *If You Give a Mouse a Cookie.* New York: Scholastic.

Shaw, N. (1986), *Sheep in a Jeep.* Boston: Houghton Mifflin.

William, S. (1989), *I Went Walking.* San Diego: Harcourt Brace Jovanovich.

A SELECTION OF FILMSTRIPS (F), CASSETTES (C), AND VIDEOS (V) FROM BOOKS MENTIONED IN THIS TEXT

Anna Banana and Me, C (Live Oak Media, Pine Plains, N.Y.)

Blueberries for Sal, F, C, V (Weston Woods, Weston, Conn.)

Caps for Sale, F, C, V (Weston Woods) C (Live Oak Media)

Crictor, F, C (Weston Woods)

The Dinosaur Who Lived in My Backyard, C (Live Oak Media)

Gilberto and the Wind, F, C (Weston Woods) C (Live Oak Media)

Goodnight Moon, F, C (Weston Woods) C (Live Oak Media)

I Like Me, F, C (Weston Woods)

It Looked Like Spilt Milk, C (Live Oak Media)

John Brown, Rose and the Midnight Cat, F, C, V (Weston Woods)

Leo the Late Bloomer, F, C (Weston Woods)

Miss Rumphius, F, C (Live Oak Media)

My Mom Travels a Lot, F, C (Live Oak Media)

The Mysterious Tadpole, F, C, V (Weston Woods)

Noah's Ark, F, C, (Weston Woods)

Owl Moon, F, C, V (Weston Woods)

Pancakes for Breakfast, F (Weston Woods)

Pinkerton, Behave, F, C (Weston Woods)

A Rainbow of My Own, F, C (Live Oak Media)

Red Riding Hood, F, C, V (Weston Woods)

Strega Nona, F, C, V (Weston Woods)

Titch, F, C (Weston Woods)

The Trip, F, C, V (Weston Woods)

Where the Wild Things Are, F, C, V (Weston Woods)

Wilfrid Gordon McDonald Partridge, F, C (Weston Woods)

Wynken, Blynken and Nod, C (Live Oak Media)

❧ Photo and Illustration Credits

Illustration, page 37: Reprinted with the permission of Macmillan Publishing Company from TITCH by Pat Hutchins. Copyright © 1971 by Pat Hutchins.

Photo, page 40: From LEO THE LATE BLOOMER by Robert Kraus. Text copyright © 1971 by Robert Kraus. Selection reprinted by permission of HarperCollins Publishers.

Illustration, page 53: From BLUEBERRIES FOR SAL by Robert McCloskey. Copyright © 1948 by Robert McCloskey, renewed 1976 by Robert McCloskey. Used by permission of Viking Penguin, a division of Penguin Books USA Inc.

Illustration, page 81: Illustration from LOUIE by Ezra Jack Keats. Copyright © 1975 by Ezra Jack Keats. By permission of Greenwillow Books, a division of William Morrow & Company, Inc.

Illustration, page 85: THE HATING BOOK by Charlotte Zolotow; text copyright © 1969 by Charlotte Zolotow, illustrations copyright (1969) by Ben Shecter. Selection reprinted by permission of HarperCollins Publishers.

Photo, page 105: From HARRY THE DIRTY DOG by Gene Zion. Text copyright © 1956 by Eugene Zion. Pictures copyright © 1956 by Margaret Bloy Graham. Selection reprinted by permission of HarperCollins Publishers.

Photo, page 124: From THE MYSTERIOUS TADPOLE by Steven Kellogg. Copyright © 1977 by Steven Kellogg. Used by permission of Dial Books for Young Readers, a division of Penguin Books USA Inc.

Illustration, page 192: From the book WHERE DOES THE TRAIL LEAD? by Burton Albert, illustrated by Brian Pinkney, copyright © 1991. Used by permission of the publisher, Simon & Schuster Books for Young Readers, New York.

Illustration, page 202: Used with the permission of the author, Nadine Bernard Westcott.

Illustration, page 227: Reprinted with the permission of Macmillan Publishing Company from MAEBELLE'S SUITCASE by Tricia Tusa. Copyright © 1987 by Tricia Tusa.

Illustration, page 238: From IS YOUR MAMA A LLAMA? by Deborah Guarino. Reprinted by permission of Scholastic, Inc.

Finding Friends

(Chapter 3)

D. J. Zeigler

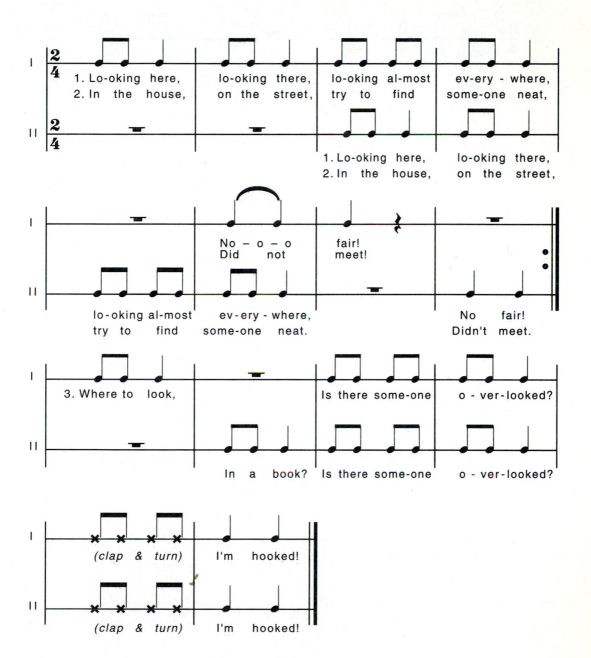

Frog Rap

(Chapter 5)

D. J. Zeigler

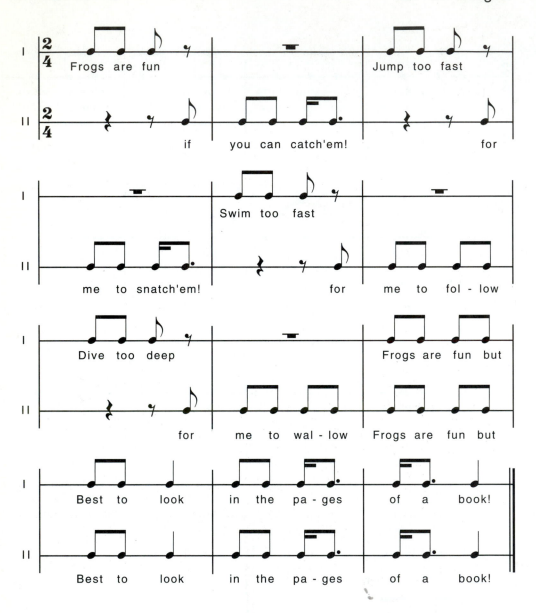

Poof!

(Chapter 7)

Group I–Children; Group II–Witch

D. J. Zeigler

C

I can be a prin-cess on a cas - tle wall

W

Poof!

C

I can be a hand-some prince climb-ing up the wall

W

Poof!

C

W

I can be a wick-ed witch, with pow-er o - ver all: Poof!

C

Oh - h - h, no! *(clap)* I'd ra - ther be
(turn)

W

C

me! *(clap)* POOF!

W

(witch collapses into heap on last POOF!)

249

Which Is Better?

(Chapter 11)

D. J. Zeigler

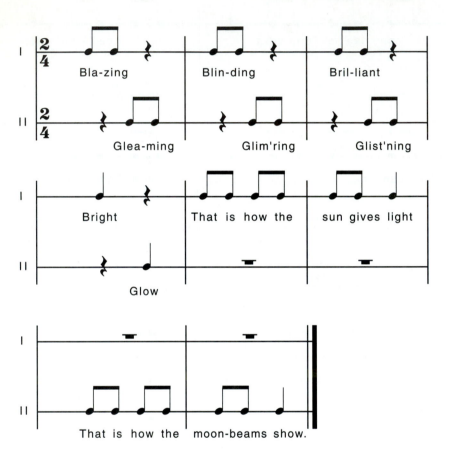

Argument

(Chapter 12)

D. J. Zeigler

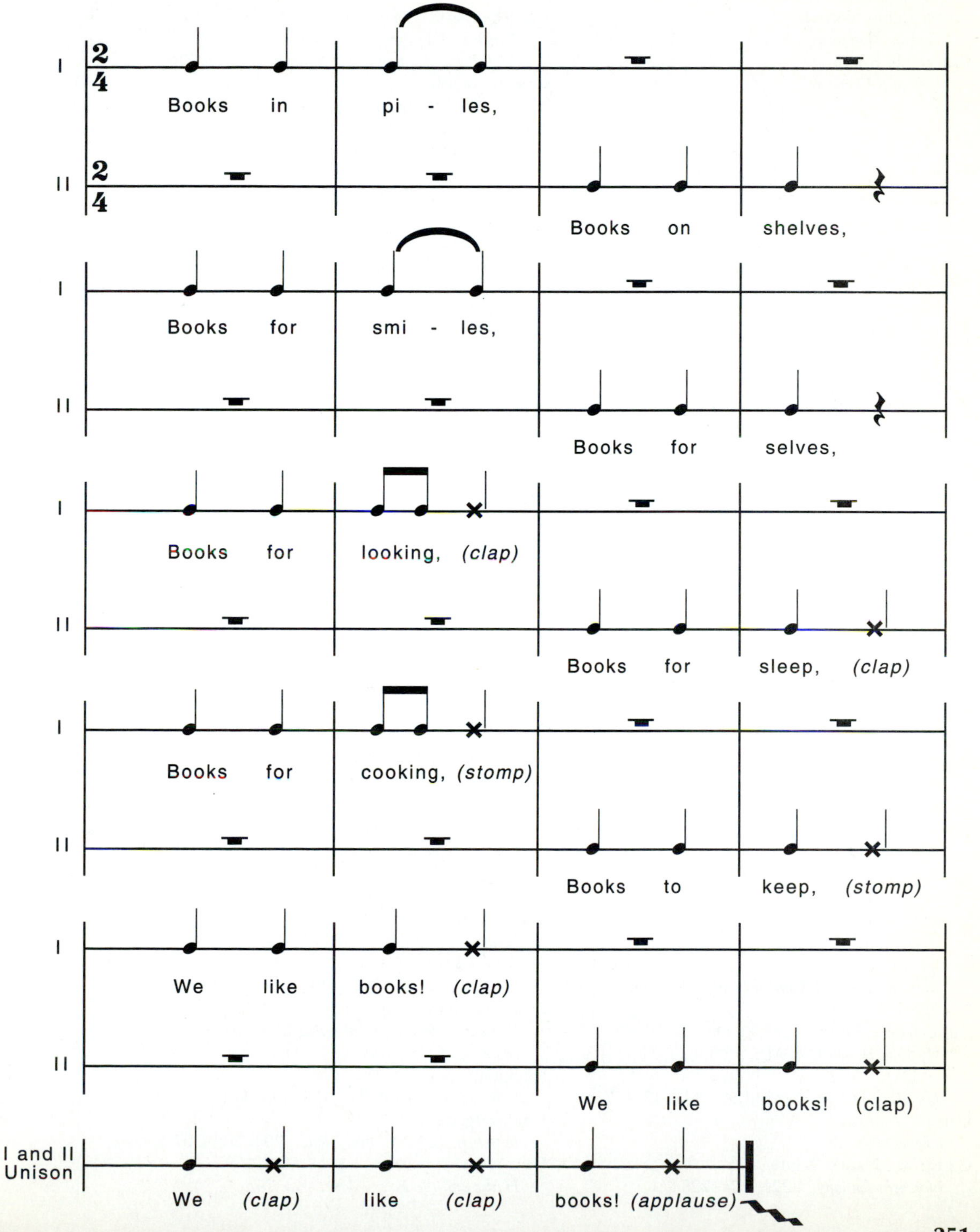

BOOK EXTENSION ACTIVITIES

23